WITH CLIVE IN INDIA

WITH CLIVE IN INDIA

OR, THE BEGINNINGS OF AN EMPIRE

G. A. HENTY

GYAN

Published by

Gyan Publishing House
5, Ansari Road
Daryaganj, New Delhi-110002
Phone: 011-47034999, 9811692060
E-mail: books@gyanbooks.com

Distribution Network
gyanbooks.com
India, USA, Canada, UK, Australia

ISBN: 978-93-7097-544-6 (PB)

First Published, 1894

2nd Impression 2025

Printed at: Gyan Press, Delhi.

WITH CLIVE IN INDIA
Author G. A. Henty

A BRUSH WITH PRIVATEERS

WITH CLIVE IN INDIA

OR THE

BEGINNINGS OF AN EMPIRE

BY

G. A. HENTY

AUTHOR OF "A TALE OF WATERLOO," AND "IN THE REIGN OF TERROR."

WITH FULL-PAGE ILLUSTRATIONS BY GORDON BROWNE

NEW YORK

CHARLES SCRIBNER'S SONS

1894

PREFACE.

MY DEAR LADS,—In the following pages I have endeavored to give you a vivid picture of the wonderful events of the ten years, which at their commencement saw Madras in the hands of the French—Calcutta at the mercy of the Nabob of Bengal—and the English influence apparently at the point of extinction in India—and which ended in the final triumph of the English both in Bengal and Madras. There were yet great battles to be fought, great efforts to be made, before the vast Empire of India fell altogether into British hands; but these were but the sequence of the events I have described.

The historical details are, throughout the story, strictly accurate, and for them I am indebted to the history of these events written by Mr. Orme, who lived at that time, to the *Life of Lord Clive*, recently published by Lieutenant-colonel Malleson, and to other standard authorities. In this book I have devoted a somewhat smaller space to the personal adventures of my hero than in my other historical tales, but the events themselves were of such a thrilling and exciting nature that no deeds of fiction could surpass them. I hope and believe then that you will follow the career of my hero, Charlie Marryat, with as much interest as you have manifested in the adventures of the many characters to whom I have hitherto introduced you.

A word as to the orthography of the names and places. An entirely new method of spelling Indian words has lately been invented by the Indian authorities. This is no doubt more correct than the rough and ready orthography of the early traders, and I have therefore adopted it for all little-known words. But there are Indian names which have become household words in England, and should never be changed, and as it would be considered a gross piece of pedantry and affectation on the part of a tourist on the Continent, who should, on his return, say he had been to Genova, Firenze and Wien, instead of Genoa, Florence and Vienna, it is, I consider, an even worse offence to transform Arcot, Cawnpoor and Lucknow, into Arkat, Kahnpur and Laknao. I have tried, therefore, so far as possible, to give the names of well-known personages and places in the spelling familiar to Englishmen, while the new orthography has been elsewhere adopted.

Yours very sincerely,

G. A. HENTY.

CONTENTS.

Chap.		Page
I.	Leaving Home,	9
II.	The Young Writer,	21
III.	A Brush with Privateers,	34
IV.	The Pirates of the Pacific,	47
V.	Madras,	58
VI.	The Arrival of Clive,	72
VII.	The Siege of Arcot,	85
VIII.	The Grand Assault,	99
IX.	The Battle of Kavaripak,	112
X.	The Fall of Seringham,	126
XI.	An Important Mission,	139
XII.	A Murderous Attempt,	153
XIII.	An Attempt at Murder,	166
XIV.	The Siege of Ambur,	180
XV.	The Pirates' Hold,	193
XVI.	A Tiger Hunt,	207
XVII.	The Capture of Gheriah,	221
XVIII.	The "Black Hole" of Calcutta,	238
XIX.	A Daring Escape,	251
XX.	The Rescue oe the White Captive,	264
XXI.	The Battle outside Calcutta,	277
XXII.	Plassey,	290
XXIII.	Plassey,	303
XXIV.	Mounted Infantry,	314
XXV.	Besieged in a Pagoda,	327
XXVI.	The Siege of Madras,	339
XXVII.	Masulipatam,	352
XXVIII.	The Defeat of Lally,	365
XXIX.	The Siege of Pondicherry,	378
XXX.	Home,	391

ILLUSTRATIONS.

PAGE

A Brush with Privateers, ... *Frontispiece*, 37

Clive leading the Storming Party at Devikota, . 64

Tim Kelly Discoursing on Horrible Reptiles, . . 89

The Bazaars of Trichinopoli, ... 124

Charlie's Mission to Rajah Boorhau, ... 147

The Fate of the Assassins, ... 168

"If you attack us, we will blow up the Magazine," 205

How Charlie dealt with his Superior Officers, 240

"I am here, Dear!" he said in a whisper, . 265

Charlie surprised by the French at Trinavady, 329

The sudden Conversion of a faithless Ally, . . 357

Welcome Home! 394

WITH CLIVE IN INDIA.

CHAPTER I.

LEAVING HOME.

A LADY in deep mourning was sitting crying bitterly by a fire in small lodgings in the town of Yarmouth. Beside her stood a tall lad of sixteen. He was slight in build, but his schoolfellows knew that Charlie Marryat's muscles were as firm and hard as those of any boy in the school. In all sports requiring activity and endurance rather than weight and strength he was always conspicuous. Not one in the school could compete with him in long-distance running, and when he was one of the hares there was but little chance for the hounds. He was a capital swimmer and one of the best boxers in the school. He had a reputation for being a leader in every mischievous prank; but he was honorable and manly, would scorn to shelter himself under the semblance of a lie, and was a prime favorite with his masters as well as his schoolfellows. His mother bewailed the frequency with which he returned home with blackened eyes and bruised face; for between Dr. Willet's school and the fisher lads of Yarmouth there was a standing feud, whose origin dated so far back that none of those now at school could trace it. Consequently fierce fights often took place in the narrow rows, and sometimes the fisher boys would be driven back on to the broad quay shaded by trees, by the river, and there being reinforced from the craft along the side would reassume the offensive and drive their opponents back into the main street.

It was but six months since Charlie had lost his father, who was the officer in command at the coast-guard station, and his scanty pension was now all that remained for the support of his widow and children. His mother had talked his future prospects over many times with Charlie. The latter was willing to do anything, but could suggest nothing. His father had but little naval interest, and had for years been employed on coast-guard service. Charlie agreed that although he should have liked of all things to go to sea, it was useless to think of it now, for he was past the age at which he could have entered as a midshipman. The matter had been talked over four years before with his father; but the latter had pointed out that a life in the navy without interest is in most cases a very hard one. If a chance of distinguishing himself happened promotion would follow; but if not, he might be for years on shore, starving on half-pay and waiting in vain for an appointment, while officers with more luck and better interest went over his head.

Other professions had been discussed but nothing determined upon, when Lieutenant Marryat suddenly died. Charlie, although an only son, was not an only child, as he had two sisters both younger than himself. After a few months of effort Mrs. Marryat found that the utmost she could hope to do with her scanty income was to maintain herself and daughters and to educate them until they should reach an age when they could earn their own living as governesses, but that Charlie's keep and education were beyond her resources. She had, therefore, very reluctantly written to an uncle whom she had not seen for many years; her family having objected very strongly to her marriage with a penniless lieutenant in the navy. She informed him of the loss of her husband, and that although her income was sufficient to maintain herself and her daughters, she was most anxious to start her son, who was now sixteen, in life, and therefore begged him to use his influence to obtain for him a situation of some sort. The letter which she now held in her hand was the answer to the appeal.

"My dear Niece," it began,—"Since you, by your own foolish conduct and opposition to all our wishes, separated yourself from your family and went your own way in life, I have heard little of you, as the death of your parents so shortly afterwards deprived me of all sources of information. I regret to hear of the loss which you have suffered. I have already taken the necessary steps to carry out your wishes. I yesterday dined with a friend who is one of the directors of the Hon. East India Company, and at my request he has kindly placed a writership in the Company at your son's service. He will have to come up to London to see the board next week, and will probably have to embark for India a fortnight later. I shall be glad if he will take up his abode with me during the intervening time. I shall be glad also if you will favor me with a statement of your income and expenses, with such details as you may think necessary. I inclose four five-pound bank-notes, in order that your son may obtain such garments as may be imme diately needful for his appearance before the board of directors and for his journey to London. I remain, my dear niece, yours sincerely,

"JOSHUA TUFTON."

"It is cruel," Mrs. Marryat sobbed—"cruel to take you away from us and send you to India, where you will most likely die of fever, or be killed by a tiger, or stabbed by one of those horrid natives, in a fortnight."

"Not so bad as that, mother, I hope," Charlie said sympathizingly, although he could not repress a smile; "other people have managed to live out there and have come back safe."

"Yes," Mrs. Marryat said sobbing; "I know how you will come back. A little, yellow, shrivelled up old man with no liver, and a dreadful temper, and a black servant. I know what it will be."

This time Charlie could not help laughing. "That's looking too far ahead altogether, mother. You take the two extremes. If I don't die in a fortnight I am to live to be a shrivelled old man. I'd rather take a happy medium, and look forward to coming back before my liver is all gone, or my temper all destroyed, with lots of money to make you and the girls comfortable. There is only one thing, I wish it had been a cadetship instead of a writership."

"That is my only comfort," Mrs. Marryat said. "If it had been a cadetship I should have written to say that I would not let you go. It is bad enough as it is; but if you had had to fight, I could not have borne it."

Charlie did his best to console his mother by telling her how every one who went to India made fortunes, and how he should be sure to come back with plenty of money, and that when the girls grew up he should be able to find rich husbands for them; and at last he succeeded in getting her to look at matters in a less gloomy light. "And I'm sure, mother," he said, "uncle means most kindly. He sends twenty pounds, you see, and says that that is for immediate necessities; so I have no doubt he means to help to get my outfit, or at any rate to advance money which I can repay him out of my salary. The letter is rather stiff and business-like, of course, but I suppose that's his way; and you see he asks about your income, so perhaps he means to help for the girls' education. I should go away very happy if I knew that you would be able to get on comfortably. Of course it's a long way off, mother, and I should have liked to stay at home to be a help to you and the girls; but one can't have all one wishes. As far as I am concerned myself, I would rather go out as a writer there, where I shall see strange sights and a strange country, than be stuck all my life at a desk in London. What is uncle like?"

"He is a short man, my dear, rather stiff and pompous, with a very stiff cravat. He used to give me his finger to shake when I was a child, and I was always afraid of him. He married a most disagreeable woman only a year or two before I married myself. But I heard she died not very long afterwards;" and so Mrs. Marryat got talking of her early days and relations, and was quite in good spirits again by the time her daughters returned from school, and she told them what she was now coming to regard as the good fortune which had befallen their brother. The girls were greatly affected. They adored their brother, and the thought that he was going away for years was terrible to them. Nothing that could be said pacified them in the slightest degree, and they did nothing but cry until they retired to bed. Charlie was much affected by their sorrow; but when they had retired he took his hat and went out to tell the news of his approaching departure to some of his chums.

The next day Mrs. Marryat wrote thanking her uncle for his kindness, and saying that Charlie would go round to London by the packet which sailed on the following Monday, and would, if the wind were fair and all went well, reach London on the Wednesday. School was, of course, at once given up, and the girls also had a holiday till their brother's departure. When the necessary clothes were ordered there was little more to do, and Charlie spent the time when his boy friends were in school, in walking with the girls along the shore, talking to them of the future, of the presents he would send them home, and of the life he should lead in India; while at other times he went out with his favorite schoolfellows, and joined in one last grand battle with the smack boys.

On Monday morning, after a sad farewell to his family, Charlie embarked on board the *Yarmouth Belle*, a packet which performed the journey to and from London once a fortnight. She was a roomy lugger built for stowage rather than speed, and her hold was crammed and her deck piled with packages of salted fish. There were five or six other persons also bound for London, the journey to which was in those days regarded as an arduous undertaking. As soon as the *Yarmouth Belle* issued from the mouth of the river she began to pitch heavily, and Charlie, who from frequently going out with his father in the revenue cutter, was a good sailor, busied himself in doing his best for his afflicted fellow-passengers.

Towards evening the wind got up, and shifting ahead the captain dropped anchor off Lowestoft. The next morning was finer, and the *Yarmouth Belle* continued her way. It was not, however, till Thursday afternoon that she dropped anchor in the Pool. Charlie was soon on shore, and giving his trunk to a porter desired him to lead the way to Bread Street, in which his uncle resided, for in the last century such things as country villas were almost unknown, and the merchants of London for the most part resided in the houses where they carried on their business. Keeping close to the porter to see that he did not make off with his trunk, for Charlie had received many warnings as to the extreme wickedness of London, he followed him through the busy streets, and arrived safely at his uncle's door. It was now dusk, and Charlie on giving his name was shown upstairs to a large room which was lighted by a fire blazing in the hearth. Standing with his back to this was a gentleman whom he at once recognized from his mother's description as her uncle, although he was a good deal more portly than when she had seen him last.

"So you are my grand-nephew," he said, holding out what Charlie considered to be a very limp and flabby hand towards him.

"Yes, uncle," Charlie said cheerfully; "and we are very much obliged to you, mamma and I, for your kindness."

"Humph!" the old gentleman grunted. "And how is it," he asked severely, "that you were not here yesterday? My niece's letter led me to expect that you would arrive yesterday."

"We came as fast as we could, uncle," Charlie laughed; "but of course the time depends upon the wind. The captain tells me that he has been as much as three weeks coming round."

Mr. Tufton grunted again as if to signify that such unpunctuality was altogether displeasing to him. "You are tall," he said, looking up at Charlie, who stood half a head above him, "and thin, very thin. You have a loose way of standing which I don't approve of."

"I'm sorry I'm loose, sir," Charlie said gravely, "if you do not approve of it; but you see running about and playing games makes one lissom. I suppose, now that's all over and I am going to spend my time in writing, I shall get stiffer."

"I hope so, I hope so," Mr. Tufton said encouragingly, and as if stiffness were one of the most desirable things in life. "I like to see young men with a sedate bearing. And you left my niece and grand-nieces well, I hope?"

"Quite well, thank you, sir," Charlie said; "but, of course, a good deal upset with parting from me."

"Yes," Mr. Tufton said; "I suppose so. Women are so emotional. Now there's nothing I object to more than emotion."

As Charlie thought that this was probably the case, he was silent, although the idea vaguely occurred to him that he should like to excite a little emotion in his uncle by the sudden insertion of a pin, or some other such means. The silence continued for some little time, and then Mr. Tufton said, "I always dine at two o'clock; but as probably you are hungry—I have observed that boys always are hungry—some food will be served you in the next room. I had already given my housekeeper orders. No doubt you will find it prepared. After that you may like to take a walk in the streets. I have supper at nine, by which hour you will, of course, have returned."

Charlie, as he ate his meal, thought to himself that his uncle was a pompous old gentleman, and that it would be very hard work getting on with him for the next three weeks. However he consoled himself by the thought "Kind is as kind does," after all, and I expect the old gentleman is not as crusty as he looks. Charlie had handed to Mr. Tufton a letter which his mother had given him, and when he returned from a ramble through the streets he found that gentleman sitting by the fire with lights upon a small table beside him. Upon this Mrs. Marryat's letter lay open.

"So you have soon become tired of the streets of London, grand-nephew?" he said.

"There is not much to see, sir. The lamps do not burn very brightly, and the fog is coming on. I thought that if it grew thicker I might lose my way, and in that case I might not have been in at the hour you named for supper."

"Humph!" the other gentleman grunted. "So

your mother has taught you to be punctual to meals. But, no; boys' appetites teach them to be punctual then if never at any other time. And why, sir," he asked severely, "did my niece not write to me before?"

"I don't know, sir," Charlie said. "I suppose she did not like—that is, she didn't think—that is—"

"Think, sir! like, sir!" said his uncle. "What right had she either to think or to like? Her duty clearly was to have made me acquainted at once with all the circumstances. I suppose I had a right to say whether I approved of my grand-nieces going tramping about the world as governesses or not. It isn't because a woman chooses by her folly to separate herself from her family that they are to be deprived of their rights in a matter of this kind. Eh, sir, what do you say to that?" and Mr. Tufton looked very angry indeed.

"I don't know, sir," Charlie said. "I have never thought the matter over."

"Why, sir, suppose she had made you a tinker, sir, and you turned out a thief, as likely as not you would have done, and you'd been hung, sir, what then? Am I to have such discredit as this brought upon me without my having any option in the matter?"

"I suppose not, sir," Charlie said. "I hope I shouldn't have turned out a thief even if I'd been a tinker; but perhaps it was because my mother feared that this might be the case that she did give you the option."

His uncle looked at him keenly; but Charlie, though with some difficulty, maintained the gravest face. "It is well she did so," Mr. Tufton said; "very well. If she had not done so, I should have known the reason why. And you, sir, do you like the thought of going to India?"

"Yes, uncle, I like the thought very much, though I would rather, if I may say so, have gone as a cadet."

"I thought so," Mr. Tufton said sarcastically; "I was

sure of it. You wanted to wear a red coat and a sword, and to swagger about the streets of Calcutta, instead of making an honorable living and acquiring a fortune."

"I don't think, sir," Charlie said, "that the idea of the red coat and sword entered into my mind; but it seemed to me the choice of a life of activity and adventure against one as a mere clerk."

"Had you entered the military service of the Company, even if you didn't get shot, you could only hope to rise to the command of a regiment, ranking with a civilian very low down on the list. The stupidity of boys is unaccountable. It's a splendid career, sir, that I have opened to you; but if I'd known that you had no ambition I would have put you into my own counting-house, though there, that wouldn't have done either, for I know you would have blotted the ledger and turned all the accounts topsy-turvy. And now sir, supper is ready;" and the old gentleman led the way into the next room.

Upon the following day Charlie was introduced by his uncle to the director who had given him his nomination, and was told by him that the board would sit upon the following day, and that he must call at the India House at eleven o'clock. The ordeal was not a formidable one. He was shown into a room where eight or ten elderly gentlemen were sitting round a large table. Among these was his friend of the day before. He was asked a question or two about his age, his father's profession, and his place of education. Then the gentleman at the head of the table nodded to him, and said he could go, and instructions would be sent to him, and that he was to prepare to sail in the *Lizzie Anderson*, which would leave the docks in ten days' time, and that he would be for the present stationed at Madras. Much delighted at having got through the ordeal so easily, Charlie returned to his uncle's. He did not venture to penetrate into the latter's counting-house, but awaited his coming upstairs to dinner, to tell him the news.

"Humph!" said his uncle; "it is lucky they did not find out what a fool you were at once. I was rather afraid that even the two minutes would do it. After dinner I will send my clerk round with you to get the few things which are necessary for your voyage. I suppose you will want to, what you call amuse yourself, to see the beasts at Exeter Change, and the play-houses. Here are two sovereigns; don't get into loose company, and don't get drinking, sir, or out of the house you go."

Charlie attempted to express his thanks, but his uncle stopped him abruptly. "Hold your tongue, sir; I am doing what is right; a thing, sir, Joshua Tufton always has done, and doesn't expect to be thanked for it. All I ask you is, that if you rob the Company's till and are hung, don't mention that you are related to me."

After dinner was over, Charlie went out under the charge of an old clerk and visited tailors' and outfitters' shops, and found that his uncle's idea of the few necessaries for a voyage differed very widely from his own. The clerk in each case inquired from the tradesmen what was the outfit which gentlemen going to India generally took with them, and Charlie was absolutely appalled at the magnitude of the orders. Four dozen shirts, ten dozen pairs of stockings, two dozen suits of white cotton cloth, and everything else in proportion. Charlie in vain remonstrated, and even implored the clerk to abstain from ordering what appeared to him such a fabulous amount of things, and begged him at any rate to wait until he had spoken to his uncle. The clerk, however, replied that he had received instructions that the full usual outfit was to be obtained, and that Mr. Tufton never permitted his orders to be questioned. Charlie was forced to submit, but he was absolutely oppressed with the magnitude of his outfit, to carry which six huge trunks were required.

"It is awful," Charlie said to himself, "positively awful. How much it will all come to, goodness only knows; three or four hundred pounds at least."

In those days before steam was thought of, and the journey to India was often of six months' duration, men never came home more than once in seven years, and often remained in India from the day of their arrival until they finally retired, without once revisiting England. The outfits taken out were therefore necessarily much larger than at the present time, when a run home to England can be accomplished in three weeks, and there are plenty of shops in every town in India where all European articles of necessity or luxury can be purchased. After separating from the clerk Charlie felt altogether unable to start out in search of amusement. He wandered about vaguely till supper-time, and then attempted to address his uncle on the subject. "My dear uncle," he began, "you've been so awfully kind to me that I really do not like to trespass upon you. I am positively frightened at the outfit your clerk has ordered; it is enormous. I'm sure I can't want so many things possibly, and I would really rather take a much smaller outfit, and then, as I want them I can have more things out from England and pay for them myself."

"You don't suppose," Mr. Tufton said sternly, "that I'm going to have my nephew go out to India with the outfit of a cabin boy. I ordered that you were to have the proper outfit of a gentleman, and I requested my clerk to order a considerable portion of the things to be made of a size which will allow for your growing, for you look to me as if you were likely enough to run up into a lanky giant of six feet high. I suppose he has done as I ordered him. Don't let me hear another word on the subject."

CHAPTER II.

THE YOUNG WRITER.

FOR the next four days Charlie followed his uncle's instructions and amused himself. He visited Exeter Change, took a boat and rowed down the river to Greenwich, and a coach and visited the palace of Hampton Court. He went to see the coaches make their start in the morning for all places in England, and marvelled at the perfection of the turn-outs. He went to the playhouses twice, in the evening, and saw Mr. Garrick in his performance as Richard the Third. On the fifth day a great surprise awaited him. His uncle at breakfast had told him briefly that he did not wish him to go out before dinner, as some one might want to see him, and Charlie, supposing that a messenger might be coming down from the India House, waited indoors, and an hour later he was astonished when the door of the room opened and his mother and sisters entered. With a shout of gladness and surprise Charlie rushed into their arms.

"My dear mother, my dear girls, this is an unexpleasure indeed! Why, what has brought you here?"

"Didn't you know we were coming, Charlie? didn't uncle tell you?" they exclaimed.

"Not a word," Charlie said. "I never dreamt of such a thing. What, has he called you up here to stay till I go?"

"Oh, my dear, he has been so kind," his mother said, "and so funny! He wrote me such a scolding letter, just as if I had been a very naughty little girl. He said he wasn't going to allow me to bring disgrace upon him by living in wretched lodgings at Yarmouth, nor by his grand-nieces being sent out as governesses. So he ordered me at once, ordered me, Charlie, as if I had no will of my own, to give up the lodgings and to take our places in the coach yesterday morning. He said we were not to shame him by appearing here in rags, and he sent me a hundred pounds, every penny of which, he said, was to be laid out in clothes. As to the future, he said it would be his duty to see that I brought no further disgrace upon the family."

"Yes, and he's been just as kind to me, mother. As I told you when I wrote, he had ordered an enormous outfit, which will, I am sure, cost hundreds of pounds. He makes me go to the playhouses and all sorts of amusements, and all the time he has been so kind he scolds, and grumbles, and predicts that I shall be hanged."

"I'm sure you won't," Kate, his youngest sister, said indignantly. "How can he say such a thing!"

"He doesn't mean it," Charlie laughed; "it's only his way. He will go on just the same way with you, I have no doubt; but you mustn't mind, you know, and musn't laugh, but must look quite grave and serious. Ah! here he is. Oh, uncle, this is kind of you!"

"Hold your tongue, sir," said his uncle, "and try and learn not to speak to your elders unless you are addressed. Niece Mary," he said, kissing her upon the forehead, "I am glad to see you again. You are not so much changed as I expected. And these are my grand-nieces, Elizabeth and Kate, though why Kate I don't know. It is a fanciful name and new to the family, and I am surprised that you didn't call her Susanna, after your grandmother."

Kate made a little face at the thought of being called Susanna. However, a warning glance from Charlie closed her lips just as she was about to express her decided preference for her own name. Mr. Tufton kissed them both, muttering to himself:

"I suppose I ought to kiss them. Girls always expect to be kissed at every opportunity. What are you laughing at, grand-niece?"

"I don't think girls expect to be kissed except by people they like," Kate said; "but we do like kissing you, uncle," throwing her arms round his neck and kissing him heartily; "because you have been so kind to Charlie and have brought us up to see him again."

"You have disarranged my white tie, niece," Mr. Tufton said, extricating himself from Kate's embrace. "Niece Mary, I fear that you have not taught your daughters to restrain their emotions, and there is nothing so dreadful as emotional women."

"Perhaps I have not taken so much pains with their education in that way as in some others," Mrs. Marryat said smiling. "But of course, uncle, if you object to be kissed, the girls will abstain from doing so."

"No," Mr. Tufton said thoughtfully. "It is the duty of nieces to kiss their uncles, in moderation—in moderation, mind, and it is the duty of the uncles to receive those salutations, and I do not know that the duty is altogether an unpleasant one. I am myself unaccustomed to be kissed, but it is an operation to which I may accustom myself in time."

"I never heard it called an operation, uncle," Lizzie said demurely; "but I now understand the meaning ot the phrase of a man's undergoing a painful operation. I used to think it meant cutting off a leg, or something of that sort, but I see its much worse."

Her uncle looked at her steadily.

"I am afraid, grand-niece, that you intend to be sarcastic. This is a hateful habit in a man, worse in a woman. Cure yourself of it as speedily as possible, or Heaven help the unhappy man who may some day be your husband. And now," he said, "ring the bell. The housekeeper will show you to your rooms. My nephew will tell you what are the hours for meals. Of course you will want to be gadding about with him. You will understand that there is no occasion to be in to meals; but if you are not present when they are upon the table you will have to wait for the next. I cannot have my house turned upside down by meals being brought up at all sorts of hours. You must not expect me, niece, to be at your beck and call during the day, as I have my business to attend to; but of an evening I shall, of course, feel it my duty to accompany you to the playhouse. It will not do for you to be going about with only the protection of a hair-brained boy."

The remainder of Charlie's stay in London passed most pleasantly. They visited all the sights of town, Mr. Tufton performing what he called his duty with an air of protest, but showing a general thoughtfulness and desire to please his visitors, which was very apparent even when he grunted and grumbled the most.

On the evening before he started he called Charlie down into his counting-house.

"To-morrow you are going to sail," he said, "and to start in life on your own account, and I trust that you will, as far as possible, be steady and do your duty to your employers. You will understand that although the pay of a writer is not high there are opportunities for advancement. The Company have the monopoly of the trade of India, and in addition to their great factories at Bombay, Calcutta, and Madras they have many other trading stations. Those who by their good conduct attract the attention of their superiors rise to positions of trust and emolument. There are many who think that the Company will in time enlarge its operations, and as they do so, superiot opportunities will offer themselves, and since the subject of India has been prominently brought before my notice I have examined the question and am determined to invest somewhat largely in the stock of the Company, a step which will naturally give me some influence with the board. That influence I shall, always supposing that your conduct warrants it, exercise on your behalf. As we are now at war with France, and it is possible that the vessel in which you are proceeding may be attacked by the way, I have thought it proper that you should be armed. You will, therefore, find in your cabin a brace of pistols, a rifle, and a double-barrel shot-gun, which last, I am informed, is a useful weapon at close quarters. Should your avocations in India permit your doing so, you will find them useful in the pursuit of game. I hope that you will not be extravagant; but as a matter of business I find that it is useful to be able to give entertainments to persons who may be in a position to benefit or advance you. I have, therefore, arranged that you will draw from the factor at Madras the sum of two hundred pounds annually in addition to your pay. It is clearly my duty to see that my nephew has every fair opportunity for making his way. Now, go upstairs at once to your mother. I have letters to write, and am too busy for talking."

So saying, with a peremptory wave of his hand he dismissed his nephew.

"Well, mother," Charlie said after telling her of his uncle's generosity, "thank goodness you will be all right now anyhow. No doubt uncle intends to do something for you and the girls, though he has said nothing at present beyond the fact that you are not to be in wretched lodgings and they are not to go out as governesses. But even if he should change his mind, and I don't think he ever does that, I shall be able to help you. Oh, he is kind, isn't he?"

The parting was far less sad than that which had taken place at Yarmouth. Charlie was now assured that his mother and sisters would be comfortable and well cared for in his absence; while his mother, happy in the lightening of her anxiety as to the future of her daughters and as to the prospects of her son, was able to bear with better heart the thought of their long separation.

Mrs. Marryat and the girls accompanied him on board ship. Mr. Tufton declined to join the party, under the plea that in the first place he was busy, and in the second that he feared there would be an emotional display. He sent however, his head clerk with them, to escort the ladies on their return from the docks.

The *Lizzie Anderson* was a fine ship of the largest size, and she was almost as clean and trim as a man-of-war. She carried twelve cannon, two of them thirty-two pounders, which were in those days considered large pieces of ordnance. All the ships of the Company, and, indeed, all ocean-going merchantmen of the day, were armed, as the sea swarmed with privateers and the black flag of the pirates was still occasionally to be seen. The girls were delighted with all they saw, as, indeed, was Charlie, for accustomed as they were only to the coasting vessels which frequented the port of Yarmouth, this floating castle appeared to them a vessel of stupendous size and power.

This was Charlie's first visit also to the ship, for his uncle had told him that all directions had been given, that the trunks with the things necessary for the voyage would be found in his cabin at the time of starting, and the rest of the luggage in the hold. Everything was in order, and Charlie found that his cabin companion was a doctor in the service returning to

Madras. He was a pleasant man of some five or six and thirty, and assured Mrs. Marryat that he would soon make her son at home on board ship, and would, moreover, put him up to the ways of things upon his arrival in India. There were many visitors on board saying good-bye to their friends, and all sat down to lunch, served in the saloon. When this was over the bell rang for visitors to go ashore. There was a short scene of parting in which Charlie was not ashamed to use his handkerchief as freely as did his mother and sisters.

Five minutes later the great vessel passed through the dock gates. Charlie stood at the stern waving his handkerchief as long as he could catch a glimpse of the figures of his family, and then, as with her sails spread and the tide gaining strength every minute beneath her, the vessel made her way down the river, he turned round to examine his fellow passengers. These were some twenty in number, and for the most part men. Almost all were, in some capacity or other, civil or military, in the service of the Company; for at that time their monopoly was a rigid one, and none outside its boundary were allowed to trade in India. The Company was indeed solely a great mercantile house of business. They had their own ships, their own establishments, and bought and sold goods like other traders. They owned a small extent of country round their three great trading towns, and kept up a little army composed of two or three white regiments, and as many composed of natives, trained and disciplined like Europeans, and known as Sepoys. Hence the clergyman, the doctor, a member of the council of Madras, four or five military officers, twice as many civilians, and three young writers besides Charlie, were all in the employment of the Company.

"Well, youngster," a cheery voice said beside him, "take your last look at the smoke of London, for it will be a good many years before you see it again, my lad. You've blue skies and clear ones where you're going, except when it rains, and when it does there is no mistake about it."

The speaker was the captain of the *Lizzie Anderson*, a fine sailor-like man of some fifty years, of which near forty had been spent in the service of the Company.

"I'm not a Londoner," Charlie said smiling, "and have no regret for leaving its smoke. Do you think we shall make a quick voyage?"

"I hope so," the captain said, "but it all depends upon the wind. A finer ship never floated than the *Lizzie Anderson;* but the Company don't build their vessels for speed, and it's no use trying to run when you meet a Frenchman. Those fellows understand how to build ships, and if they could fight them as well as they build them we should not long be mistress of the sea."

Most of the people on board appeared to know each other, and Charlie felt rather lonely till the doctor came up and began to chat with him. He told him who most of his fellow passengers were:

"That gentleman there, walking on the other side of the deck as if not only the ship but the river and banks on both sides belonged to him, is one of the council. That is his wife over there with a companion holding her shawl for her. That pretty little woman next to her is the wife of Captain Tibbets, the tall man leaning against the bulwarks. Those two sisters are going out to keep house for their uncle, one of the leading men in Madras, and, I suppose, to get husbands, which they will most likely do before they have been there many weeks. They look very nice girls. But you soon get acquainted with them all. It is surprising how soon people get friendly on board ship, though, as a rule, they quarrel like cats and dogs before they get to the end of it."

"What do they quarrel about?" Charlie asked surprised.

"Oh, about anything or nothing," the doctor said. "They all get heartily sick of each other and of the voyage, and they quarrel because they have nothing else to do. You will see we shall be as happy a party as possible till we get about as far as the Cape. After that the rows will begin, and by the time we get to India half the people won't speak to each other. Have you been down the river before? That's Gravesend. I see the captain is getting ready to anchor. So, I suppose the tide has nearly run out. If this wind holds we shall be fairly out at sea when you get up to-morrow. You snore, I hope?"

"No, sir, I don't think so," Charlie said.

"I hoped you did," the doctor said, "because I'm told I do sometimes. However, as I usually smoke a cigar on deck the last thing, I hope you will be fairly asleep before I am. If at any time I get very bad and keep you awake you must shake me."

Charlie said it took a good deal to keep him awake, and that he should probably get accustomed to it ere long. "It's better to do that," he said with a laugh, "than to keep on waking you for the next four or five months."

A week later the *Lizzie Anderson* was running down the Spanish coast with all sail set. She was out of sight of land, and so far had seen nothing likely to cause uneasiness. They had met many vessels homeward bound from the Mediterranean, and one or two big ships which the captain pronounced to be Indiamen. That morning, however, a vessel was seen coming out from the land. She seemed to Charlie's eyes quite a small vessel, and he was surprised to see how often the captain and officers turned their glasses towards her.

"I fancy our friend over there is a French privateer," the doctor remarked to him; "and I should not be surprised if we found ourselves exchanging shots with her before many hours are over."

"But she's a little bit of a thing," Charlie said. "Surely she would never venture to attack a ship like ours."

"It's the size of the guns, not the size of the ship, that counts, my boy. She has the advantage of being able to sail three feet to our two, and probably, small as she is, she carries half as many men again as we do. However, we carry heavy metal, and can give a good account of ourselves. Those thirty-twos will astonish our friend if she comes within range."

The stranger was a large schooner, and the tautness of the spars and rigging showed that she was in beautiful order. She crossed the line upon which the merchantman was sailing some two miles in her rear, and then bearing up followed in her wake.

Charlie stood near the captain, who, instead of watching her, was sweeping the horizon with his glass. Presently he paused and gazed intently at a distant object.

"I thought so," he said to the first officer. "I fancied that fellow wasn't alone. He would hardly have ventured to try his strength with us if he had been. Send a man up to the tops and let him see what he can make her out to be. I can only see her topmasts, but I can make out no yards."

Presently the look-out came down and reported that the distant vessel appeared to be a large fore-and-aft schooner bearing down upon them.

"She will not be up for two hours yet," the captain said. "It will be getting dark then. It is not likely they will engage at night, but they will keep close and show their teeth at daybreak."

It soon became known that the belief of the captain was that the vessel in their wake, and that which could be seen approaching on the beam, were French privateers, and soon all were preparing in their own way for what might happen. The sailors cleared the decks and loosed the guns. The gentlemen went below and shortly returned bringing up rifles and fowling-pieces. Small-arms and cutlasses were brought up and piled round the masts.

"Why don't you put on more sail, sir?" Mr. Ashmead, the member of the council, said to the captain. "My wife, sir, objects to the sound of firearms, and I must really beg that you will increase your speed. As it is we are losing rather than gaining upon that vessel behind. The duty of the ships of the Company is to try not to fight."

"If they can help it," the captain added quietly. "Not to fight if they can help it, Mr. Ashmead. But unfortunately, the choice upon the present occasion, lies with the gentlemen yonder and not with us. It is not of the slightest use adding to the sail we carry, for at our very best speed those schooners could sail round and round us. As night comes on I intend to shorten sail and put the ship into fighting trim. In the morning I shall again increase it, but I shall not make any attempt to escape a combat which it depends entirely on those privateers to bring on or not as they choose. I am sorry that Mrs. Ashmead should be exposed to the unpleasantness of listening to the explosion of firearms, and that my other lady passengers should be exposed to the danger which cannot but arise more or less from a naval conflict. However, I hope, sir, that there need be no great anxiety as to the result. The Company has given us a heavy armament, and you may be sure that we shall all do our best."

Seeing the gentlemen go below for their guns Charlie asked one of the other young writers, a lad of about his own age, named Peters, with whom he had become friendly, to go below with him. He had not yet examined the arms that his uncle had given him, for he had not thought of them since he saw the gun-cases under his berth on his first arrival on board ship. He found the doctor already in his cabin putting together a heavy double-barrelled gun.

"Well, youngster," he said, "so we're likely to have a brush. I see you have a couple of gun cases under your berth. You are a good deal better provided than most lads who go out as writers. Ah! that's a beautiful piece of yours," he said, as Charlie unlocked one of the cases and took out a rifle, a small bore and a heavy barrel, and beautifully finished. "With a greased patch and a heavy charge that ought to carry a bullet far and true. Have you had any practice?"

"Not with this gun, sir. I used sometimes to practise shooting at gulls with a musket on board the cutter my father commanded, and I got to be a fair shot with it."

"Then you ought to be able to do good work with such a piece as that. What is in the other case? Ah! that's a beauty too," he said as he examined the double-barrelled gun. "Made extra strong and heavy, I see, so as to carry bullets. You'll find your shoulder ache at first, but you'll get accustomed to it in time. I'm always in favor of heavy barrels. They shoot stronger and straighter than your light guns, are not so liable to get bent or bruised if a stupid servant drops one across a stone, and, after all, two or three pounds difference in weight does not make any material difference when you're accustomed to it. Although, I grant a heavy gun does not come quite so quickly up to the shoulder for a snap shot."

"Now, Peters," Charlie said, "you take the double-barrel; I will use the rifle. Mine will come into play first, but, as my uncle said when he gave it me, yours will do most execution at close quarters."

At dusk the schooners, having exchanged some signals by flags, took up their positions, one on each quarter of the ship, at a distance of some two miles.

"Do not you think," Charlie asked his friend the doctor, "that they are likely to try and board us to-night?"

"No," the doctor said. "These privateers generally depend upon their long guns. They know that we shall be on the watch all night, and that in a hand-to-hand fight they would lose a considerable number of men, while by keeping at a distance and maintaining a fire with their long guns, they rely upon crippling their opponents, and then ranging up under their stern, pouring in a fire at close quarters until they surrender. Another thing is that they prefer daylight, as they can then see whether any other vessel is approaching. Were one of our cruisers to hear a cannonade in the night she would come down and might take them unaware. No, I think you will see that at daylight, if the coast is clear, they will begin."

Such was evidently the captain's opinion also, as he ordered sail to be still further shortened, and all, save the watch on deck, to turn in at once. The lights were all extinguished, not that the captain had any idea of evading his pursuers, but that he wished to avoid offering them a mark for their fire should they approach in the darkness.

CHAPTER III.

A BRUSH WITH PRIVATEERS.

THE night passed quietly. Once or twice lights were seen as the schooners showed a lantern for a moment to notify their exact position to each other. As soon as dawn broke every man on board the *Lizzie Anderson* was at his post. The schooners had drawn up a little, but were still under easy sail. The moment that the day grew clear enough for it to be perceived that no other sail could be seen above the horizon, fresh sail was spread upon the schooners and they began rapidly to draw up. On the previous evening the four heavy guns had been brought aft, and the Indiaman could have made a long running fight with her opponents had the captain been disposed. To this, however, he objected strongly, as his vessel was sure to be hulled and knocked about severely, and perhaps some of his masts cut down. He was confident in his power to beat off the two privateers, and he therefore did not add a stitch of canvas to the easy sail under which he had been holding on all night. Presently a puff of smoke shot out from the bow of the schooner from the weather quarter, followed almost instantaneously by one from her consort. Two round shot struck up the water, the one under the Indiaman's stern, the other under her forefoot.

"The rascals are well within range," the captain

said quietly. "See, they are taking off canvas again. They intend to keep at that distance and hammer away at us. Just what I thought would be their tactics."

Two more shots were fired by the schooners. One flew over the deck between the masts and plunged harmlessly in the sea beyond, the other struck the hull with a dull crash.

"It is lucky the ladies were sent into the hold," the captain said; "that shot has gone right through their cabin. Now, my lads, have you got the sights well upon them? Fire!"

The four thirty-two pounders spoke out almost at the same moment, and all gazed over the bulwarks anixously to watch the effect, and a cheer arose as it was seen how accurate had been the aim of the gunners. One shot struck the schooner to windward in the bow, a foot or two above the water-level; another went through her foresail close to the mast.

"A foot more, and you would have cut his foremast asunder."

The vessel to leeward had been struck by only one shot, the other passing under her stern. She was struck just above her deck line, the shot passing through the bulwark, and, as they thought on board the merchantman, narrowly missing if not actually striking the mainmast.

"There is some damage done," Dr. Rae said, keeping his glass fixed on the vessel; "there is a good deal of running about on deck there."

It was evident that the display of the heavy metal carried by the Indiaman was an unpleasant surprise to the privateers. Both lowered sail and ceased firing, and there was then a rapid exchange of signals between them.

"They don't like it," the captain said laughing; "they see that they cannot play the game they expected, and that they've got to take as well as to give. Now it depends upon the sort of stuff their captains are made of, whether they give it up at once or come straight up to close quarters. Ah! they mean fighting."

As he spoke a cloud of canvas was spread upon the schooners, and sailing more than two feet to the merchantman's one they ran quickly down towards her, firing rapidly as they came. Only the merchantman's heavy guns replied, but these worked steadily and coolly and did considerable damage. The bowsprit of one of their opponents was shot away. The sails of both vessels were pierced in several places, and several rugged holes were knocked in their hulls.

"If it were not that I do not wish to sacrifice any of the lives on board unnecessarily," the captain said, "I would let them come alongside and try boarding. We have a strong crew, and with the sixty soldiers we should give them such a reception as they do not dream of. However, I will keep them off if I can. Now, Mr. James, he said to the first officer, "I propose to give that vessel to leeward a dose; they are keeping about abreast, and by the course they are making will range alongside at about a cable's length. When I give the word pour a broadside with the guns to port upon that weather schooner. At that moment, gentlemen," he said turning to the passengers, "I shall rely upon you to pick off the steersman of the other vessel, and to prevent another taking his place. She steers badly now, and the moment her helm is free she'll run up into the wind. As she does so I shall bear off, run across her bow, and rake her deck with grape as we pass. Will you, Mr. Barlow, order your men to be in readiness to open fire with musketry upon her as we pass?"

The schooners were now running rapidly down upon the Indiaman. They were only able to use the guns in their bows, and the fire of the Indiaman from the heavy guns on her quarter was inflicting more damage than she received.

"Let all hands lie down on deck," the captain ordered, "they will open with their broadside guns as they come up. When I give the word let all the guns on the port side be trained at the foot of her mainmast, and fire as you get the line. On the starboard side lie down till I give the word."

It was a pretty sight as the schooners, throwing the water high up from their sharp cut-waters, came running along heeling over under the breeze. As they ranged alongside their topsails came down, and a broadside from both was poured into the Indiaman. The great ship shook as the shot crashed into her, and several sharp cries told of the effect which had been produced. Then the captain gave the word, and a moment afterward an irregular broadside, as the captain of each gun brought his piece to bear, was poured into the schooner from the guns on the port side. As the privateer heeled over her deck could be plainly seen, and the shot of the Indiaman, all directed at one point, tore up a hole around the foot of the mainmast. In an instant the spar tottered and with a crash fell alongside. At the same moment three of the passengers took a steady aim over the bulwark at the helmsman of the other privateer, and simultaneously with the reports of their pieces the man was seen to fall. Another sprang forward to take his place, but again the rifles spoke out, and he fell beside his comrade. Freed from the strain which had counteracted the pressure of her mainsail the schooner flew up into the wind. The Indiaman held on her course for another length and then her helm was put up, and she swept down across the bows of the privateer. Then the men leaped to their feet, the soldiers lined the bulwarks, and as she passed along a few yards only distant from her foe, each gun poured a storm of grape along her crowded deck while the troops and passengers kept up a continuous fire of musketry.

"That will do," the captain said quietly; "now we may keep her on her course, they have had more than enough of it."

There was no doubt of that, for the effect of the iron storm had been terrible, and the decks of the schooner were strewn with dead and dying. For a time after the merchantman had borne upon her course the sails of the schooner flapped wildly in the wind, and then the foremast went suddenly over the side.

"I should think you could take them both, Captain Thompson," one of the passengers said.

"They are as good as taken," the captain answered, "and would be forced to haul down their flags if I were to wear round and continue the fight. But they would be worse than useless to me. I should not know what to do with their crews, and should have to cripple myself by putting very strong prize crews upon them, and so run the risk of losing my own ship and cargo. No, my business is to trade and not to fight. If any one meddle with me I am ready to take my own part; but the Company would not thank me if I were to risk the safety of this ship and her valuable cargo for the sake of sending home a couple of prizes which might be recaptured as they crossed the bay, and would not fetch any great sum if they got safely in port."

An examination showed that the casualties on board the *Lizzie Anderson* amounted to three killed and eight wounded. The former were sewn in hammocks with a round shot at their feet and dropped overboard, the clergyman reading the burial service. The wounded were carried below and attended to by the ship's surgeon and Dr. Rae. The ship's decks were washed and all traces of the conflict removed. The guns were again lashed in their places, carpenters were lowered over the side to repair damages, and when the ladies came on deck an hour after the conflict was over, two or three ragged holes in the bulwarks and a half dozen in the sails were the sole signs that the ship had been in action, save that some miles astern could be seen the two crippled privateers with all sails lowered at work to repair damages. Two or three days afterwards Charlie Marryat and his friend Peters were sitting beside Dr. Rae, when the latter said:

"I hope that we sha'n't find the French in Madras when we get there."

"The French in Madras!" Charlie exclaimed in surprise. "Why, sir, there's no chance for that, is there?"

"A very great chance," the doctor said; "don't you know that they captured the place three years ago?"

"No, sir; I'm ashamed to say that I know nothing at all about India except that the Company have trading stations at Bombay, Madras, and Calcutta."

"I will tell you about it," the doctor said; "it is as well that you should understand the position of affairs at the place to which you are going. You must know that the Company hold the town of Madras and a few square miles of land around it as tenants of the Nawab of the Carnatic, which is the name of that part of India. The French have a station at Pondicherry, eighty-six miles to the sou'west of Madras. This is a larger and more important town than Madras, and of course the greatest rivalry prevails between the English and French. The French are much more powerful than the English and exercise a predominating influence throughout the Carnatic. The French governor, Monsieur Dupleix, is a man of very great ability and far-seeing views. He has a considerable force of French soldiers at his command, and by the aid which he has given to the nawab upon various occasions he has obtained a predominating influence in his councils.

"When war was declared between England and France in the year '44, the English squadron under Commodore Barnet was upon the coast, and the Company sent out orders to Mr. Morse, the governor of Madras, to use every effort to destroy the French settlement, of whose rising power they felt the greatest jealousy. Dupleix, seeing the force that could be brought against him, and having no French ships on the station, although he was aware that a fleet under Admiral La Bourdonnais was fitting out and would arrive shortly, dreaded the contest, and proposed to Mr. Morse that the Indian colonies of the two nations should remain neutral and take no part in the struggle in which their respective countries were engaged. Mr. Morse, however, in view of the orders he had received from the Company, was unable to agree to this. Dupleix then applied to the nawab, who at his request forbade his European tenants to make war on land with each other, an order which they were obliged to obey.

"In July, 1746, La Bourdonnais arrived with his fleet. and chased the small English squadron from the Indian seas. Dupleix now changed his tactics, and regardless of the injunction which he himself had obtained from the nawab he determined to crush the English at Madras. He supplied the fleet with men and money and ordered the admiral to sail for Madras. The fleet arrived before the town on the 14th of September, landed a portion of its troops, six hundred in number, with two guns, a short distance along the coast, and on the following day disembarked the rest, consisting of a thousand French troops, four hundred Sepoys, and three hundred African troops, and summoned Madras to surrender. Madras was in no position to offer any effectual resistance. The fort was weak and indefensible. The English inhabitants consisted only of a hundred civilians and two hundred soldiers. Governor Morse endeavored to obtain from the nawab the protection which he had before granted to Dupleix, a demand which the nawab at once refused. I was there at the time and quite agreed with the governor that it was useless to attempt resistance to the force brought against us. The governor, therefore, surrendered on the 21st. The garrison and all the civilians in the place not in the service of the Company were to become prisoners of war, while those in the regular service of the Company were free to depart, engaging only not to carry arms against the French until exchanged. These were the official conditions; but La Bourdonnais, infludence by jealousy of Dupleix, and by the promise of a bribe of forty thousands pounds, made a secret condition with Mr. Morse by which he bound himself to restore Madras in the future, upon the payment of a large sum of money. This agreement Dupleix, whose heart was set upon the total expulsion of the English, refused to ratify.

"A good many of us considered that by this breach of the agreement we were released from our parole not to carry arms against the French, and a dozen or so of us in various disguises escaped from Madras and made our way to Fort St. David, a small English settlement twelve miles south of Pondicherry. I made the journey with a young fellow named Clive, who had come out as a writer about two years before. He was a fine young fellow, as unfitted as you are, I should think, Marryat, for the dull life of a writer, but full of energy and courage. At Fort St. David we found two hundred English soldiers and a hundred Sepoys, and a number of us having nothing to do at our own work volunteered to aid in the defence.

"After Dupleix had conquered Madras, the nawab awoke to the fact of the danger of allowing the French to become all-powerful by the destruction of the English, and ordered Dupleix to restore the place. Dupleix refused, and the nawab sent his son, Maphuz Khan, to invest the town. Dupleix at once despatched a detachment of two hundred and thirty French and seven hundred Sepoys, commanded by an engineer officer named Paradis, to raise the siege. On the 2d of November the garrison of Madras sallied out and drove away the cavalry of Maphuz Khan, and on the 4th, Paradis attacked his army and totally defeated it.

"This, lads, was a memorable battle; it is the first time that European and Indian soldiers have come into contest, and it shows how immense is the superiority of Europeans. What Paradis did then, opens all sorts of possibilities for the future, and it may be that either we or the French are destined to rise from mere trading companies to be rulers of Indian states. Such, I know, is the opinion of young Clive, who is a very longheaded and ambitious young fellow. I remember his saying to me one night when we were with difficulty holding our own in the trenches, that if we had but a man of energy and intelligence at the head of our affairs in Southern India we might ere many years passed be masters of the Carnatic. I own that it appears to me more likely that the French will be in that position, and that we shall not have a single establishment left there; but time will show.

"Having defeated Maphuz Khan, Dupleix resolved to make a great effort to expel us from Fort St. David, our sole footing left in Southern India, and he despatched an army of nine hundred Frenchmen, six hundred Sepoys, and a hundred Africans, with six guns and six mortars, against us. They were four to one against us and we had hot work, I can tell you. Four times they tried to storm the place, and each time we drove them back, till at last they gave it up in disgust at the end of June, having besieged us for six months. Soon after this Admiral Boscawen with a great fleet and an army arrived from England, and on the 19th of August, besieged Pondicherry. The besieging army was six thousand strong, of whom three thousand seven hundred and twenty were English. But Pondicherry resisted bravely, and after two months the besiegers were forced to retire, having lost in attacks or by fever one thousand and sixty-five men. At the end of the siege, in which I had served as a medical officer, I returned to England. A few months after I left, peace was made between England and France, and by its terms Dupleix had to restore Madras to the English. I hear that fighting has been going on ever since, the English and French engaging as auxiliaries to rival native princes, and especially that there was some hot fighting round Davikota. However we shall hear about that when we get there."

"And what do you think will be the result of it all, Dr. Rae?"

"I think that undoubtedly sooner or later either the French or ourselves will be driven out; which it will be remains to be seen. If we are expelled, the effect of our defeat is likely to operate disastrously at Calcutta if not at Bombay. The French will be regarded as a powerful people whom it is necessary to conciliate, while we shall be treated as a nation of whom they need have no fear, and whom they can oppress accordingly. If we are successful and absolutely obtain possession of the Carnatic, our trade will vastly increase, fresh posts and commands of all sorts will be established, and there will be a fine career open to you young fellows in the service of the Company."

After rounding the Cape of Good Hope the ship encountered a series of very heavy gales, which drove her far out of her course up the eastern coast of Africa. In the last gale her foremast was carried away, and she put in to a small island to refit. She had also sprung a leak, and a number of stores were landed to enable her to be taken up into shallow water and heeled over in order that the leak might be got at.

The captain hurried on the work with all speed.

"Had it not been for this," Charlie heard him say to Mr. Ashmead, "I would have rigged a jury-mast and proceeded; but I can't stop the leak from the inside without shifting a great portion of the cargo, and our hold is so full that this would be difficult in the extreme. But I own that I do not like delaying a day longer than necessary here. The natives have a very bad reputation, besides which it is suspected that one if not more pirates have their rendezvous in these seas. Several of our merchantmen have mysteriously disappeared without any gale having taken place which would account for their loss. The captain of a ship which reached England two or three days before we sailed, brought news that when she was within a fortnight's sail of the Cape the sound of guns was heard one night, and that afterwards a ship was seen on fire low down on the horizon. He reached the spot soon after daybreak and found charred spars and other wreckage, but though he cruised about all day he could find no signs of any boats. Complaints have been made to government, and I hear that there is an intention of sending two or three sloops out here to hunt the pirates up; but that will be of no use to us."

Upon the day of their arrival at the island a native sailing boat was seen to pass across the mouth of the bay. When half across she suddenly tacked round and sailed back in the direction from which she had come.

Before proceeding to lighten the ship the captain had taken steps to put himself in a position of defence. For some distance along the centre of the bay the ground rose abruptly at a distance of some thirty yards from the shore, forming a sort of natural terrace; behind this a steep hill rose. The terrace, which was forty feet above the water level, extended for about a hundred yards, when the ground on either side of the plateau dropped away as steeply as in front. The guns were the first things taken out of the ship, and, regardless of the remonstrances of the passengers at what they considered to be a waste of time, Captain Thompson had the whole of them taken up on the terrace. A small battery was thrown up by the sailors at the two corners, and in each of these two of the thirty-two pounders were placed. The broadside guns were ranged in line along the centre of the terrace.

"Now," the captain said, when at the end of the second day the preparations were completed by the transport of a quantity of ammunition from the ship's magazine to the terrace, "I feel comfortable. We can defend ourselves here against all the pirates of the South Seas. If they don't come we shall only have lost our two days' work, and shall have easy minds for the remainder of our stay here, which we should not have had if we had been at the mercy of the first of those scoundrels who happened to hear of our being laid up."

The next morning the work of unloading the ship began, the bales and packages being lowered from the ship as they were brought up from the hold into boats alongside, and then taken to the shore and piled there at the foot of the slope. This occupied three days, and at the end of that time the greater portion of the cargo had been removed. The ship, now several feet lighter in the water than before, was brought broadside to shore until her keel touched the ground. Then the remaining cargo was shifted, and by the additional aid of tackle and purchases on shore fastened to her masts, she was heeled over until her keel nearly reached the level of the water. It was late one evening when this work was finished, and the following morning the crew were to begin to scrape her bottom, and the carpenters were to repair the leak, and the whole of the seams under water were to be corked and repitched.

Hitherto all had remained on board; but previous to the ship being heeled over, tents constructed of the sails were erected on the terrace, beds and other articles of necessity landed, and the passengers, troops and crew, took up their temporary abode there.

CHAPTER IV.

THE PIRATES OF THE PACIFIC.

A REGULAR watch was set both on the plateau and on board ship. Towards morning one of the watch on board hailed the officer above.

"I have fancied, sir, for some time that I heard noises. It seems to me like the splash of a very large number of oars."

"I have heard nothing," the officer said; "but you might hear sounds down there coming along on the water before I do. I will go down to the water's edge and listen."

He did so, and was at once convinced that the man's ears had not deceived him. Although the night was perfectly still and not a breath of wind was stirring, he heard a low rustling sound like that of the wind passing through the dried leaves of a forest in autumn.

"You are right, Johnson, there is something going on out at sea beyond the mouth of the bay. I will call the captain at once."

Captain Thompson on being aroused also went down to the water-side to listen, and at once ordered the whole party to get under arms. He requested Mr. Barlow, the young lieutenant in charge of the troops, to place half his men across each end of the plateau. The back was defended by a cliff which rose almost perpendicularly from it to a height of some hundred feet, the plateau being some thirty yards in depth from the sea face to its foot. The male passengers were requested to divide themselves in two parties, and to join the soldiers in defending the position against flank attacks. The guns were all loaded, and the sailors then set to work dragging up bales of goods from below. and placing them so as to form a sort of breastwork before the guns along the sea face.

The noise at sea had by this time greatly increased, and although it was still too dark to see what was passing, Captain Thompson said that he had no doubt whatever that the boats had one or more large ships in tow.

"Had it not been for that," he said, "they would long ago have been here. I expect that they hoped to catch us napping, but the wind fell and delayed them. They little dream how well we are prepared. Did they know of our fort here, I question whether they would have ventured upon attacking us at all, but would have waited till we were well at sea, and then our chance would have been a slight one. Well, gentlemen, you will allow that the two days were not wasted. I think now the pirates are well inside the bay. In half an hour we shall have light enough to see them. There, listen! there's the splash of their anchors. There, again! I fancy there are two ships moored broadside on, stem and stern."

All this time the work on shore had been conducted in absolute silence, and the pirates could have had no intimation that their presence was discovered. Presently against the faintly dawning light in the east the masts of two vessels could be seen. One was a large ship, the other a brig. Almost at the same time the rough sound of boats' keels grounding on the shore could be heard.

"Just as I thought," the captain whispered; "they have guessed that some of us will be ashore, and will make a rush upon us here when the ships open fire."

The word was passed along the guns that every one was to be double-shotted and that their fire was at first to be directed at the brig. They were to aim between wind and water, and strive to sink her as speedily as possible. As the light gradually grew brighter the party on the plateau anxiously watched for the moment when, the hull of the Indiaman becoming plain to the enemy, these would open fire upon it, and so give the signal for the fight. At the first alarm the tents had all been levelled, and a thick barricade of bales erected round a slight depression of the plateau at the foot of the cliff in its rear. Here the ladies were placed for shelter.

As the light increased it could be seen that in addition to the two ships were a large number of native dhows. Presently from the black side of the ship a jet of fire shot out, and at the signal a broadside was poured into the Indiaman by the two vessels. At the same moment with a hideous yell hundreds of black figures leaped to their feet on the beach and rushed towards the, as yet unseen, position of the English. The captain shouted "Fire!" and the twenty guns on the plateau poured their fire simultaneously into the side of the brig. The captain then gave orders that two of the light guns should be run along the terrace to take position on the flanks, and aid the soldiers against the attacks. This time Charlie had lent his rifle to Peters, and was himself armed with his double-barrel gun.

"Steady, boys," Mr. Hallam, the ensign who commanded the soldiers at the side where Charlie was stationed, cried; "don't fire a shot till I give the word, and then aim low."

With terrific yells the throng of natives, waving curved swords, spears, and clubs, rushed forward.

The steep ascent checked them, but they rushed up until within ten yards of the line of soldiers on its brow. Then Mr. Hallam gave the word to fire, and the soldiers and passengers poured a withering volley into them. At so short a distance the effect was tremendous. Completely swept away, the leading rank fell down among their comrades, and these for a moment recoiled. Then gathering themselves together they again rushed forward, while those in their rear discharged volleys of arrows over their heads.

Among the defenders every man now fought for himself, loading and firing as rapidly as possible. Sometimes the natives nearly gained a footing on the crest, but each time the defenders with clubbed muskets beat them back again. The combat was, however, doubtful, for their assailants were many hundred strong, when the defenders were gladdened with a shout of "Make way, my hearties. Let us come to the front and give them a dose."

In a moment two ship's guns loaded to the muzzle with bullets were run forward, and poured their contents among the crowded masses below. The effect was decisive. The natives, shaken by the resistance they had already experienced and appalled by the destruction wrought by the cannon, turned and fled along the shore, followed by the shots of the defenders, and by two more rounds of grape which the sailors poured into them before they could reach their boats. Similar success had attended the defenders of the other flank of the position, and all hands now aided in swinging round the guns which had done such good service, to enable them to bear their share in the fight with the ships. In the middle of the fight the party had heard a great cheer from those working the seaward guns, and they now saw its cause. The brig had disappeared below the water, and the sailors were now engaged in a contest with the ship. The pirates fought their guns well, but they were altogether overmatched by the twenty guns playing upon them from a commanding position. Already the dhows were hoisting their sails, and one of the cables of the ship suddenly disappeared in the water, while a number of men sprang upon the ratlins.

"Fire at the masts," Captain Thompson shouted; "cripple her if you can. Let all with muskets and rifles try to keep men out of the rigging."

The ship was anchored within three hundred yards of the shore, and although the distance was too great for anything like accurate fire, several of the men dropped as they ran up the shrouds. The sailors worked their guns with redoubled vigor, and a great shout arose as the mainmast, wounded in several places, fell over the side.

"Sweep her decks with grape," the captain shouted, "and she's ours. Mr. James, take all the men that can be spared from the guns, man the boats, and make a dash for the ship at once. I see the men are leaving her. They're crowding over the side into their boats. Most likely they'll set fire to her. Set all your strength putting it out. We will attend to the other boats."

It was evident now that the pirates were deserting the ship. They had fallen into a complete trap, and instead of the easy prey on which they calculated, found themselves crushed by the fire of a heavy battery in a commanding position. Captain Thompson, seeing that the guns of the ship were silent and that all resistance had ceased, now ordered the sailors to turn their guns on the dhows and sink as many as possible. These, crowded together in their efforts to escape, offered an easy mark for the gunners, whose shot tore through their sides smashing and sinking them in all directions. In ten minutes the last of those that floated had gained the mouth of the bay and, accompanied by the boats crowded with the crews of the two pirate vessels, made off, followed by the shot of the thirty-two pounders until they had turned the low promontory which formed the head of the bay. Long ere this Mr. James and the boats' crews had gained the vessel, and were engaged in combating the fire, which had broken out in three places.

The boats were sent back to shore and returned with Captain Thompson and the rest of the sailors, and this reinforcement soon enabled them to get the mastery of the flames. The ship was found to be the *Dover Castle*, a new and very fast ship of the Company's service, of which all traces had been lost since she left Bombay two years before. She was now painted entirely black, and a snake had been added for her figure-head. The original name, however, still remained upon the binnacle and ship's bell. Her former armament had been increased, and she now carried thirty guns, of which ten were thirty-two pounders. A subsequent search showed that her hold was stored with valuable goods, which had, by the marks upon the bales, evidently belonged to several ships which she had no doubt taken and sunk after removing the pick of their cargoes.

The prize was a most valuable one, and the captain felt that the board of directors would be highly delighted at the recovery of their ship, and still more by the destruction of the two bands of pirates. The deck of the ship was thickly strewn with dead. Among them was the body of a man who by his dress was evidently the captain. From some of the pirates who still lived, Captain Thompson learned that the brig was the original pirate, that she had captured the *Dover Castle*, that from her and subsequent prizes they had obtained sufficient hands to man both ships, all who refused to join being compelled to walk the plank. These were the only two pirate ships in those seas, so far as the men knew. Their rendezvous was at a large native town on the mainland, at the mouth of a river three days' sail distant. The news of the Indiaman being laid up refitting at the island was brought by the native craft they had seen on the day after their arrival, and upon its being known the natives had insisted in joining in the attack. The pirate captain, whose interest it was to keep well with them, could not refuse to allow them to join, although he would gladly have dispensed with their aid, believing his own force to be far more than sufficient to capture the vessel, which he supposed to be lying an easy prize at his hands.

Another ten days were spent in getting the cargo and guns on board the *Lizzie Anderson*, and in fitting out both ships for sea. Then Mr. James and a portion of the crew being placed on board the prize, they sailed together for India. The *Dover Castle* proved to be much the faster sailor, but Captain Thompson ordered her to reduce sail and to keep about a mile in his wake, as she could at any time close up when necessary; and the two together would be able to oppose a determined front even to a French frigate, should they meet with one on their way.

The voyage passed without incident, save that when rounding the southern point of Ceylon a sudden squall from the land struck them. The vessel heeled over suddenly, and a young soldier who was sitting on the bulwarks to leeward was jerked backwards and fell into the water. Charlie Marryat was on the quarter-deck, leaning against the rail, watching a shoal of flying-fish passing at a short distance. In the noise and confusion caused by the sudden squall, the creaking of cordage, the flapping of sails, and the shouts of the officers to let go the sheets, the fall of the soldier was unnoticed, and Charlie was startled by perceiving in the water below him the figure of a struggling man. He saw at once that he was unable to swim. Without an instant's hesitation Charlie threw off his coat and kicked off his shoes, and with a loud shout of "Man overboard!" sprang from the taffrail and with a few vigorous strokes was alongside the drowning man. He seized him by the collar and held him at a distance. "Now," he said, "don't struggle, else I'll let you go. Keep quiet and I can hold you up till we're picked up."

In spite of the injunction the man strove to grasp him, but Charlie at once let go his hold and swam a pace back as the man sunk. When he came up he seized him again, and again shouted, "Keep quite quiet, else I'll leave go."

This time the soldier obeyed him, and turning him on his back and keeping his face above water, Charlie looked around at the vessel he had left. The Indiaman was still in confusion. The squall had been sudden and strong. The sheets had been let go, the canvas was flapping in the wind, and the hands were aloft reducing sail. She was already some distance away from him. The sky was bright and clear, and Charlie, who was surprised at seeing no attempt to lower a boat, saw a signal run up to the masthead. Looking the other way he saw at once why no boat had been lowered. The *Dover Castle* was but a quarter of a mile astern. Carrying less sail than her consort, she had been better prepared for the squall, and was running down upon him at a great rate. A moment later a boat was swung out on davits and several men climbed into it. The vessel kept on her course until scarcely more than her own length away. Then she suddenly rounded up into the wind, and the boat was let fall and rowed rapidly towards him.

All this time Charlie had made no effort beyond what was necessary to keep his own head and his companion's face above the water. He now lifted the soldier's head up, and shouted to him that aid was at hand. In another minute they were dragged into the boat. This was soon alongside the ship, and three minutes later the *Dover Castle* was pursuing her course in the track of the *Lizzie Anderson*, having signalled that the pair had been rescued. Charlie found that the soldier was an Irish lad of some nineteen years old. His name, he said, was Tim Kelly, and as soon as he had recovered himself sufficiently to speak he was profuse in his professions of gratitude to his preserver. Tim, like the majority of the recruits in the Company's service, had been enlisted while in a state of drunkenness, had been hurried on board a guard-ship, where, when he recovered, he found a number of other unfortunates like himself. He had not been permitted to communicate with his friends on shore, but had been kept in close confinement until he had been put in uniform and conveyed on board the *Lizzie Anderson* half an hour before she sailed. The Company's service was not a popular one. There was no fighting in India, and neither honor, glory, nor promotion to be won. The climate was unsuited to Europeans, and few indeed of those who sailed from England as soldiers in the Company's service ever returned. The Company then were driven to all sorts of straits to keep up even the small force which they then maintained in India, and their recruiting agents were by no means particular as to the means they employed to make up the tale of recruits.

The vessels did not again communicate until they came to anchor in Madras roads, as the wind was fair and Captain Thompson anxious to arrive at his destination. During these few days Tim Kelly had followed Charlie about like a shadow. Having no duties to perform on board, he asked leave to act as Charlie's servant; and Charlie was touched by the efforts which the grateful fellow made to be of service to him. Upon their arrival they saw to their satisfaction that the British flag was waving over the low line of earthworks which constitute the British fort. Not far from this, near the water's edge, stood the white houses and stores of the Company's factors and behind these again were the low hovels of the black town. The prospect was not an inviting one, and Charlie wondered how on earth a landing was to be effected through the tremendous surf which broke upon the shore. He soon found that until the wind went down and the surf moderated somewhat, no communication could be effected. The next morning, however, the wind lulled, and a crowd of curious native boats were seen putting off from the shore.

Charlie had, after the vessel anchored, rejoined his ship with Tim Kelly, and he now bade good-bye to all on board; for only the doctor, two civilians, and the troops were destined for Madras, all the rest going on in the ship to Calcutta, after she had discharged that portion of her cargo intended for Madras. Charlie had during the last twelve hours been made a great deal of, on account of the gallantry he had displayed in risking his life for that of the soldier. Peters and one of the other young writers were also to land, and taking his seat with these in a native boat, paddled by twelve canoe men, he started for the shore. As they approached the line of surf Charlie fairly held his breath, for it seemed impossible that the boat could live through it. The boatmen, however, ceased rowing outside the line of broken water, and lay on their paddles for three or four minutes. At last a wave larger than any of its predecessors was seen approaching. As it passed under them the steersman gave a shout. In an instant the rowers struck their paddles into the water and the boat dashed along with the speed of a racehorse on the crest of the wave. There was a crash. For a moment the boat seemed to the lads engulfed in white foam, and then she ran high up upon the beach. The rowers seized the boys and leaping out carried them beyond the reach of the water before the next wave broke upon them, and then triumphantly demanded a present for their skilful management. This the lads were glad to give, for they considered that their escape had been something miraculous.

For a while they stood on the shore watching other boats with the soldiers and baggage coming ashore, and then being accosted by a gentleman in the employment of the Company, followed him to the residence of the chief factor. Here they were told that rooms would be given them in one of the houses erected by the Company for the use of its employés, that they would mess with the other clerks residing in the same house, and that at nine o'clock in the morning they would report themselves as ready for work.

Charlie and his friends amused themselves by sauntering about in the native town, greatly surprised by the sights and scenes which met their eyes; for in those days very little was known of India in England. They were, however, greatly disappointed. Visions of oriental splendor, of palaces and temples, of superbly dressed chiefs with bands of gorgeous retainers had floated before their mind's eye. Instead of this they saw squalid huts, men dressed merely with a rag of cotton around them, everywhere signs of squalor and poverty. Madras, however, they were told that evening, was not to be taken as a sample of India. It was a mere collection of huts which had sprung up round the English factories. But when they went to a real Indian city they would see a very different state of things.

CHAPTER V.

MADRAS.

AFTER the young writers had seen the native town they returned to the beach and spent the afternoon watching the progress of landing the cargo of the *Lizzie Anderson*. They were pleased to see their own luggage safely ashore, as it would have been greatly damaged had the boat containing it been swamped, a misfortune which happened to several of the boats laden with cargo. It was very amusing each time that one of these boats arrived to see a crowd of natives rush down into the water waist deep, seize it and drag it up beyond the next wave. Many of them would be knocked down, and some swept out by the retreating wave, only to return on the next roller. All could swim like fish, and any of these events were greeted with shouts of laughter by the rest. When the packages were landed a rope was put around them, and through this a long bamboo pole was inserted, which would be lifted on to the shoulders of two, four, or six porters, according to its weight, and these would go off at a hobbling sort of trot with their burden to the factory. Their own baggage was taken up to the quarters allotted to them, and at the hour named for dinner the new-comers met for the first time those with whom they were to be associated.

All were dressed in white suits, and Charlie was

struck with the pallor of their faces and the listless air of most of them. The gentleman to whom they had first been introduced made them acquainted with the others.

"How refreshingly healthy and well you look!" a young man of some six-and-twenty years old, named Johnson, said. "I was something like that when I first came out here, though you'd hardly think it now. Eight years of stewing in this horrible hole takes the life and spirits out of anyone. However, there's one consolation, after eight or ten years of quill-driving in a stuffy room one becomes a little more one's own master, and one's duties begin to be a little more varied and pleasant. One gets a chance of being sent up occasionally with goods or on some message or other to one of the native princes and then one gets treated like a prince, and sees that India is not necessarily so detestable as we have contrived to make it here. The only bearable time of one's life is the few hours after dinner, when one can sit in a chair in the veranda and smoke and look at the sea. Some of the fellows play billiards and cards; but if you will take my advice you won't go in for that sort of thing. It takes a lot out of one, and fellows that do it are, between you and me, in the bad books of the big-wigs. Besides, they lose money, get into debt, and all sorts of mischief comes of it."

The speaker was sitting between Charlie and Peters, and was talking in a tone of voice which would not be overheard by the others.

"Thank you," Charlie said. "I for one will certainly take your advice. I suppose one can buy ponies here. I should think a good ride every morning early, before work, would do one good."

Yes, it is not a bad thing," Johnson said. A good many fellows do it when they first come out here; but after a time they lose their energy, you see, though some do keep it up. What appetites you fellows have! It does one good to see you eat."

"I have not the least idea what we are eating," Charlie said laughing; "but it's really very nice whatever it is. But there seems an immense quantity of pepper, or hot stuff of some kind or other, which one would have thought, in this tremendous heat, would have made one hotter instead of cooler."

"Yes," their new friend answered. "No doubt all this pepper and curry do heat the blood; but you see it is done to tempt the appetite. Meat here is fearfully coarse and tasteless. Our appetites are poor, and were it not for these hot sauces we should eat next to nothing. Will you have some bananas?"

"They are nice and cool," Peters said as, having peeled the long fruit as he saw his companion doing, he took a bite of one; "but they have very little taste."

"Most of our fruit is tasteless," Johnson said, "except, indeed, the mango and mangostine. They are equal to any English fruit in flavor, but I would give them all for a good English apple. Its sharpness would be delicious here; and now, as you have done, if you will come and sit in the veranda of my room we will smoke a cigar and have something cool to drink, and I will answer as well as I can the questions you've asked me about the state of things here."

When they had seated themselves in the extremely comfortable cane chairs in a veranda, facing the sea, and had lit their cigars, their friend began:

"Madras isn't much of a place now; but you should have seen it before the French had it. Our chiefs think of nothing but trade, and care nothing how squalid and miserable is the place in which they make money. The French have larger ideas. They transformed this place, cleared away that portion of the native town which surrounded the factory and fort, made wide roads, formed an esplanade, improved and strengthened the fortifications, forbade the natives to throw all their rubbish and offal on the beach, and made, in fact, a decent place of it. We hardly knew it when we came back, and whatever the Company may have thought, we were thoroughly grateful for the French occupation. One good result, too, is that our quarters have been greatly improved; for not only did the French build several new houses, but at present all the big men, the council and so on, are still living at Fort St. David, which is still the seat of administration. So you see we have got better quarters; we are rid of the stenches and nuisances of the native town; the plague of flies which made our life a burden is abated; and we can sit here and enjoy the cool sea breeze without its being poisoned before it reaches us by the heaped-up filth on the beach. It must have wrung Dupleix's heart to give up the place over which they expended so much pains, and after all it didn't do away with the fighting. In April we sent a force from Fort St. David—before we came back here,—four hundred and thirty white soldiers and a thousand Sepoys, under the command of Captain Cope, to aid a fellow who had been turned out of the rajahship of Tanjore. I believe he was a great blackguard, and the man who had taken his place was an able ruler liked by the people."

"Then why should we interfere on behalf of the other?" Charlie asked.

"My dear Marryat," their host said compassionately, "you are very young yet, and quite new to India. You will see after a time that right has nothing at all to do with the dealings of the Company in their relations to the native princes. We are at present little people living here on sufferance among a lot of princes and powers who are enemies and rivals of each other. We have, moreover, as neighbors another European colony considerably stronger than we are. The consequence is, the question of right cannot enter into the considerations of the Company. It may be said that for every petty kingdom in Southern India there are at least two pretenders, very often half a dozen. So far we have not meddled much in their quarrels, but the French have been much more active that way. They always side with one or other of these pretenders, and when they get the man they support into power, of course he repays them for their assistance. In this manner, as I shall explain to you presently, they have virtually made themselves masters of the Carnatic outside the walls of Fort St. David, and this place.

"Well, our people thought to take a leaf out of the French book, and as the ex-rajah offered us in payment for our aid the possession of Devikota, a town at the mouth of the river Kolrun, a place likely to be of great use to us, we agreed to assist him. Cope with the land forces had marched to the border of the Tanjore territory, and the guns and heavy baggage were to go by sea; but, unfortunately, we had a tremendous gale just after they sailed. The admiral's flag-ship, the *Namur*, of seventy-four guns, the *Pembroke*, of sixty, and the hospital ship, *Apollo*, were totally lost, and the rest of the fleet scattered in all directions. Cope entered the Tanjore territory, but found the whole population attached to the new rajah. It was useless for him, therefore, to march upon Tanjore, which is a really strong town, so he marched down to Devikota, where he hoped to find some of the fleet. Not a ship, however, was to be seen, and as without guns Cope could do nothing, he returned here, as we had just taken possession again.

"Then he went to Fort St. David, and there was a great discussion among the big-wigs. It was clear from what Cope said that our man had not a friend in his own country. Still, as he pointed out, Devikota was a most important place for us. Neither Madras nor Fort St. David has a harbor, and Devikota, therefore, where the largest ships could run up the river and anchor, would be of immense utility to us. As this was really the reason for which we had gone into the affair it was decided to repeat the attempt. By this time Major Lawrence, who commands the whole of the Company's forces in India, and who had been taken a prisoner in one of the French sorties at the siege of Pondicherry, has been released, so he was put at the head of the expedition, and the whole of the Company's English troops, eight hundred in all, including the artillery, and fifteen hundred Sepoys, started on board ship for Devikota. I must tell you that Lawrence is a first-rate fellow, the only really good officer we have out here, and the affair couldn't have been in the hands of a better man.

"The ships arrived safely at the mouth of the Kolrun, and the troops were landed on the bank of the river opposite the town, where Lawrence intended to erect his batteries, as, in the first place, the shore behind the town was swampy, and in the second the Rajah of Tanjore, who had got news of our coming, had his army encamped there to support the place. Lawrence got his guns in position and fired away, across the river, at the earthen wall of the town. In three days he had a breach. The enemy didn't return our fire, but occupied themselves in throwing up an entrenchment across the side of the fort. We made a raft and crossed the river, but the enemy's matchlock men peppered us so severely that we lost thirty English and fifty Sepoys in getting over. The enemy's entrenchment was not finished, but in front of it was a deep rivulet which had to be crossed.

"Lawrence gave the command of the storming party to Clive. He is one of our fellows, a queer, restless sort of chap, who was really no good here, for he hated his work and always seemed to think himself a martyr. He was not a favorite among us, for he was often gloomy and discontented, though he had his good points. He was straightforward and manly, and he put down two or three fellows here who had been given to bully the young ones, in a way that astonished them. He would never have made a good servant of the Company, for he so hated his work that when he had been out here about a year he tried to blow out his brains. He snapped the pistol twice at his head, but it didn't go off though it was loaded all right. Strange, wasn't it? So he came to the conclusion that he wasn't meant to kill himself, and went on living till something should turn up."

"Yes," Charlie said; "Dr. Rae spoke to us about him during the voyage. He knew him at the siege of Fort St. David, and Pondicherry."

"Yes," Johnson said. "He came out there quite in a new light. He got transferred into the military service, and was always in the middle of the fighting. Major Lawrence had a very high opinion of him, and so selected him to lead the storming party. It really seems almost as if he had a charmed life. Lawrence gave him thirty-three English soldiers and seven hundred Sepoys. The rest of the force were to follow as soon as Clive's party gained the entrenchments. Clive led the way with his Europeans, with the Sepoys supporting behind, and got across the rivulet with a loss of only four men. He waited on the other bank till he saw the Sepoys climbing up, and then again led the English on in advance towards the unfinished part of the entrenchment. The Sepoys, however, did not move, but remained waiting for the main body to come up. The enemy let Clive and his twenty-nine men get on some distance in advance, and then their cavalry, who had been hidden by a projec-

CLIVE LEADING THE STORMING PARTY AT DEVIKOTA.

tion of the fort, charged suddenly down on him. They were upon our men before they had time to form, and in a minute twenty-six of them were cut to pieces. Clive and the other three managed to get through the Tanjore horsemen and rejoin the Sepoys. That was almost as narrow a shave for his life as with the pistol. Lawrence now crossed with his main body and advanced.

"Again the Tanjore horsemen charged; but this time we were prepared, and Lawrence let them come on till within a few yards, and then gave them a volley which killed fourteen and sent the rest scampering away. Lawrence pushed forward. The garrison, panic-stricken at the defeat of their cavalry, abandoned the breach and escaped to the opposite side of the town, and Devikota was ours. A few days later we captured the fortified temple of Uchipuran. A hundred men were left there, and these were afterwards attacked by the Rajah of Tanjore with five thousand men, but they held their own and beat them off. A very gallant business that! These affairs showed the rajah that the English could fight, a point which, hitherto, the natives had been somewhat sceptical about. They were afraid of the French, but they looked upon us as mere traders. He had, too, other things to trouble him as to the state of the Carnatic, and so hastened to make peace. He agreed to pay the expenses of the war, and to cede us Devikota and some territory round it, and to allow the wretched ex-rajah, in whose cause we had pretended to fight, a pension of four hundred a year, on condition that we kept him shut up in one of our forts. Not a very nice business on our side, was it? Still we had gained our point, and, with the exception of the ex-rajah, who was a bad lot after all, no one was discontented.

"When the peace was signed our force returned to Fort St. David. While they had been away there had been a revolution in the Carnatic. Now this was rather a complicated business; but as the whole situation at present turns upon it, and it will not improbably cause our expulsion from Southern India, I will explain it to you as well as I can. Now you must know that all Southern India, with the exception of a strip along the west coast, is governed by a viceroy, appointed by the emperor at Delhi. He was called the Subadar of the Deccan. Up till the end of 'forty-eight Nizam Ul-Mulk was viceroy. About that time he died, and the emperor appointed his grandson, Muzaffar Jung, who was the son of a daughter of his, to succeed him. But the subadar had left five sons. Four of these lived at Delhi, and were content to enjoy their life there. The second son, however, Nazir Jung, was an ambitious man, who had rebelled even against his father. Naturally he rebelled against his nephew. He was on the spot when his father died while the new subadar was absent. Nazir, therefore, seized the reins of government and all the resources of the state. The emperor has troubles enough of his own at Delhi, and Muzaffar had no hope of aid from him. He therefore went to Satarah, the court of the Marattas, to ask for their assistance. There he met Chunda Sahib. This man was the nephew of the last nawab of the Carnatic, Dost Ali. Dost Ali had been killed in a battle with them in 1739; and they afterwards captured Trichinopoli, and took Chunda Sahib, who commanded there, prisoner, and had since kept him at Satarah. Had he been at liberty he would no doubt have succeeded his uncle, whose only son had been murdered; but as he was at Satarah the Subadar of the Deccan bestowed the government of the Carnatic upon Anwarud-din.

"Chunda Sahib and Muzaffar Jung put their heads together and agreed to act in concert. Muzaffar, of course, desired the subadarship of the Deccan, to which he had been appointed by the court of Delhi. Chunda Sahib wanted the nawabship of the Carnatic, and advised his ally to abandon his intention of asking for Maratta aid, and to ally himself with the French. A correspondence ensued with Dupleix, who, seeing the immense advantage it would be to him to gain what would virtually be the position of patron and protector of the Subadar of the Deccan and the Nawab of the Carnatic, at once agreed to join them. Muzaffar raised thirty thousand men, and Chunda Sahib six thousand--it is always easy in India to raise an army with a certain amount of money and lavish promises—marched down and joined a French force of four hundred strong, commanded by D'Auteuil. The nawab advanced against them, but was utterly defeated at Ambur, the French doing pretty well the whole of the work. The nawab was killed, and one of his sons, Maphuz Khan, taken prisoner. The other, Muhummud Ali, bolted at the beginning of the fight. Arcot, the capital of the Carnatic, surrendered next day.

"Muzaffar Jung proclaimed himself Subadar of the Deccan, and appointed Chunda Sahib Nawab of the Carnatic. Muzaffar Jung conferred upon Dupleix the sovereignty of eighty-one villages adjoining the French territory. Muzaffar, after paying a visit to Pondicherry, remained in the camp with his army, twenty miles distant from that place. Chunda Sahib remained as the guest of Dupleix at Pondicherry.

"On the receipt of the news of the battle of Ambur, Mr. Floyer, who is governor at Fort St. David, sent at once to Chunda Sahib to acknowledge him as nawab, which, in the opinion of every one here, was a very foolish step. Muhummud Ali had fled to Trichinopoli, and sent word to Mr. Floyer that he could hold the place, and even reconquer the Carnatic, if the English would assist him. I know that Admiral Boscawen, who was with the fleet at Fort St. David, urged Mr.

Floyer to do so, as it was clear that Chunda Sahib would be a mere tool in the hands of the French. When Chunda Sahib delayed week after week at Pondicherry, Mr. Floyer began to hesitate, but he could not make up his mind, and Admiral Boscawen, who had received orders to return home, could no longer act in contravention to them, and was obliged to sail.

"The instant the fleet had left, and we remained virtually defenceless, Chunda Sahib, supplied with troops and money by Dupleix, marched out from Pondicherry and joined Muzaffar Jung with the avowed intention of marching upon Trichinopoli. Had he done this at once he must have taken the place, and it was a question of weeks and days only of our being turned altogether out of Southern India. Nothing, indeed, could have saved us. Muzaffar Jung and Chunda Sahib, however, disregarding the plan which Dupleix had marked out for them, resolved, before marching on Trichinopoli, to conquer Tanjore, which is the richest city in Southern India. The rajah had only a few weeks before made peace with us, and he now sent messengers to Nazir Jung, Muzaffar's rival in the Deccan, and to the English, imploring their assistance. Both parties resolved at once to grant it, for alone both must have been overwhelmed by the alliance between the two Indian princes and the French, and their only hope of a successful resistance to this combination was in saving Trichinopoli.

"The march of these allies upon Tanjore opened the road to Trichinopoli, and Captain Cope with a hundred and twenty men were at once despatched to reinforce Muhammud Ali's garrison. Of this little force he sent off twenty men to the aid of the Rajah of Tanjore, and these under cover of the night, passed through the lines of the besiegers and into the city, which was strongly fortified and able to stand a long siege. The English at once entered into a treaty with

Nazir Jung, promising him six hundred English troops to assist him in maintaining his sovereignty of the Deccan, and in aiding to place Muhammud Ali in the nawabship of the Carnatic. Tanjore held out bravely. For some weeks the rajah had thrown dust in the eyes of Chunda Sahib by pretending to negotiate. Then when the allies attacked he defended the city for fifty-two days, at the end of which one of the gates of the town had been captured, and the city was virtually at the mercy of the besiegers; he again delayed them by entering into negotiations for surrender. In vain Dupleix continued to urge Chunda Sahib to act energetically and to enter Tanjore.

"Chunda Sahib, however, although he has a good head for planning, is irresolute in action. His troops were discontented at the want of pay. The French contingent also was demoralized from the same cause. The troops feared to engage in a desperate struggle in the streets of a town abounding with palaces, each of which was virtually a fortress, especially as it was known that Nazir Jung was marching with all speed to fall upon their rear. So at last the siege was broken up, and the army fell back upon Pondicherry.

"Meanwhile Cope's detachment of a hundred men, with six thousand native horsemen, escorted Muhammud Ali to join Nazir Jung at Valdaur, fifteen miles from Pondicherry. Lawrence was busy at work at Fort St. David, organizing a force to go to his aid. Dupleix saw that it was necessary to aid his allies energetically. The army on its return from the siege of Tanjore was reorganized, the French contingent increased to two thousand men, and a supply of money furnished from his private means.

"The army set out to attack Nazir Jung and his ally at Valdaur. When the battle began, however, the French contingent mutinied and refused to fight; and the natives, panic-stricken by the desertion of their allies, fell back on Pondicherry. Chunda Sahib accompanied his men, Muzaffar Jung surrendered to his uncle, the usurper. In three or four days the discipline of the French army was restored, and on the 13th of April it attacked and defeated a detachment of Nazir Jung's army, and a few days later captured the strong temple of Tiruvadi, sixteen miles from Fort St. David.

"Some months passed before the French were completely prepared; but on September the first, D'Auteuil, who commanded the French, and Chunda Sahib attacked the army of the native princes, twenty thousand strong, and defeated it utterly, the French not losing a single man. Muhammud Ali, with only two attendants, fled to Arcot, and the victory rendered Chunda Sahib virtual master of the Carnatic. Muzaffar Jung, after his surrender to his uncle, had been loaded with chains, and remained a prisoner in the camp, where, however he managed to win over several of the leaders of his uncle's army. Gingee was stormed by a small French force, and the French officer there entered into a correspondence with the conspirators, and it was arranged that when the French army attacked Nazir Jung these should declare against him.

"On the 15th December the French commander, with eight hundred Europeans, three thousand Sepoys, and ten guns, marched against Nazir Jung, whose army of twenty-five thousand men opposed him. These. however, he defeated easily. While the battle was going on, the conspirators murdered Nazir Jung, released Muzaffar Jung, and saluted him as subadar. His escape was a fortunate one, for his uncle had ordered him to be executed that very day. Muzaffar Jung proceeded to Pondicherry, where he was received with great honors. He nominated Dupleix Nawab of the Carnatic and neighboring countries, with

Chunda Sahib as his deputy, conferred the highest dignities upon him, and granted the French possession of all the lands and forts they had conquered. He arranged with Dupleix a plan for common action, and agreed that a body of French troops should remain permanently at his capital."

CHAPTER VI.

THE ARRIVAL OF CLIVE.

"I HAVE nearly brought down the story to the present time," Mr. Johnson said. "One event has taken place, however, which was of importance. Muzaffar Jung set out for Hyderabad accompanied by a French contingent under Bussy. On the way the chiefs who had conspired against Nazir Jung mutinied against his successor. Muzaffar charged them with his cavalry; two of the three chief conspirators were killed, and while pursuing the third Muzaffar was himself killed. Bussy at once released from confinement a son of Nazir Jung, proclaimed him Subadar of the Deccan, escorted him to Hyderabad, and received from him the cession of considerable fresh grants of territory to the French. The latter were now everywhere triumphant, and Trichinopoli and Tanjore were, with the three towns held by the English, the sole places which resisted their authority. Muhammud Ali deeming further resistance hopeless had already opened negotiations with Dupleix for the surrender of Trichinopoli. Dupleix agreed to his conditions; but when Muhammud Ali found that Count Bussy with the flower of the French force had been despatched to Hyderabad, he gained time by raising fresh demands which would require the ratification of the subadar.

"Luckily for us Mr. Floyer had been recalled and

his place taken by Mr. Saunders, who is, every one says, a man of common sense and determination. Muhammud Ali urged upon him the necessity for the English to make common cause with him against the enemy, for if Trichinopoli fell it would be absolutely impossible for the English to resist the French and their allies. Early this year, then, Mr. Saunders assured him that he should be assisted with all our strength, and Muhammud Ali thereupon broke off the negotiations with the French. Most unfortunately for us Major Lawrence had gone home to England on sick leave. Captain Gingen, who now commands our troops, is a wretched substitute for him; Captain Cope is no better.

"Early this year Mr. Saunders sent Cope with two hundred and eighty English and three hundred Sepoys to Trichinopoli. Benefiting by the delay which was caused before Dupleix, owing to the absence of his best troops at Hyderabad, could collect an army, Cope laid siege to Madura, but was defeated and had to abandon his guns. Three thousand of Muhammud Ali's native troops thereupon deserted to the enemy. The cause of the English now appeared lost. Dupleix planted the white flags, emblems of the authority of France, in the fields within sight of Fort St. David. With immense efforts Mr. Saunders put into the field five hundred English troops, a thousand Sepoys, a hundred Africans, and eight guns under the command of Captain Gingen, whose orders were to follow the movements of the army with which D'Auteuil and Chunda Sahib were marching against Trichinopoli.

"Luckily Chunda Sahib, instead of doing so at once, moved northwards to confirm his authority in the towns of North and South Arcot, and to raise additional levies. Great delay was caused by this. On arriving before the important fortress of Valkonda,

Chunda Sahib found before it the troops of Captain Gingen, who had been reinforced by sixteen hundred troops from Trichinopoli. The governor of the place not knowing which party was the stronger, refused to yield to either, and for a fortnight the armies lay at a short distance from each other, near the fortress, with whose governor both continued their negotiations. Gingen then lost patience and attacked the place, but was repulsed, and the governor at once admitted the French within the fortress. The next day the main body of the French attacked us, the guns of the fortress opening fire upon us at the same time. Our men, a great portion of whom were recruits just joined from England, fell into a panic and bolted, abandoning their allies and leaving their guns, ammunition, and stores in the hands of the enemy. Luckily D'Auteuil was laid up with gout. If he had pressed on there remained only the two or three hundred men under Cope to offer the slightest resistance. Trichinopoli must have fallen at once, and we, without a hundred soldiers here, should have had nothing to do but pack up and go. As it was, Gingen's beaten men were allowed to retreat quietly towards Trichinopoli.

"The next day D'Auteuil was better and followed in pursuit, and Gingen had the greatest difficulty in reaching Trichinopoli. There at the present moment we lie shut up, a portion of our force only remaining outside the walls. The place itself is strong. The town lies round a lofty rock on which stands the fortress, which commands the country for some distance round. Still there is no question that the French could take it if they attacked it. Our men are utterly dispirited with defeat. Cope and Gingen have neither enterprise nor talent. At present the enemy, who are now under the command of Colonel Law, who has succeeded D'Auteuil, are contenting themselves with beleaguering the place. But as we have no troops whatever to send to its rescue, and Muhammud Ali has no friends elsewhere to whom to look for aid, it is a matter of absolute certainty that the place must fall, and then Dupleix will only have to request us to leave, and we shall have nothing else to do but to go at once. So I should advise you not to trouble yourself to unpack your luggage, for in all probability another fortnight will see us on board ship.

"There, that's a tremendous long yarn I've been telling you, and not a pleasant one. It's a history of defeat, loss of prestige and position. We have been out-fought and out-diplomatized, and have made a mess of everything we put our hand to. I should think you must be tired of it. I am; I haven't done so much talking for years."

Charlie and Peters thanked their new acquaintance warmly for the pains he had taken in explaining the various circumstances and events which had led to the present unfortunate position, and Charlie asked, as they stood up to say good-night to Mr. Johnson, "What has become of Clive all this time?"

"After the conquest of Devikota," Mr. Johnson said, "the civilians in the service were called back to their posts; but to show that they recognized his services the authorities allowed Clive to attain the rank of captain, which would have been bestowed upon him had he remained in the military service, and they appointed him commissary to the army, a post which would take him away from the office-work he hated. Almost directly afterwards he got a bad attack of fever and was forced to take a cruise in the Bay of Bengal. He came back in time to go with Gingen's force; but after the defeat of Valkonda he resigned his office, I suppose in disgust, and returned to Fort St. David. In July some of the Company's ships came in with some reinforcements. There were no military officers left at Fort St. David, so Mr. Pigct, a member of the council, started with a large convoy of stores, escorted by eighty English and three hundred Sepoys. Clive volunteered to accompany them. They had to march thirty or forty miles to Verdachelam, a town close to the frontier of Tanjore, through which the convoy to Trichinopoli would be able to pass unopposed, but the intervening country was hostile to the English. However, the convoy passed unmolested, and after seeing it safely to that point Pigot and Clive set out to return with an escort of twelve Sepoys. They were at once attacked, and for miles a heavy fire was kept up on them. Seven of the escort were killed, the rest reached Fort St. David in safety. Pigot's report of Clive's conduct, strengthened by that previously made by Major Lawrence, induced the authorities to transfer him permanently to the army. He received a commission as captain and was sent off, with a small detachment remaining at St. David's to Devikota. There he placed himself under Captain Clarke, who commanded, and the whole body, numbering altogether a hundred English, fifty Sepoys, with a small field-piece, marched up to Trichinopoli, and I hear managed to make its way in safety. He got in about a month ago."

"And what force have we altogether, here and at St. David's, in case Trichinopoli falls?"

"What with the detachment that came with you, and two others which arrived about ten days back, we have altogether about three hundred and fifty men. What on earth could these do against all the force of the nawab, the subadar, and three or four thousand French troops?"

The prospect certainly seemed gloomy in the extreme, and the young writers retired to their beds on this the first night of their arrival in India, with the conviction that circumstances were in a desperate position. The next day they set to work, and at its end agreed that they should bear the loss of their situations, and their expulsion from the country, with more than resignation. It was now August, the heat was terrible, and as they sat in their shirt-sleeves at their desks, bathed in perspiration, at their work of copying invoices, they felt that any possible change of circumstances would be for the better. The next day, and the next, still further confirmed these ideas. The nights were nearly as hot as the days. Tormented by mosquitos they tossed restlessly in their beds for hours, dozing off towards morning and awaking unrefreshed and worn out.

When released from work at the end of the third day Charlie and Peters strolled down together to the beach and bewailed their hard fate. "There are two ships coming from the south," Charlie said presently. "I wonder whether they're from England or Fort St. David!"

"Which do you hope they will be?" Peters said.

"I hope they're from St. David's," Charlie answered. "Even if they made a quick voyage they couldn't have left England many weeks after us, and although I should be glad to get news from home, I am still more anxious just at present for news from St. David's. Between ourselves I long to hear of the fall of Trichinopoli. Everyone says it is certain to take place before long, and the sooner it does the sooner we shall be out of this frightful place."

After dinner they again went down to the beach and were joined by Dr. Rae, who chatted with them as to the ships, which were now just anchoring. These had already signalled that they were from St. David's, and that they had on board Mr. Saunders the governor and a detachment of troops. Already the soldiers from the *Lizzie Anderson*, aided by a number of natives, were at work pitching tents in the fort for the reception of the new-comers, and conjecture was busy on shore among the civilians as to the object of bringing troops from St. David's to Madras, that is, directly away from the scene of action.

"It is one of two things," Dr. Rae said: "either Trichinopoli has surrendered and they are evacuating Fort St. David, or they have news that the nawab is marching to attack us here. I should think it to be the latter, for Fort St. David is a great deal stronger than this place, though the French did strengthen it during their stay here. If, then, the authorities have determined to abandon one of the two towns, and to concentrate all their force for the defence of the other, I should have thought they would have held on to St. David's. There is a boat being lowered from one of the ships, so we shall soon have news."

A signal from the ship announced that the governor was about to land, and the principal persons at the factory assembled on the beach to receive him. Dr. Rae and the two young writers stood a short distance from the party. As the boat was beached Mr. Saunders sprang out and, surrounded by those assembled to meet him, walked at once towards the factory. An officer got out from the boat and superintended the debarkation of the baggage, which a number of coolies at once placed on their heads and carried away. The officer was following them when his eye fell upon Dr. Rae. "Ah! Doctor," he said, "how are you? When did you get out again from England?"

"Only three or four days since, Captain Clive. I did not recognize you at first. I am glad to see you again."

"Yes, I have cast my slough," Captain Clive said laughing, "and have, thank God, exchanged my pen for a sword, for good."

"You were able to fight, though, as a civilian," Dr. Rae said laughing.

"Yes, we had some tough fighting behind the ramparts of St. David's and in the trenches before Pondicherry; but we shall have sharper work still before us, or I am mistaken."

"What! are they going to attack us here?" Dr. Rae exclaimed.

"Oh no, just the other way," Captain Clive said; "we are going to carry the war into their quarters. It is a secret yet, and must not go farther." And he included the two writers in his look.

"These are two fresh comers, Captain Clive. They came out in the same ship with me. This is Mr. Marryat, this Mr. Peters. They are both brave young gentlemen, and had an opportunity of proving it on the way out, for we were twice engaged. The first time with privateers; the second, a very sharp affair, with pirates. That ship lying off there is a pirate we captured."

"Aha!" Captain Clive said, looking keenly at the lads. "Well, young gentlemen, and how do you like what you have seen of your life here?"

"We hate it, sir," Charlie said; "we would both of us a thousand times rather enlist under you as private soldiers. Oh, sir, if there is any expedition going to take place, do you think there is a chance of our being allowed to go as volunteers?"

"I will see about it," Captain Clive said, smiling. "Trade must be dull enough here at present, and we want every hand that can hold a sword or a musket in the field. You are sure you can recommend them?" he said, turning to Dr. Rae with a smile.

"Most warmly," the doctor said; "they both showed great coolness and courage in the affairs I spoke of. Have you any surgeons with you, Captain Clive? If not, I hope that I shall go with any expedition that will take place. The doctor here is just recovering from an attack of fever and will not be fit for weeks for the fatigues of active service. May I ask who is to command the expedition?"

"I am," Clive said quietly. "You may well look surprised that an officer who has but just joined should have been selected; but in fact there is no one else. Cope and Gingen are both at Trichinopoli, and even if they were not—" he paused, and a shrug of the shoulders expressed his meaning clearly. "Mr. Saunders is good enough to feel some confidence in my capacity, and I trust that I shall not disappoint him. We are going—but this, mind, is a profound secret till the day we march—to attack Arcot. It is the only possible way of relieving Trichinopoli."

"To attack Arcot?" Dr. Rae said, astonished. "That does indeed appear a desperate enterprise with such a small body as you have at your command, and these, entirely new recruits. But I recognize the importance of the enterprise. If you should succeed it will draw off Chunda Sahib from Trichinopoli. It's a grand idea, Captain Clive, a grand idea, though I own it seems to me a desperate one."

"In desperate times we must take desperate measures, Doctor," Captain Clive said. "Now I must be going on after the governor. I shall see you tomorrow. I will not forget you, young gentlemen." So saying he proceeded to the factory.

It was afterwards known that the proposal to effect a diversion by an expedition against Arcot was the proposal of Clive himself. Upon arriving at Trichinopoli he had at once seen that all was lost there. The soldiers were utterly dispirited and demoralized; they had lost all confidence in themselves and their officers, who had also lost confidence in themselves. At Trichinopoli nothing was to be done, and it must be either starved out, or fall an easy prey should the enemy advance to the assault. Clive had then, after a few days' stay, made his way out from the town and proceeded to Fort St. David, where he had laid before the governor the proposal which he believed to be the only possible measure which could save the English in India.

The responsibility thus set before Mr. Saunders was a grave one. Upon the one hand he was asked to detach half of the already inadequate garrisons of Fort St. David and Madras upon an enterprise which, if unsuccessful, must be followed by the loss of the British possessions, of which he was governor; he would have to take this great risk, not upon the advice of a tried veteran like Lawrence, but on that of a young man, only a month or two back a civilian; and it was to this young man, untried in command, that the leadership of this desperate enterprise must be intrusted. Upon the other hand, if he refused to take this responsibility the fall of Trichinopoli, followed by the loss of the three English ports, was certain. But for this no blame or responsibility could rest upon him. Many men would have chosen the second alternative; but Mr. Saunders had since Clive's return seen a good deal of him, and had been impressed with a strong sense of his capacity, energy, and good sense. Mr. Pigot, who had seen Clive under the most trying circumstances, was also his warm supporter; and Mr. Saunders at last determined to adopt Clive's plan, and to stake the fortunes of the English in India on this desperate venture.

Accordingly, leaving a hundred men only at Fort St. David, he decided to carry the remainder to Madras, and that Clive, leaving only fifty behind as a garrison there, should, with the whole available force, march upon Arcot.

The next morning, as Charlie and Peters were at breakfast, a native entered with a letter from the chief factor to the effect that their services in the office would be dispensed with, and that they were, in accordance with their request, to report themselves to Captain Clive as volunteers. No words can express the joy of the two lads at receiving the intelligence, and they created so much noise in the exuberance of their delight that Mr. Johnson came in from the next room to see what was the matter.

"Ah!" he said, when he heard the cause of the uproar; "when I first came out here I should have done the same, and should have regarded the certainty of being knocked on the head as cheerfully as you do. Eight years out here takes the enthusiasm out of a man, and I shall wait quietly to see whether we are to be transferred to Calcutta or shipped back to England."

A quarter of an hour later, Charlie and Peters joined Captain Clive in the camp.

"Ah!" he said, "my young friends, I'm glad to see you. There is plenty for you to do at once. We shall march to-morrow, and all preparations have to be made. You will both have the rank of ensign while you serve with me. I have only six other officers, two of whom are civilians who, like yourselves, volunteered at St. David's. They are of four or five years' standing, and as they speak the language they will serve with the Sepoys under one of my military officers; another officer, who is also an ensign, will take the command of the three guns. The Europeans are divided into two companies; one of you will be attached to each. The remaining officer commands both."

During the day the lads had not a moment to themselves, and were occupied until late at night in superintending the packing of stores and tents, and the following morning, the 26th of August, 1751, the force marched from Madras. It consisted of two hundred of the Company's English troops, three hundred Sepoys, and three small guns. They were led, as has been said, by eight European officers, of whom only Clive and another had ever heard a shot fired in action, four of the eight being young men in the civil service who had volunteered. Charlie was glad to find that among the company to which he was appointed was the detachment which had come out with him on board ship and the moment these heard that he was to accompany them as their officer, Tim Kelly pressed forward and begged that he might be allowed to act as Charlie's servant, a request which the lad readily complied with.

The march the first day was eighteen miles, a distance which in such a climate was sufficient to try to the utmost the powers of the young recruits. The tents were soon erected, each officer having two or three native servants, that number being indispensable in India. Charlie and Peters had one tent between them which was shared by two other officers, as the column had moved in the lightest order possible in India.

"Sure, Mr. Marryatt," Tim Kelly said to him confidentially, "that black hathen of a cook is going to pison ye. I have been watching him, and there he is putting all sorts of outlandish things into the mate. He's been pounding them up on stones, for all the world like an apothecary, and even if he manes no mischief, the food isn't fit to set before a dog, let alone a Christian and a gintleman like yourself. If you give the word, sir, I knock him over with the butt end of my musket, and do the cooking for you meself."

"I'm afraid the other officers wouldn't agree to that, Tim," Charlie said laughing. "The food isn't so bad as it looks, and I don't think an apprenticeship among the Irish bogs is likely to have turned you out a first-rate cook, Tim, except, of course, for potatoes."

"Shure, now, yer honor, I can fry a rasher of bacon with any man."

"Perhaps you might do that, Tim, but as we've no bacon here, that won't help us. No, we must put up with the cook, and I don't think any of us will be the worse for the dinner."

On the morning of the 29th Clive reached Conjeveram, a town of some size, forty-two miles from Madras. Here Clive gained the first trustworthy intelligence as to Arcot. He found the garrison outnumbered his own force by two to one, and that although the defences were not in a position to resist an attack by heavy guns, they were capable of being defended against any force not so provided. Clive at once despatched a messenger to Madras, begging that two eighteen-pounders might be sent after him, and then without awaiting their coming he marched forward against Arcot.

CHAPTER VII.

THE SIEGE OF ARCOT.

FROM Conjeveram to Arcot is twenty-seven miles, and the troops, in spite of a delay caused by a tremendous storm of thunder and lightning, reached the town in two days. The garrison, struck with panic at the sudden coming of a foe when they deemed themselves in absolute security, at once abandoned the fort, which they might easily have maintained until Chunda Sahib was able to send a force to relieve it. The city was incapable of defence after the fort had been abandoned, and Clive took possession of both without firing a shot. He at once set to work to store up provisions in the fort in which he found eight guns and an abundance of ammunition, as he foresaw the likelihood of his having to stand a siege there; and then, leaving a garrison to defend it in his absence, marched on the 4th of September with the rest of his forces against the enemy, who had retired from the town to the mud fort of Timari, six miles south of Arcot. After a few discharges with their cannon they retired hastily, and Clive marched back to Arcot. Two days later, however, he found that they had been reinforced, and as their position threatened his line of communications he again advanced towards them. He found the enemy about two thousand strong drawn up in a grove under cover of the guns of the fort. The grove was inclosed by a bank and ditch, and some fifty yards away was a dry tank inclosed by a bank higher than that which surrounded the grove. In this the enemy could retire when dislodged from their first position.

Charlie's heart beat fast when he heard the order given to advance. The enemy outnumbered them by five to one, and were in a strong position. As the English advanced, the enemy's two field-pieces opened upon them. Only three men were killed, and, led by their officers, the men went at the grove at the double. The enemy at once evacuated it and took refuge in the tank, from behind whose high bank they opened fire upon the English. Clive at once divided his men into two columns, and sent them round to attack the tank upon two sides. The movement was completely successful. At the same moment the men went with a rush at the banks, and upon reaching the top opened a heavy fire upon the crowded mass within. These at once fled in disorder. Clive then summoned the fort to surrender; but the commander, seeing that Clive had no battering train, refused to do so, and Clive fell back upon Arcot again until his eighteen-pounders should arrive.

For the next eight days the troops were engaged in throwing up defences, and strengthening and victualling the fort. The enemy gaining confidence gathered to the number of three thousand and encamped three miles from the town, proclaiming that they were about to besiege; and at midnight on the 14th Clive sallied out, took them by surprise, and dispersed them. The two eighteen-pounders for which Clive had sent to Madras were now well upon the road, under the protection of a small body of Sepoys, and were approaching Conjeveram. The enemy sent a considerable body of troops to cut off the guns, and Clive found that the small number which he had sent out to meet the approaching party would not be sufficient. He therefore resolved to take the whole force, leaving only sufficient to garrison the fort. The post which the enemy occupied was a temple near Conjeveram, and as this was twenty-seven miles distant, the force would be obliged to be absent for at least two days. As it would probably be attacked and might have to fight hard, he decided on leaving only thirty Europeans and fifty Sepoys within the fort. He appointed Dr. Rae to the command of the post during his absence, and placed Charlie and Peters under his orders.

"I wonder whether they will have any fighting," Charlie said, as the three officers looked from the walls of the fort after the departing force.

"I wish we had gone with them," Peters put in; "but it will be a long march in the heat."

"I should think," Dr. Rae said, "that they are sure to have fighting. I only hope they may not be attacked at night. The men are very young and inexperienced, and there is nothing tries new soldiers so much as a night attack. However, from what I hear of their own wars, I believe that night attacks are rare among them. I don't know that they have any superstition on the subject, as some African people have, on the ground that evil spirits are about at night; but the natives are certainly not brisk after nightfall. They are extremely susceptible to any fall of temperature, and as you have, of course, noticed, sleep with their heads covered completely up. However, we must keep a sharp lookout here to-night."

"You don't think that we are likely to be attacked, sir, do you?"

"It is possible we may be," the doctor said. "They will know that Captain Clive has set out from here with the main body and has left only a small garrison. Of course they have spies and will know that there are only eighty men here, a number insufficient to defend one side of this fort, to say nothing of the whole circle of the walls. They have already found out that the English can fight in the open, and their experience at Timari will make them shy of meeting us again. Therefore it is just possible that they may be marching in this direction to-day, while Clive is going in the other, and that they may intend carrying it with a rush. I should say, to-day let the men repose as much as possible; keep the sentries on the gates and walls, but otherwise let them all have absolute quiet. You can tell the whites, and I will let the Sepoys know, that they will have to be in readiness all night, and that they had better therefore sleep as much as possible to-day. We will take it by turns to be on duty, one going round the walls and seeing that the sentries are vigilant, while the others sit in the shade and doze off if they can. We must all three keep on the alert during the night."

Dr. Rae said that he himself would see that all went well for the first four hours, after which Charlie should go on duty; and the two subalterns accordingly made themselves as comfortable as they could in their quarters, which were high up in the fort and possessed a window looking over the surrounding country.

"Well, Tim, what is the matter with *you*?" they asked that soldier as he came in with an earthenware jar of water which he placed to cool in the window; "you look pale."

"And it's pale I feel, your honor, with the life frightened fairly out of me a dozen times a day. It was bad enough on the march, but this place just swarms with horrible reptiles. Shure an' it's a pity that the holy St. Patrick didn't find time to pay a visit to India. If he'd driven the varmint into the sea for them, as he did in Ireland, the whole population would have become Christians out of pure gratitude.

TIM KELLY DISCOURSING ON HORRIBLE REPTILES.

Why, yer honor, in the cracks and crevices of the stones of this ould place there are bushels and bushels of 'em. There are things they call centipades, with a million legs on each side of them, and horns big enough to frighten ye; of all sizes up to, as long as my hand and as thick as my finger, and they say that a bite from one of them will put a man in a raging fever, and maybe kill him. Then there are scorpions, the savagest looking little bastes ye ever saw, for all the world like a little lobster with his tail turned over his back, and a sting at the end of it. Then there's spiders, some of 'em nigh as big as a cat."

"Oh, nonsense, Tim!" Charlie said; "I don't think from what I've heard that there's a spider in India whose body is as big as a mouse."

"It isn't their body, yer honor, it's their legs. They're just cruel to look at. It was one of 'em that gave me a turn a while ago. I was just lying on my bed smoking my pipe, when I saw one of the creatures as big as a saucer, I'll take my oath, walking towards me with his wicked eye fixed full on me. I jumped off the bed and on to a bench that stood handy. 'What are ye yelling about, Tim Kelly?' said Corporal Jones to me. 'Here's a riotous baste here, corporal,' says I, 'that's meditating an attack on me.' 'Put your foot on it, man,' says he. 'It's mighty fine,' says I, 'and I in my bare feet.' So the corporal tells Pat Murphy, my right-hand man, to tackle the baste. I could see Pat didn't like the job ayther, yer honor, but he's not the boy to shrink from his duty; so he comes and he takes post on the form be my side, and just when the cratur is making up his mind to charge us both, Pat jumps down upon him and squelched it. Shure, yer honor, the sight of such bastes is enough to turn a Christian man's blood."

"The spider had no idea of attacking you, Kelly,"

Peters said laughing; "it might possibly bite you in the night, though I do not think it would do so, or if you took it up in your fingers."

"The saints defind us, yer honor! I'd as soon think of taking a tiger by the tail. The corporal, he's an Englishman, and lives in a country where they've got snakes and reptiles; but it's hard on an Irish boy, dacently brought up within ten miles of Cork's own town, to be exposed to the like. And do ye know, yer honor, when I went out into the town yesterday, what should I see but a man sitting down against a wall with a little bit of a flute in his hand and a basket by his side. Well, yer honor, I thought maybe he was going to play a tune, when he lifts up the top of the basket and then began to play. Ye may call it music, yer honor, but there was nayther tune nor music in it. Then all of a suddint two sarpents in the basket lifts up their heads, with a great ear hanging down on each side, and began to wave themselves about."

"Well, Tim, what happened then?" Charlie asked, struggling with his laughter.

"Shure it's little I know what happened after, for I just took to my heels, and I never drew breath till I was inside the gates."

"There was nothing to be frightened at, Tim," Charlie said; "it was a snake-charmer. I have never seen one yet, but there are numbers of them all over India. Those were not ears you saw, but the hood. The snakes like the music and wave their heads about in time to it. I believe that although they are a very poisonous snake and their bite is certain death, there is no need to be afraid of them, as the charmers draw out their poison fangs when they catch them."

"Do they, now?" Tim said in admiration; "I wonder what the regimental barber would say to a job like that now. He well nigh broke Dan Sullivan's jaw yesterday in getting out a big tooth, and then swore at the poor boy for having such a powerful strong jaw. I should like to see his face if he was asked to pull out a tooth from one of them dancing sarpents. I brought ye in some fruits, yer honors. I don't know what they are, but you may trust me they're not poison. I stopped for half an hour beside the stall till I saw some of the people of the country buying and eating them. So then I judged that they were safe for yer honors."

"Now, Tim, you'd better go and lie down and get a sleep, if the spiders will let you, for you will have to be under arms all night, as it is possible that we may be attacked."

The first part of the night passed quietly. Double sentries were placed at each of the angles of the walls. The cannons were loaded and all ready for instant action. Dr. Rae and his two subalterns were upon the alert, visiting the posts every quarter of an hour to see that the men were vigilant. Towards two o'clock a dull sound was heard, and although nothing could be seen the men were at once called to arms and took up the post to which they had already been told off on the walls. The noise continued. It was slight and confused, but the natives are so quiet in their movements that the doctor did not doubt that a considerable body of men were surrounding the place, and that he was about to be attacked. Presently one of the sentries over the gateway perceived something approaching. He challenged, and immediately afterwards fired. The sound of his gun seemed to serve as the signal for an assault, and a large body of men rushed forward at the gate, while at two other points a force ran up to the foot of the walls and endeavored to plant ladders.

The garrison at once collected at the points of

attack, a few sentries only being left at intervals on the wall to give notice should any attempt be made elsewhere. From the walls a heavy fire of musketry was poured upon the masses below, while from the windows of all the houses around, answering flashes of fire shot out, a rain of bullets being directed at the battlements. Dr. Rae himself commanded at the gate; one of the subalterns at each of the other points assailed. The enemy fought with great determination; several times the ladders were planted and the men swarmed up them, but as often these were hurled back upon the crowd below. At the gate the assailants endeavored to hew their way with axes through it, but so steady was the fire directed from the loopholes which commanded it upon those so engaged, that they were each time forced to recoil with great slaughter. It was not until nearly daybreak that the attack ceased, and the assailants, finding that they could not carry the place by a *coup de main*, fell back.

The next day the main body of the British force returned with the convoy. News arrived the following day that the enemy were approaching to lay siege to the place. The news of the capture of Arcot had produced the effect which Clive had anticipated from it. It alarmed and irritated the besiegers of Trichinopoli, and inspired the besieged with hope and exultation. The Maratta chief of Gutti and the Rajah of Mysore, with whom Muhammud Ali had for some time been negotiating, at once declared in his favor. The Rajah of Tanjore and the chief of Pudicota, adjoining that state, who had hitherto remained strictly neutral, now threw in their fortunes with the English, and thereby secured the communications between Trichinopoli and the coast.

Chunda Sahib determined to lose not a moment in recovering Arcot, knowing that its recapture would at once cool the ardor of the new native allies of the English, and that with its capture that last hope of the besieged in Trichinopoli would be at an end. Continuing the siege, he despatched three thousand of his best troops with a hundred and fifty Frenchmen to reinforce the two thousand men already near Arcot under the command of his son Riza Sahib. Thus the force about to attack Arcot amounted to five thousand men, while the garrison under Clive's orders had, by the losses in the defence of the fort, by fever and disease, been reduced to one hundred and twenty Europeans and two hundred Sepoys, while four out of the eight officers were *hors de combat*.

The fort which this handful of men had to defend was in no way capable of offering a prolonged resistance. Its walls were more than a mile in circumference and were in a very bad state of repair. The rampart was narrow and the parapet low, and the ditch in many places dry. The fort had two gates. These were in towers standing beyond the ditch, and connected with the interior by a causeway across it. The houses in the town in many places came close up to the walls, and from their roofs the ramparts of the forts were commanded.

On the 23d September Riza Sahib with his army took up his position before Arcot. Their guns had not, however, arrived, with the exception of four mortars, but they at once occupied all the houses near the fort, and from the walls and upper windows kept up a heavy fire on the besieged. Clive determined to make an effort at once to drive them from this position, and he accordingly, on the same afternoon, made a sortie. So deadly a fire, however, was poured into the troops as they advanced that they were unable to make any way, and were forced to retreat into the fort again after suffering heavy loss.

On the night of the 24th, Charlie Marryat, with twenty men carrying powder, was lowered from the walls, and an attempt was made to blow up the houses nearest to them; but little damage was done, for the enemy were on the alert, and they were unable to place the powder in effective positions, and with a loss of ten of their number the survivors with difficulty regained the fort. For the next three weeks the position remained unchanged. So heavy was the fire which the enemy, from their commanding position, maintained, that no one could show his head for a moment without running the risk of being shot. Only a few sentinels were kept upon the walls to prevent the risk of surprise, and these had to remain stooping below the parapet. Every day added to the losses.

Captain Clive had a series of wonderful escapes, and indeed the men began to regard him with a sort of superstitious reverence, believing that he had a charmed life. One of his three remaining officers, seeing an enemy taking deliberate aim at him through a window, endeavored to pull him aside. The native changed his aim and the officer fell dead. On three other occasions sergeants who accompanied him on his rounds were shot dead by his side, yet no ball touched him. Provisions had been stored in the fort, before the commencement of the siege, sufficient for sixty days, and of this a third was already exhausted when on the 14th of October the French troops serving with Riza Sahib received two eighteen-pounders and seven smaller pieces of artillery. Hitherto the besiegers had contented themselves with harassing the garrison night and day, abstaining from any attack which would cost them lives until the arrival of their guns. Upon receiving these they at once placed them in a battery which they had prepared on the northwest of the fort and opened fire. So well was this battery placed, and so accurate the aim of its gunner, that the very first shot dismounted one of the eighteen-pounders in the fort; the second again struck the gun and completely disabled it. The besieged mounted their second heavy gun in its place, and were preparing to open fire on the French battery, when a shot struck it also and dismounted it. It was useless to attempt to replace it, and it was during the night removed to a portion of the walls not exposed to the fire of the enemy's battery. The besiegers continued their fire, and in six days had demolished the wall facing their battery, making a breach of fifty feet wide.

Clive, who had now only the two young subalterns serving under him, worked indefatigably. His coolness and confidence of bearing kept up the courage of his little garrison, and every night, when darkness hid them from the view of the enemy's sharpshooters, the men labored to prepare for the impending attack. Works were thrown up inside the fort to command the breach. Two deep trenches were dug, one behind the other, the one close to the wall, the other some distance farther back. These trenches were filled with sharp iron three-pointed spikes and palisades erected extending from the ends of the ditches to the ramparts, and a house pulled down in the rear to the height of a breastwork, behind which the garrison could fire at the assailants as they endeavored to cross the ditches. One of the three field-pieces Clive had brought with him he mounted on a tower, flanking the breach outside. Two he held in reserve, and placed two small guns, which he had found in the fort when he took it, on the flat roof of a house in the fort commanding the inside of the breach.

From the roofs of some of the houses around the fort the besiegers beheld the progress of these defences; and Riza Sahib feared, in spite of his enormously superior numbers, to run the risk of a repulse. He knew that the amount of provisions which Clive had stored was not large, and thinking that famine would inevitably compel his surrender, shrank from incurring the risk of disheartening his army by the slaughter which an unsuccessful attempt to carry the place must entail. He determined at any rate to increase the probability of success and utilize his superior forces by making an assault at two points simultaneously. He therefore erected a battery on the south-west, and began to effect a breach on that side also.

Clive on his part had been busy endeavoring to obtain assistance. His native emissaries, penetrating the enemy's lines, carried the news of the situation of affairs in the fort to Madras, Fort St. David, and Trichinopoli. At Madras a few fresh troops had arrived from England, and Mr. Saunders, feeling that Clive must be relieved at all cost, however defenceless the state of Madras might be, despatched on the 20th of October a hundred Europeans and a hundred Sepoys under Lieutenant Innis. These after three days marching arrived at Trivatoor, twenty-two miles from Arcot. Riza Sahib had heard of his approach and sent a large body of troops with two guns to attack him. The contest was too unequal. Had the British force been provided with field-pieces they might have gained the day, but after fighting with great bravery they were forced to fall back with a loss of twenty English and two officers killed and many more wounded, while the Sepoys suffered equally severely.

One of Clive's messengers reached Murari Reo, the Maratta chief of Gutti. This man was a ferocious freebooting chief, daring and brave himself, and admiring those qualities in others. Hitherto his alliance with Muhammud Ali was little more than nominal, for he had dreaded bringing upon himself the vengeance of Chunda Sahib and the French, whose ultimate success in the strife appeared certain. Clive's march upon Arcot, and the heroic defence which the handful of men there were opposing to overwhelming numbers, excited his highest admiration. As he afterwards said, he had never before believed that the English could fight, and when Clive's messenger reached him he at once sent back a promise of assistance. Riza Sahib learned almost as soon as Clive himself that the Marattas were on the move. The prospects of his communications being harassed by these daring horsemen filled him with anxiety. Murari Reo was encamped with six thousand men at a spot thirty miles to the west of Arcot, and he might at any moment swoop down upon the besiegers. Although, therefore, Riza Sahib had for six days been at work effecting a new breach, which was now nearly open to assault, he sent on the 30th of October a flag of truce with an offer to Clive of terms if he would surrender Arcot. The garrison were to be allowed to march out with their arms and baggage, while to Clive himself he offered a large sum of money. In case of refusal he threatened to storm the fort and put all its defenders to the sword. Clive returned a defiant refusal, and the guns again opened on the second breach.

On the 9th of November the Marattas began to show themselves in the neighborhood of the besieging army. The force under Lieutenant Innis had been reinforced, and was now under the command of Captain Kilpatrick, who had a hundred and fifty English troops with four field-guns. This was now advancing. Four days later the new breach had attained a width of thirty yards, but Clive had prepared defences in the rear similar to those at the other breach; and the difficulties of the besiegers would here be much greater, as the ditch was not fordable. The fifty days which the siege had lasted had been terrible ones for the garrison. Never daring to expose themselves unnecessarily during the day, yet ever on the alert to repel an attack, laboring at night at the defences with their numbers daily dwindling, and the prospect of an assault becoming more and more imminent, the work of the little garrison was terrible, and it is to the defences of Lucknow and Cawnpore, a hundred years later, that we must look to find a parallel in English warfare for their endurance and bravery. Both Charlie Marryat and Peters had been wounded, but in neither case were the injuries severe enough to prevent their continuing on duty. Tim Kelly had his arm broken by a ball, while another bullet cut a deep seam along his cheek and carried away a portion of his ear. With his arm in splints and a sling, and the side of his face covered with strappings and plaster, he still went about his business.

"Ah! yer honors," he said one day to his masters, "I've often been out catching rabbits, with ferrets to drive 'em out of their holes, and sticks to knock 'em on the head as soon as they showed themselves; and it's a divarshun I was always mightily fond of, but I never quite intered into the feelings of the rabbits. Now I understand them complately, for ain't we rabbits ourselves. The officers, saving your presence, are the ferrets who turn us out of our holes on duty, and the niggers yonder with their muskets and their matchlocks are the men with sticks ready to knock us on the head directly we show ourselves. If it plase Heaven that I ever return to the ould country again, I'll niver lend a hand at rabbiting to my dying day."

CHAPTER VIII.

THE GRAND ASSAULT.

THE 14th of November was a Mahommedan festival, and Riza Sahib determined to utilize the enthusiasm and fanatic zeal which such an occasion always excites among the followers of the Prophet, to make his grand assault upon Arcot, and to attack at three o'clock in the morning. Every preparation was made on the preceding day, and four strong columns told off for the assault. Two of these were to attack by the breaches, the other two at the gates. Rafts were prepared to enable the party attacking by the new breach to cross the moat, while the columns advancing against the gates were to be preceded by elephants, who, with iron plates on their foreheads, were to charge and batter down the gates.

Clive's spies brought him news of the intended assault, and at midnight he learned full particulars as to the disposition of the enemy. His force was now reduced to eighty Europeans and a hundred and twenty Sepoys. Every man was told off to his post and then, sentries being posted to arouse them at the approach of the enemy, the little garrison lay down in their places to get two or three hours sleep before the expected attack. At three o'clock the firing of three shells from the mortars into the fort gave the signal for assault. The men leaped up and stood to their arms, full of confidence in their ability to resist the attack. Soon the shouts of the advancing columns testified to the equal confidence and ardor of the assailants.

Not a sound was heard within the walls of the fort until the elephants advanced toward the gates. Then suddenly a stream of fire leaped out from loophole and battlement. So well directed and continuous was the fire, that the elephants, dismayed at the outburst of fire and noise, and smarting from innumerable wounds turned and dashed away, trampling in their flight multitudes of men in the dense columns packed behind them. These, deprived of the means upon which they had relied to break in the gates, turned and retreated rapidly.

Scarcely less prolonged was the struggle at the breaches. At the first breach a very strong force of the enemy marched resolutely forward. They were permitted without a shot being fired at them to cross the dry ditch, mount the shattered debris of the wall, and pour into the interior of the fort. Forward they advanced until, without a check, they reached the first trench bristling with spikes. Then, as they paused for a moment, from the breastwork in front of them, from the ramparts, and every spot which commanded the trench, a storm of musketry was poured on them, while the gunners swept the crowded mass with grape and bags of bullets. The effect was tremendous. Mowed down in heaps the assailants recoiled, and then, without a moment's hesitation turned and fled. Three times, strongly reinforced, they advanced to the attack, but were each time repulsed with severe slaughter.

Still less successful were those at the other breach. A great raft capable of carrying seventy conveyed the head of the storming party across the ditch, and they had just reached the foot of the breach when Clive, who was himself at this point, turned two field pieces upon them with deadly effect. The raft was upset and smashed, and the column, deprived of its intended means of crossing the ditch, desisted from the attack.

Among those who had fallen at the great breach was the commander of the storming party, a man of great valor. Four hundred of his followers had also been killed, and Riza Sahib, utterly disheartened at his repulse at all points, decided not to renew the attack. He had still more than twenty men to each of the defenders; but the obstinacy of their resistance and the moral effect produced by it upon his troops, the knowledge that the Maratta horse were hovering in his rear, and that Kilpatrick's little column was close at hand, determined him to raise the siege. After the repulse of the assault the heavy musketry fire from the houses around the fort was continued. At two in the afternoon he asked for two hours truce to bury the dead. This was granted, and on its conclusion the musketry fire was resumed and continued until two in the morning. Then suddenly it ceased. Under cover of the fire Riza Sahib had raised the siege and retired with his army to Vellore.

On the morning of the 15th Clive discovered that the enemy had disappeared. The joy of the garrison was immense. Every man felt proud and happy in the thought that he had taken his share in a siege which would not only be memorable in English history till the end of time, but which had literally saved India to us. The little band made the fort re-echo with their cheers when the news came in. Caps were thrown high in the air, and the men indulged in every demonstration of delight. Clive was not a man to lose time. The men were at once formed up and marched into the abandoned camp of the enemy, where they found four guns, four mortars, and a great quantity of ammunition. A cloud of dust was seen approaching, and soon a mounted officer riding forward announced the arrival of Captain Kilpatrick's detachment.

Not a moment was lost, for Clive felt the importance of at once following up the blow inflicted by the repulse of the enemy. Three days were spent in continuous labor in putting the fort of Arcot again in a position of defence; and leaving Kilpatrick in charge there, he marched out with two hundred Europeans, seven hundred Sepoys, and three guns, and attacked and took Timari, the little fort which before baffled him. This done he returned towards Arcot to await the arrival of a thousand Maratta horse which Murari Reo had promised him. When these arrived, however they proved unwilling to accompany him. Upon their way they had fallen in with a portion of Riza Sahib's retreating force and had been worsted in the attack; and as the chance of plunder seemed small while the prospect of hard blows was certain, the freebooting horsemen refused absolutely to join in the pursuit of the retreating enemy. Just at this moment the news came in that reinforcements from Pondicherry were marching to meet Riza Sahib at Arni, a place seventeen miles south of Arcot, twenty south of Vellore. It was stated that with these reinforcements a large sum of money was being brought for the use of Riza Sahib's army. When the Marattas heard the news, the chance of booty at once altered their intentions, and they declared themselves ready to follow Clive. The greater portion of them however, had dispersed plundering over the country, and great delay was caused before they could be collected. When six hundred of them had been brought together Clive determined to wait no longer, but started at once for Arni.

The delay enabled Riza Sahib, marching down from Vellore, to meet his reinforcements, and when Clive, after a forced march of twenty miles, approached Arni, he found the enemy, composed of three hundred

French troops, two thousand five hundred Sepoys, and two thousand horsemen, with four guns, drawn up before it. Seeing their immense superiority in numbers these advanced to the attack.

Clive determined to await them where he stood. The position was an advantageous one. He occupied a space of open ground some three hundred yards in width. On his right flank was a village. On the left a grove of palm-trees. In front of the ground he occupied were rice fields, which, it being the wet season, were very swampy and altogether impracticable for guns. These fields were crossed by a causeway which led to the village, but as it ran at an angle across them, those advancing upon it were exposed to the fire of the English front. Clive posted the Sepoys in the village, the Maratta horsemen in the grove, and the two hundred English with the guns on the ground between them. The enemy advanced at once. His native cavalry with some infantry marched against the grove, while the French troops with about fifteen hundred infantry moved along the causeway against the village.

The fight began on the English left. There the Maratta cavalry fought bravely. Issuing from the palm grove they made repeated charges against the greatly superior forces of the enemy. But numbers told, and the Marattas, fighting fiercely, were driven back into the palm grove, where they with difficulty maintained themselves. In the meantime the fight was going on at the centre. Clive opened fire with his guns on the long column marching almost across his front to attack the village. The enemy, finding themselves exposed to a fire which they were powerless to answer, quitted the causeway, and formed up in the rice fields fronting the English position. The guns protected only by a few Frenchmen and natives, remained on the causeway. Clive now despatched two of his guns and fifty English to aid the hard-pressed

Marattas in the grove, and fifty others to the village with orders to join the Sepoys there, to dash forward on to the causeway and charge the enemy's guns.

As the column issued from the village along the causeway at a rapid pace the French limbered up their guns and retired at a gallop. The infantry, dispirited at their disappearance, fell back across the rice fields, an example which their horsemen on their right, already dispirited by the loss which they were suffering from the newly arrived English musketry and the discharges of the field-pieces, followed without delay. Clive at once ordered a pursuit. The Marattas were despatched after the enemy's cavalry, while he himself with his infantry advanced across the causeway and pressed upon the main body. Three times the enemy made a stand, but each time failed to resist the impetuosity of the pursuers, and the night alone put a stop to the pursuit, by which time the enemy were completely routed.

The material loss had not been heavy, for but fifty French and a hundred and fifty natives were killed or wounded; but the army was broken up, the *morale* of the enemy completely destroyed, and it was proved to all Southern India, which was anxiously watching the struggle, that the English were in the field of battle superior to their European rivals. This assurance alone had an immense effect. It confirmed in their alliance with the English many of the chiefs whose friendship had hitherto been lukewarm, and brought over many waverers to our side. In the fight eight Sepoys and fifty of the Maratta cavalry were killed or disabled, the English did not lose a single man. Many of Riza Sahib's soldiers came in during the next few days and enlisted in the British force. The Marattas captured the treasure the prospect of which had induced them to join in the fight, and the governor of Arni agreed to hold the town for Muhammud Ali. Clive moved on at once to Conjeveram, where thirty French troops and three hundred Sepoys occupied the temple, a very strong building. Clive brought up two eighteen-pounders from Madras and pounded the walls, and the enemy seeing that the place must fall, evacuated it in the night and retired to Pondicherry. North Arcot being now completely in the power of the English, Clive returned to Madras, and then sailed to Fort St. David to concert measures with Mr. Saunders for the relief of Trichinopoli. This place still held out, thanks rather to the feebleness and indecision of Colonel Law, who commanded the besiegers, than to any effort on the part of the defenders.

Governor Dupleix, at Pondicherry, had seen with surprise the result of Clive's dash upon Arcot. He had, however, perceived that the operations there were wholly secondary, and that Trichinopoli was still the all-important point. The fall of that place would more than neutralize Clive's successes at Arcot, and he, therefore, did not suffer Clive's operations to distract his attention here. Strong reinforcements and a battering train were sent forward to the besiegers, and by repeated messages he endeavored to impress upon Law and Chunda Sahib the necessity of pressing forward the capture of Trichinopoli. But Dupleix was unfortunate in his instruments. Law was always hesitating and doubting. Chunda Sahib, although clever to plan, was weak in action, indecisive at moments when it was most necessary that he should be firm. So then, in spite of the entreaties of Dupleix, he had detached a considerable force to besiege Clive. Dupleix seeing this, and hoping that Clive might be detained at Arcot long enough to allow of the siege of Trichinopoli being brought to a conclusion, had sent the three hundred French soldiers to strengthen the force of Riza Sahib. He had still an overpowering force at Trichinopoli, Law having nine hundred trained French soldiers, a park of fifty guns, two thousand Sepoys, and the army of Chunda Sahib twenty thousand strong. Inside Trichinopoli were a few English soldiers under Captain Cope and a small body of troops of Muhammud Ali; while outside the walls, between them and the besiegers, was the English force under Gingen, the men utterly dispirited, the officer without talent, resolution, or confidence.

Before leaving the troops with which he had won the battle of Arni, Clive had expressed to the two young writers his high appreciation of their conduct during the siege of Arcot, and promised them that he would make it a personal request to the authorities at Fort St. David that they might be permanently transferred from the civil to the military branch of the service; and such a request made by him was certain to be complied with. He strongly advised them to spend every available moment of their time in the study of the native language, as without that they would be useless if appointed to command a body of Sepoys. Delighted at the prospect now open to them of a permanent relief from the drudgery of a clerk's life in Madras, the young fellows were in the highest spirits; and Tim Kelly was scarcely less pleased when he heard that Charlie was now likely t. be always employed with him. The boys lost not a moment in sending down to Madras to engage the services of a native "moonshee" or teacher. They wrote to their friend Johnson asking him to arrange terms with the man who understood most English, and to engage him to remain with them some time.

A few days later Tim Kelly came in. "Plase, yer honors, there's a little shrivelled atomy of a man outside as wants to spake wid ye. He looks for all the world like a monkey wrapped up in white clothes, but he spakes English after a fashion, and has brought this letter for you. The cratur scarce looks like a human being, and I misdoubt me whether you had better let him in."

"Nonsense, Tim," Charlie said, opening the letter; "it's the moonshee we are expecting from Madras. He has come to teach us the native language."

"Moonshine, is it! by jabers, and it's a mighty poor compliment to the moon to call him so. And is it the language you're going to larn now. Shure, Mr. Charles, I wouldn't demane myself by larning the lingo of these black hathens. Isn't for them to larn the English, and mighty pleased they ought to be to get themselves to spake like Christians."

"But who's going to teach them, Tim?"

"Oh, they larn fast enough," said Tim. "You've only got to point to a bottle of water, or to the fire, or whatever else you want, and swear at them, and they understand directly. I've tried it myself over and over again."

"There, Tim, it's no use standing talking any longer; bring in the moonshee." From that moment the little man had his permanent post in a corner of the boys' room, and when they were not on duty they were constantly engaged in studying the language, writing down the names of every object they came across and getting it by heart, and learning every sentence, question, and answer which occurred to them as likely to be useful. As for Tim, he quite lost patience at this devotion to study on the part of his master, who, he declared to his comrades, went on just as if he intended to become a nigger and a hathen himself. "It's just awful to hear him, Corporal M'Bean, jabbering away in that foreign talk with that little black monkey moonshine. The little cratur atwisting his shrivelled fingers about, that looks as if the bones were coming through the skin. I wonder what the good father at Blarney, where I come from, you know, corporal, would say to sich goings-on. Faith, then, and if he were here, I'd buy a bottle of holy water and sprinkle it over the little hathen. I suspict he'd fly straight up the chimney when it touched him."

"My opinion of you, Tim Kelly," the corporal, who was a grave Scotchman, said, "is that you're just a fule. Your master is a brave young gentleman, and is a deal more sensible than most of them, who spend all their time in drinking wine and playing cards. A knowledge of the language is most useful. What would you do yourself if you were to marry a native woman and couldn't speak to her afterwards?"

"The saints defind us!" Tim exclaimed; "and what put such an idea in yer head, corporal? It's nayther more nor less than an insult to suppose that I, a dacent boy, and brought up under the teaching of Father O'Shea, should marry a hathen black woman; and if you weren't my suparior officer, corporal, I'd tach ye better manners." Fortunately at this moment Charlie's voice was heard shouting for his servant, and Tim was therefore saved from the breach of the peace which his indignation showed that he meditated.

December passed quietly, and then in January, 1752, an insurrection planned by Dupleix broke out. The governor of Pondicherry had been suffering keenly from disappointments, which, as time went on, and his entreaties and commands to Law to attack Trichinopoli were answered only by excuses and reasons for delay, grew to despair, and he resolved upon making another effort to occupy the attention of the man in whom he already recognized a great rival, and to prevent his taking steps for the relief of Trichinopoli. Law had over and over again assured him that in the course of a very few weeks that place would be driven by famine to surrender; and, as soon as Clive arrived at Fort St. David, Dupleix set about taking steps which would again necessitate his return to the north, and so give to Law the time which he asked for. Supplies of money were sent to Riza Sahib together with four hundred French soldiers. These marched suddenly upon Punemalli and captured it, seized again the fortified temple of Conjeveram, and from this point threatened both Madras and Arcot.

Had this force possessed an active and determined commander, it could undoubtedly have carried out Dupleix's instructions, captured Madras, and inflicted a terrible blow upon the English. Fortunately it had no such head. It marched indeed against Madras, plundered and burnt the factories, levied contributions, and obtained possession of everything but the fort, where the civilians and the few men who constituted the garrison daily expected to be attacked, in which case the place must have fallen. This, however, the enemy never even attempted, contenting themselves with ravaging the place outside the walls of the fort. The little garrison of Arcot, two hundred men in all, were astonished at the news that the province which they had thought completely conquered was again in flames, that the road to Madras was cut by the occupation of Conjeveram by the French, and that Madras itself was, save the fort, in the hands of the enemy. The fort itself, they knew, might easily be taken, as they were aware that it was defended by only eighty men.

The change in the position was at once manifest in the altered attitude of the fickle population. The main body of the inhabitants of Southern India were Hindoos, who had for centuries been ruled by foreign masters. The Mahommedans from the north had been their conquerors, and the countless wars which had taken place, to them signified merely whether one family or another were to reign over them. The sole desire was for peace and protection, and they, therefore, ever inclined towards the side which seemed strongest.

Their sympathies were no stronger with their Mahommedan rulers than with the French or English, and they only hoped that whatever power was strongest might conquer; and that after the hostilities were over their daily work might be conducted in peace, and their property and possessions be enjoyed in security. The capture and defence of Arcot, and the battle of Arni, had brought them to regard the English as their final victors; and the signs of deep and even servile respect which greeted the conquerors wherever they went, and which absolutely disgusted Charlie Marryat and his friend, were really sincere marks of the welcome to masters who seemed able and willing to maintain their rule over them. With the news of the successes of Riza Sahib all this changed. The natives no longer bent to the ground as the English passed them in the streets. The country people who had flocked in with their products to the markets absented themselves altogether, and the whole population prepared to welcome the French as their new masters.

In the fort the utmost vigilance was observed. The garrison labored to mend the breaches and complete the preparations for defence. Provisions were again stored up, and they awaited anxiously news from Clive. That enterprising officer was at Fort St. David, busy in making his preparations for a decisive campaign against the enemy round Trichinopoli, when the news of the rising reached him. He was expecting a considerable number of fresh troops from England, as it was in January that the majority of the reinforcements despatched by the Company arrived in India, and Mr. Saunders had written to Calcutta begging that a hundred men might be sent thence. These were now, with the eighty men at Madras, and the two hundred at Arcot, all the force that could be at his disposal, for at Fort St. David there was not a single available man. With all the efforts that Clive, aided by the authorities, could make, it was not until the middle of February that he had completed his arrangements. On the 9th the hundred men arrived from Bengal, and without the loss of a day, Clive started from Madras to form a junction with the garrison from Arcot, who, leaving only a small force to hold the fort, had moved down to meet him.

CHAPTER IX.

THE BATTLE OF KAVARIPAK.

THE troops from Arcot had already moved some distance on their way to Madras, and Clive, therefore, with the new levies, joined them on the day after his leaving Madras. The French and Riza Sahib let slip the opportunity of attacking these bodies before they united. They were well aware of their movements, and had resolved upon tactics, calculated in the first place to puzzle the English commander, to wear out his troops, and to enable them finally to surprise and take him entirely at a disadvantage. The junction with the Arcot garrison raised the force under Clive's orders to three hundred and eighty English, thirteen hundred Sepoys, and six field-guns, while the enemy at Vendalur, a place twenty-five miles south of Madras, where they had a fortified camp, had four hundred French troops, two thousand Sepoys, two thousand five hundred cavalry, and twelve guns. Hoping to surprise them there Clive marched all night. When the force approached the town they heard that the enemy had disappeared, and that they had started apparently in several directions.

The force was halted for a few hours, and then the news was obtained that the enemy had united their forces at Conjeveram, and that they had marched away from that place in a westerly direction. Doubting not that they were about to attack Arcot, which, weakened by the departure of the greater portion of its garrison, would be in no position to defend itself against a sudden *coup de main* by a strong force, Clive set his troops again in motion. The French, indeed, had already bribed some of the native soldiers within the fort, who were to reply to a signal made without if they were in a position to open the gates. However, by good fortune their treachery had been discovered, and when the French arrived they received no reply to their signal; and as Arcot would be sure to fall if they defeated Clive, they marched away without attacking it, to take up the position which they had agreed upon beforehand. It was at nine in the evening that Clive at Vendalur obtained intelligence that the enemy had assembled at Conjeveram. The troops had already marched twenty-five miles, but they had had a rest of five hours, and Clive started with them at once, and reached Conjeveram, twenty miles distant, at four in the morning. Finding that the enemy had again disappeared he ordered the troops to halt for a few hours. They had already marched forty-five miles in twenty-four hours, a great feat when it is remembered that only the Arcot garrison were in any way accustomed to fatigue, the others being newly raised levies. The greater portion of the Sepoys had been enlisted within the fortnight preceding.

"I don't know, Mr. Marryat, whether the French call this fighting; I call it playing hide and seek," Tim Kelly said. "Shure we've bin marching with only a halt of two or three hours since yisterday morning, and my poor feet are that sore that I daren't take my boots off me, for I'm shure I'd never git 'em on agin. If the French want to fight us why don't they do it square and honest, not be racing and chasing about like a lot of wild sheep."

"Have you seen the moonshee, Tim? He is with the baggage."

"Shure and I saw him," Tim said. "The cart come in just now, and there was he perched up on the top of it like a dried monkey. You don't want him to-night, shure, yer honor."

"Oh no, I don't want him, Tim. You'd better go now, and get to sleep at once if you can, we may be off again at any minute."

Arcot is twenty-seven miles from Conjeveram. Clive felt certain that the enemy had gone on to that place, but anxious as he was for its safety, it was absolutely necessary that the troops should have a rest before starting on such a march. They were therefore, allowed to rest until twelve o'clock, when, refreshed by their eight hours' halt and breakfast, they started upon their long march towards Arcot, making sure that they should not find the enemy until they reached that place. Had Clive possessed a body of cavalry, however small, he would have been able to scour the country, and to make himself acquainted with the real position of the French. Cavalry are to a general what eyes are to a man, and without these he is liable to tumble into a pitfall. Such was the case on the present occasion. Having no doubt that the enemy were engaged in attacking Arcot the troops were plodding along carelessly and in loose order, when, to their astonishment, after a sixteen-mile march, as they approached the town of Kavaripak just as the sun was setting, a fire of artillery opened upon them from a grove upon the right of the road but two hundred and fifty yards distant. Nothing is more confusing than a surprise of this kind, especially to young troops, and when no enemy is thought to be near.

The French general's plans had been well laid. He had reached Kavaripak that morning, and allowed his troops to rest all day, and he expected to obtain an easy victory over the tired men who would, unsuspicious of danger, be pressing on to the relief of Arcot.

So far his calculations had been correct, and the English marched unsuspiciously into the trap laid for them. The twelve French guns were placed in a grove, round whose sides, facing the point from which Clive was approaching, ran a deep ditch with a high bank forming a regular battery. A body of French infantry were placed in support of the guns, with some Sepoys in reserve behind the grove. Parallel with the road on the left ran a deep water-course, now empty, and in this the rest of the infantry were stationed, at a point near the town of Kavaripak, and about a quarter of a mile further back than the grove. On either side of this water-course the enemy had placed his powerful cavalry force.

For a moment when the guns opened there was confusion and panic among the British troops. Clive, however, ever cool and confident in danger, and well seconded by his officers, rallied them at once. The position was one of extreme danger. It was possible, indeed, to retreat, but in the face of an enemy superior in infantry and guns, and possessing so powerful a body of cavalry, the operation would have been a very dangerous one. Even if accomplished it would entail an immense loss of *morale* and prestige to his troops. Hitherto under his leading they had been always successful, and a belief in his own superiority adds immensely to the fighting power of a soldier. Even should the remnant of the force fight its way back to Madras the campaign would have been a lost one, and all hope of saving Trichinopoli would have been at an end.

"Steady, lads, steady," he shouted. "Form up quietly and steadily. We have beaten the enemy before, you know, and we will do so again."

While the troops, in spite of the artillery fire, fell into line, Clive rapidly surveyed the ground. He saw the enemy's infantry advancing up the water-course, and so sheltered by it as to be out of the fire of his troops. He saw their cavalry sweeping down on the other side of the water-course, menacing his left and threatening his baggage. The guns were at once brought up from the rear, but before these arrived the men were falling fast. Three of the guns he placed to answer the French battery, two of them he hurried to his left with a small body of English and two hundred Sepoys, to check the advance of the enemy's cavalry. The main body of his infantry he ordered into the water-course, which afforded them a shelter from the enemy's artillery. The baggage carts and baggage he sent half a mile to the rear, under the protection of forty Sepoys and a gun. While this was being done the enemy's fire was continuing, but his infantry advanced but slowly, and had not reached a point abreast of the grove when the British force in the water-course met them. It would not seem to be a very important matter at what point in the water-course the infantry of the two opposing parties came into collision, but matters apparently trifling in themselves often decide the fate of battles; and, in fact, had the French artillery retained their fire until their infantry were abreast of the grove, the battle of Kavaripak would have been won by them, and the British power in Southern India would have been destroyed. Clive moved confidently and resolutely among his men, keeping up their courage by cheerful words, and he was well seconded by his officers.

"Now, lads," Charlie Marryat cried to the company of which he was in command, "stick to it. You ought to be very thankful to the French for saving you the trouble of having to march another twelve miles before giving you an opportunity of thrashing them."

The men laughed and redoubled their fire on the French infantry, who were facing them in the water-course at a distance of eighty yards. Neither party liked to charge. The French commander knew that he had only to hold his position to win the day. His guns were mowing down the English artillerymen. The English party on the left of the water-course with difficulty held their own against the charges of his horsemen, and were rapidly dwindling away under the artillery fire, while other bodies of his cavalry had surrounded the baggage, and were attacking the little force told off to guard it. He knew, too, that any attempt the English might make to attack the battery, with its strong defences, must inevitably fail.

The situation was becoming desperate. It was now ten o'clock; the fight had gone on for four hours. No advantage had been gained, the men were losing confidence, and the position grew more and more desperate. Clive saw that there was but one chance of victory. The grove could not be carried in the front, but it was just possible that it might be open in the rear. Choosing a sergeant who spoke the native language well, he bade him leave the party in the water-course and make his way round to the rear of the grove, and discover whether it was strongly guarded there or not. In twenty minutes the sergeant returned with the news that there was no strong force there.

Clive at once took two hundred of his English infantry, the men who had fought at Arcot, and quietly left the water-course and made his way round towards the rear of the grove. Before he had gone far the main body in the water-course, surprised at the sudden withdrawal of the greater portion of the English force and missing the presence of Clive himself, began to lose heart. They no longer replied energetically to the fire of the French infantry. A movement of retreat began, the fire ceased, and in a minute or two they would have broken in flight. At this moment

Clive returned. As he moved forward he had marked the dying away of the English fire, and guessing what had happened, had given over the command of the column to Lieutenant Keene, the senior officer, and hurried back to the water-course. He arrived there just as the troops had commenced to run away. Throwing himself among them, with shouts and exhortations, he succeeded in arresting their flight, and by assurances that the battle was as good as won elsewhere, and that they had only to hold their ground for a few minutes longer to ensure victory, he got them to advance to their former position and to reopen fire on the French, who had, fortunately, remained inactive instead of advancing and taking advantage of the cessation of the English fire.

In the mean time Lieutenant Keene led his detachment, making a long circuit, to a point three hundred yards immediately behind the grove. He then sent forward one of his officers, Ensign Symmonds, who spoke French perfectly, to reconnoitre the grove. Symmonds had proceeded but a little way when he came upon a large number of French Sepoys, who were covering the rear of the grove, but who, as their services were not required were sheltering themselves there from the random bullets which were flying about. They at once challenged, but Symmonds answering them in French, they being unable to see his uniform in the darkness, and supposing him to be a French officer, allowed him to advance. He passed boldly forward into the grove. He proceeded nearly through it, until he came within sight of the guns, which were still keeping up their fire upon those of the English, while a hundred French infantry, who were in support, were all occupied in watching what was going on in front of them.

Symmonds returned to the detachment by a path to the right of that by which he had entered, and passed out without seeing a soul. Lieutenant Keene gave the word to advance, and, following the guidance of Mr. Symmonds, entered the grove. He advanced unobserved until within thirty yards of the enemy. Here he halted and poured a volley into them. The effect was instantaneous. Many of the French fell, and the rest, astounded at this sudden and unexpected attack, left their guns and fled. Sixty of them rushed for shelter into a building at the end of the grove, where the English surrounded them and forced them to surrender.

By this sudden stroke the battle of Kavaripak was won. The sound of the musketry fire and the immediate cessation of that of the enemy's guns, told Clive that the grove was captured. A few minutes later fugitives arriving from the grove informed the commander of the enemy's main body of infantry of the misfortune which had befallen them. The French fire at once ceased and the troops withdrew. In the darkness it was impossible for Clive to attempt a pursuit. He was in ignorance of the direction the enemy had taken; his troops had already marched sixty miles in two days, and he would, moreover, have been exposed to sudden dashes of the enemy's cavalry. Clive, therefore, united his troops, joined his baggage, which the little guard had gallantly defended against the attacks of the enemy's cavalry, and waited for morning. At daybreak not an enemy was to be seen. Fifty Frenchmen lay dead on the field and sixty were captives. Three hundred French Sepoys had fallen. There were, besides, many wounded. The enemy's artillery had been all captured. The British loss was forty English and thirty Sepoys killed, and a great number of both wounded.

The moral effect of the victory was immense. It was the first time that French and English soldiers had fought in the field against each other in India.

The French had proved to the natives that they were enormously their superiors in fighting power. Hitherto the English had not done so. The defence of Arcot had proved that they could fight behind walls, but the natives had themselves many examples of gallant defences of this kind. The English troops under Gingen and Cope had suffered themselves to be cooped up in Trichinopoli and had not struck a blow in its defence. At Kavaripak the natives discovered that the English could fight as well, or better than the French. The latter were somewhat stronger numerically than their rivals; they had double the force of artillery, were half as strong again in Sepoys, and had two thousand five hundred cavalry, while the English had not a single horseman. They had all the advantages of surprise and position, and yet they had been entirely defeated.

Thenceforth the natives of India regarded the English as a people to be feared and respected, and for the first time considered their ultimate triumph over the French to be a possibility. As the policy of the native princes had ever been to side with the strongest, the advantage thus gained to the English cause by the victory of Kavaripak was enormous.

On the following day the English took possession of the fort of Kavaripak and marched to Arcot. Scarcely had they arrived there when Clive received a despatch from Fort St. David ordering him to return there at once with all his troops, to march to the relief of Trichinopoli, where the garrison was reported to be in the sorest straits from want of provisions. The force reached Fort St. David on the 11th of March. Here preparations were hurried forward for the advance to Trichinopoli, and in three days Clive was ready to start. Just as he was about to set out a ship arrived from England, having on board some more troops, together with Major Lawrence and several officers, some of whom were captains senior to Clive. Major Lawrence, who had already proved his capacity and energy, of course took command of the expedition, and treated Clive, who had served under him at the siege of Pondicherry, and whose successes in the field had attracted his high admiration, as second in command, somewhat to the discontent of the officers senior to him in rank.

The force consisted of four hundred Europeans, eleven hundred Sepoys, and eight guns, and escorted a large train of provisions and stores. During these months which the diversion, caused by the attack of Riza Sahib and the French upon Madras, had given to the besiegers of Trichinopoli, they should have long since captured the town. In spite of all the orders of Dupleix, Law could not bring himself to attack the town, and the French governor of Pondicherry saw with dismay that the two months and a half which his efforts and energy had gained for the besiegers had been entirely wasted, and that it was probable the whole fruits of his labors would be thrown away. He now directed Law to leave only a small force in front of Trichinopoli, and to march with the whole of his army, and that of Chunda Sahib, and crush the force advancing under Lawrence to the relief of Trichinopoli. Law, however, disobeyed orders, and, indeed, acted in direct contradiction to them. He maintained six hundred French troops and many thousands of native before Trichinopoli, and sent but two hundred and fifty French, and about three hundred and fifty natives—a force altogether inferior in numbers to that which it was sent to oppose—to arrest the progress of Lawrence's advancing column.

The position which this French force was directed to occupy was the fort of Koiladi, an admirable position. As the two branches of the Kavari were here but half a mile apart, had Law concentrated all his force here he could, no doubt, have successfully opposed the English. Lawrence, however, when the guns of the fort opened upon him, replied to them by the fire of his artillery, and as the French force was insufficient to enable its commander to fight him in the open, he was enabled to take his troops and convoy in safety past the fort. When Law heard this he marched out and took his position round a lofty and almost inaccessible rock called Elmiseram, and prepared to give battle. Lawrence, however, after passing Koiladi, had been joined by a hundred English and fifty dragoons from Trichinopoli. These acted as guides, and led him by a route by which he avoided the French position, and effected a junction with two hundred Europeans and four hundred Sepoys from Trichinopoli, and with a body of Maratta cavalry under Murari Reo. Law having failed to attack the English force upon its march, now, when its strength was nearly doubled, suddenly decided to give battle, and advanced against the force which, wearied with its long march, had just begun to prepare their breakfast. The French artillery at once put the Maratta cavalry to flight.

Lawrence called the men again under arms, and sent Clive forward to reconnoitre. He found the French infantry drawn up with twenty-two guns, with large bodies of cavalry on either flank. Opposite to the centre of their position was a large caravansary, or native inn, with stone buildings attached. It was nearer to their position than to that occupied by the English, and Clive saw at once that if seized and held by the enemy's artillery, it would sweep the whole ground over which the English would have to advance. He galloped back at full speed to Major Lawrence, and asked leave at once to occupy the building. Obtaining permission he advanced with all speed to the caravansary with some guns and infantry.

The negligence of the French in allowing this move

ment to be carried out was fatal to them. The English artillery opened upon them from the cover of the inn and buildings, and to this fire the French in the open could reply only at a great disadvantage. After a cannonade lasting half an hour, the French, having lost forty European and three hundred native soldiers, fell back, the English having lost only twenty-one. Disheartened at this result, utterly disappointed at the failure which had attended his long operations against Trichinopoli, without energy or decision, Law at once raised the siege of the town, abandoning a great portion of his baggage, and destroying great stores of ammunition and supplies, crossed an arm of the Kavari, and took post in the great fortified temple of Seringam.

The delight of the troops so long besieged in Trichinopoli, inactive, dispirited, and hopeless, was extreme, and the exultation of Muhammud Ali and his native allies was no less.

Captain Cope, towards the end of the siege, had been killed in one of the little skirmishes which occasionally took place with the French.

Charlie Marryat and Peters had, owing to some of the officers senior to them being killed or invalided, and to large numbers of fresh recruits being raised, received a step in rank. They were now lieutenants, and each commanded a body of Sepoys two hundred strong. At Charlie's request Tim Kelly was detached from his company and allowed to remain with him as soldier servant. After the retreat of the French and the settling down of the English force in the lines they had occupied, Charlie and his friend entered Trichinopoli, and were surprised at the temples and palaces there. Although very inferior to Tanjore, and in no way even comparable to the cities of the northwest of India, Trichinopoli was a far more important city than any they had hitherto seen. They ascended the lofty rock and visited the fort on its summit, which looked as if in the hands of a resolute garrison, it should be impregnable to attack. The manner in which this rock, as well as that of Elmiseram and others lying in sight, rose sheer up from the plain, filled them with surprise; for although these natural rock fortresses are common enough in India, they are almost without an example in Europe. After visiting the fort they rambled through the town, and were amused at the scene of bustle in its streets and at the gay shops, full of articles new and curious to them, in the bazaars.

"They are wonderfully clever and ingenious," Charlie said. "Look what rough tools that man is working with, and what delicate and intricate work he is turning out. If these fellows could but fight as well as they work, and were but united among themselves, not only should we be unable to set a foot in India,

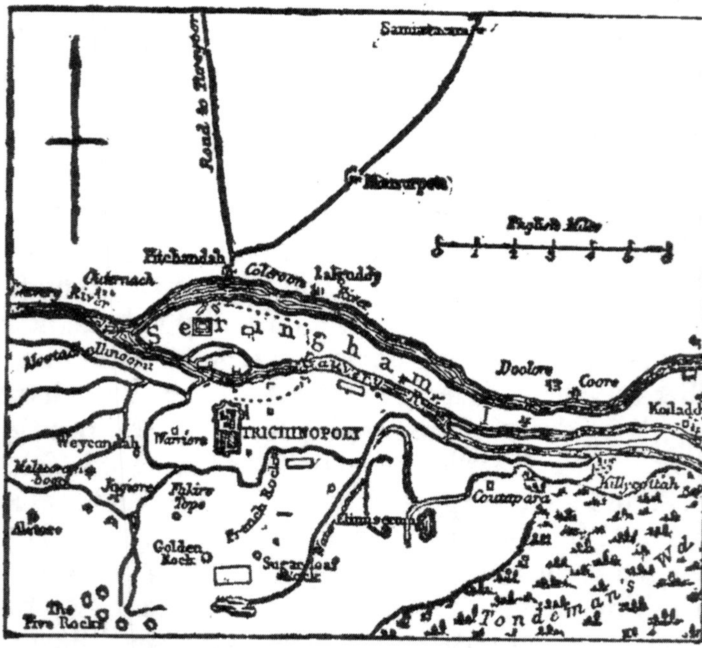

THE ENVIRONS OF TRICHINOPOLI, to illustrate the Military Operations of 1751-1753.

THE BAZAARS OF TRICHINOPOLI.

but the emperor, with the enormous armies which he would be able to raise, would be able to threaten Europe. I suppose they never have been really good fighting men. Alexander, a couple of thousand years ago, defeated them, and since then the Afghans and other northern peoples have been always overrunning and conquering them. I can't make it out. These Sepoys, after only a few weeks' training, fight almost as well as our own men. I wonder how it is that, when commanded by their own countrymen, they are able to make so poor a fight of it. We had better be going back to camp again, Peters, at any moment there may be orders for us to do something. With Major Lawrence and Clive together we are not likely to stop here long inactive."

CHAPTER X.

THE FALL OF SERINGAM.

ALTHOUGH called an island, Seringam is in fact a long narrow tongue of land running between the two branches of the river Kavari. In some places these arms are but a few hundred yards apart, and the island can therefore be defended against an attack along the land. But the retreat of the French by this line was equally difficult, as we held the narrowest part of the neck, two miles from Koiladi. Upon the south our forces at Trichinopoli faced the French across the river. Upon the other side of the Kolrun, as the northern arm of the Kavari is called, the French could cross the river and make their retreat, if necessary, in any direction. The two principal roads, however, led from Paichandah, a strong fortified position on the bank of the river, facing the temple of Seringam. Clive saw that a force crossing the river, and taking up its position on the north, would entirely cut off Law's army in the island, would intercept any reinforcements sent by Dupleix to its rescue, and might compel the surrender of the whole French army. The attempt would, of course, be a dangerous one. The French force was considerably stronger than the English, and were the latter divided into two portions, entirely cut off from each other, the central point between them being occupied by the French, the latter would have an opportunity of throwing his whole force upon one after the other. This danger would have been so great that, had the French been commanded by an able and active officer, the attempt would never have been made. Law, however, had shown amply that he had neither energy nor intelligence, and Major Lawrence therefore accepted Clive's proposal.

But to be successful it was necessary that both portions of the English force should be well commanded. Major Lawrence felt confident in his own capacity to withstand Law upon the southern bank, and in case of necessity he could fall back under the guns of Trichinopoli. He felt sure that he could, with equal certainty, confide the command of the other party to Captain Clive. There was, however, the difficulty that he was the junior captain present, and that already great jealousy had been excited among his seniors by the rank which he occupied in the councils of Lawrence. Fortunately the difficulty was settled by the native allies. Major Lawrence laid his plans before Muhammud Ali and his allies, whose co-operation and assistance were absolutely necessary. These, after hearing the proposal, agreed to give their assistance, but only upon the condition that Clive should be placed in command of the expeditionary party. They had already seen the paralyzing effects of the incapacity of some English officers. Clive's defence of Arcot and the victories of Arni and Kavaripak had excited their intense admiration, and caused them to place unbounded confidence in him. Therefore they said, "If Captain Clive commands we will go. Unless he commands we do not." Major Lawrence was glad that the pressure thus placed upon him enabled him, without incurring a charge of favoritism, to place the command in the hands of the officer upon whom he most relied.

On the night of the 6th of April Clive set out with a force composed of four hundred English, seven hundred Sepoys, three thousand Maratta cavalry, a thousand Tanjore cavalry, six light guns and two heavy ones. Descending the river he crossed the island at a point three miles to the east of Law's camping ground, and marched to Samieaveram, a town nine miles north of the island, and commanding the roads from the north and east. The movement was just made in time. Dupleix, utterly disgusted with Law, had resolved to displace him. D'Auteuil, the only officer he had of sufficient high rank to take his place, had not when previously employed betrayed any great energy or capacity. It appeared, nevertheless, that he was at any rate superior to Law. On the 10th of April, therefore, he despatched D'Auteuil with a hundred and twenty French, and five hundred Sepoys, with four guns and a large convoy to Seringam, where he was to take the command. When he arrived within fifteen miles of Samieaveram, he learned that Clive had possession of that village, and he determined upon a circuitous route by which he might avoid him. He therefore sent a messenger to Law to acquaint him with his plans in order that he might aid him by making a diversion.

Clive in the mean time had been at work. On the day after his arrival at Samieaveram, he attacked and captured the temple of Mansurpet, half way between the village and the island. The temple was lofty and stood on rising ground, and commanded a range of the country for many miles round. On its top Clive established a signal station. Upon the following day he carried the mud fort of Lalgudi, which was situated on the north bank of the river two miles to the east of Paichandah, which now remained Law's only place of exit from the island.

D'Auteuil, after sending word to Law of his intentions, marched from Utatua, where he was lying, by a road to the west which would enable him to move round Samieaveram to Paichandah. Clive captured one of the messengers and set off with his force to intercept him. D'Auteuil, however, received information by his spies of Clive's movement, and not wishing to fight a battle in the open with a superior force, fell back to Utatua, while Clive returned to Samieaveram. Law, too, had received news of Clive's movements. Here was a chance of retrieving the misfortunes of the campaign. Paichandah being still in his hands, he could sally out with his whole force and that of Chunda Sahib, seize Samieaveram in Clive's absence, and extend his hand to D'Auteuil, or fall upon Clive's rear. Instead of this he repeated the mistake he had made before Trichinopoli; and instead of marching out with his whole force, he sent only eighty Europeans, of whom forty were deserters from the English army, and seven hundred Sepoys.

The English returned from their march against D'Auteuil. The greater portion of the troops were housed in two temples, a quarter of a mile apart, known as the Large and Small Pagoda. Clive with several of his officers was in a caravansary close to the Small Pagoda. Charlie's company were on guard, and after paying a visit to the sentries and seeing that all were on the alert, he returned to the caravansary. The day had been a long one, and the march under the heat of the sun very fatiguing. There was therefore but little conversation, and Charlie, finding on his return from visiting the sentries that his leader and the other officers had already wrapped themselves in their cloaks and lain down to rest, imitated their example. Half an hour later the French column arrived at Samieaveràm. The officer in command was a daring and determined man. Before reaching the place he had heard that the English had returned, and finding that he had been forestalled, he might well have returned to Law. He determined, however, to attempt to surprise the camp. He placed his deserters in front, and when the column, arriving near the Sepoy sentinel, was challenged, the officer in command of the deserters, an Irishman, stepped forward, and said that he had been sent by Major Lawrence to the support of Captain Clive. As the other English-speaking soldiers now came up the sentry and native officer with him were completely deceived, and the latter sent a soldier to guide the column to the English quarter of the camp. Without interruption the column marched on through lines of sleeping Sepoys and Marattas until they reached the heart of the village. Here they were again challenged. They replied with a volley of musketry into the caravansary and another into the pagoda. Then they rushed into the pagoda, bayoneting all they found there.

Charlie, who had just dropped off to sleep, sprang to his feet, as did the other officers. While, confused by the noise and suddenness of the attack, others scarcely understood what was happening, Clive's clear head and ready judgment grasped the situation at once. "Gentlemen," he said calmly, "there is no firing going on in the direction of the Great Pagoda. Follow me there at once."

Snatching up their arms the officers followed him at a run. The whole village was a scene of wild confusion. The firing round the pagoda and caravansary were continuous. The Maratta horsemen were climbing into their saddles and riding away out into the plain, the Sepoys were running hither and thither. At the pagoda he found the soldiers turning out under arms, and Clive, ordering his officers to do their best to rally the native troops in good order against the enemy, at once moved forward toward the caravansary with two hundred English troops. On arriving there he found a large body of Sepoys firing away at random. Believing them to be his own men, for the

French and English Sepoys were alike dressed in white, he halted the English a few yards from them, and rushed among them, upbraiding them for their panic, striking them, and ordering them instantly to cease firing and to form in order. One of the Sepoy officers recognized Clive to be an Englishman, struck at him and wounded him with his sword.

Clive, still believing him to be one of his own men, was furious at what he considered an act of insolent insubordination, and seizing him, dragged him across to the Small Pagoda to hand him over, as he supposed, to the guard there. To his astonishment he found six Frenchmen at the gate, and these at once summoned him to surrender. Great as was his surprise, he did not for a moment lose coolness, and at once told them that he had come to beg them to lay down their arms, that they were surrounded by his whole army, and that unless they surrendered his troops would give no quarter. So impressed were the Frenchmen with the firmness of the speaker that three of them at once surrendered, while the other three ran into the temple to inform their commander.

Clive took the three men who had surrendered, and returned to the English troops he had left near the caravansary. The French Sepoys had discovered that the English were enemies, and had moved quietly off. Confusion still reigned. Clive did not imagine for a moment that so daring an assault could have been made on his camp by a small body of enemies, and expected every moment an attack by Law's whole force. The commander of the French in the pagoda was disturbed by the news brought in by the three men from the gate, and despatched eight of his most intelligent men to ascertain exactly what was going on. These, however, fell into the hands of the English, and the officer of the party, not knowing that the Small Pagoda was in the hands of the French, handed them over to a sergeant, and told him to take a party and escort his eight prisoners and the three Captain Clive had captured to that pagoda for confinement there. Upon arrival at the gate the Frenchmen at once joined their comrades, and these latter were also so bewildered at the affair that they allowed the English sergeant and his guard to march off again unmolested.

By this time, owing to the absence of all resistance elsewhere, Clive had learnt that the whole of the party who had entered the camp were in the Lesser Pagoda, and, as he was still expecting momentarily to be attacked by Law's main army, he determined to rid himself of this enemy in his midst. The pagoda was very strong and only two men could enter abreast. Clive led his men to the attack, but so well did the French defend themselves that after losing an officer and fifteen men, Clive determined to wait till morning.

The French officer, knowing that he was surrounded, and beyond the reach of all assistance, resolved upon cutting a way through, and at daylight his men sallied out from the temple. So fierce, however, was the fire with which the English received him that twelve of his men were instantly killed, and the rest ran back into the temple.

Clive, hoping that their commander would now surrender without further effusion of blood, advanced to the gateway and entered the porch to offer terms. He was himself so faint from the loss of blood from his wounds that he could not stand alone, but leaned against a wall, supported by two sergeants. The officer commanding the deserters came out to parley, but, after heaping abuse upon Clive, levelled his musket and discharged it at him.

He missed Clive, but killed the two sergeants who were supporting him.

The French officer in command, indignant at this

conduct, rushed forward at once to disavow it, and stated that he had determined to defend the post to the last, solely for the sake of the deserters, but that the conduct of their officer had released him from that obligation, and he now therefore surrendered at once. The instant day broke and Clive saw that Law was not, as he expected, at hand, he despatched the Maratta horse in pursuit of the French Sepoys. These were overtaken and cut to pieces, and not one man of the force which Law had despatched against Clive returned to the island. The English loss was heavy. The greater portion of the occupants of the Small Pagoda were bayonetted by the French when they entered, and as fifteen others were killed in the attack, it is probable that at least one-fourth of the English force under Clive were killed. Clive's own escapes were extraordinary. In addition to those of being killed by the French Sepoys, among whom he ran by mistake, and of death at the hands of the treacherous deserter, he had one almost as close when the French fired their volley into the caravansary. A box at his feet was shattered, and a servant who slept close to him was killed.

Some days passed after this attack without any fresh movement on either side. Major Lawrence then determined to drive back D'Auteuil. He did not despatch Clive against him, as this would involve the risk that Law might again march out to surprise Samieaveram. He therefore directed Clive to remain at that place and watch the island while he sent a force of a hundred and fifty English, four hundred Sepoys, five hundred Marattas, with four guns to attack D'Auteuil from his own force, under Captain Dalton. This officer in the advance marched his troops near Samieaveram, and, making as much show with them as he could, impressed D'Auteuil with the idea that the force was that of Clive. Accordingly he broke up his camp at Utatua in the night, abandoned his stores, and retreated hastily upon Valconda. Dalton them marched to Samieaveram, and placed his force at Clive's disposal, and, to prevent any disputes arising as to precedence and rank, offered himself to serve under him as a volunteer.

Not only D'Auteuil but Law was deceived by Dalton's march. From the lofty towers of Seringam he saw the force marching towards Utatua, believed that Clive with his whole force had left Samieaveram, and did now what he should have before done, crossed the river with all his troops. Clive's lookout on the temple of Mansurpet perceived what was going on and signalled the news to Clive, who at once set out with his whole force, and, before Law was prepared to issue out from Paichandah, Clive was within a mile of that place. Law might still have fought with a fair chance of success, as he was far stronger than his enemy, but he was again the victim of indecision and want of energy, and, covered by Paichandah, he fell back across the river again.

On the 15th of May Clive captured Paichandah, and then determined to give a final blow to D'Auteuil's force, which had, he learned, again set out to endeavor to relieve Law. He marched to Utatua to intercept him. D'Auteuil, hearing of his coming, instantly fell back again to Valconda. The native chief of this town, however, seeing that the affairs of the French were desperate, and willing, like all his countrymen, to make his peace with the strongest, had already accepted bribes from the English, and upon D'Auteuil's return closed the gates and refused to admit him. Clive soon arrived and D'Auteuil, caught between two fires, surrendered with his whole force.

Had Law been a man of energy he had yet a chance of escape. He had still seven or eight hundred French troops with him, two thousand Sepoys, and four thousand of Chunda Sahib's troops. He might then have easily crossed the Kavari at night and fallen upon Lawrence, whose force there now was greatly inferior to his own. Chunda Sahib in vain begged him to do so. His hesitation continued until, three days after the surrender of D'Auteuil, a battering train reached Lawrence, whereupon Law at once surrendered, his chief stipulation being that the life of Chunda Sahib should be spared. This promise was not kept. The unfortunate prince had preferred to surrender to the Rajah of Tanjore, who had several times intrigued secretly with him, rather than to Muhammud Ali or the English, whom he regarded as his implacable enemies. Had he placed himself in our hands his life would have been safe. He was murdered by the treacherous rajah within twenty-four hours of his surrender.

With the fall of Seringam terminated the contest for the supremacy of the Carnatic between the English and French, fighting respectively on behalf of their puppets, Muhammud Ali and Chunda Sahib. This stage of the struggle was not a final one, but both by its circumstances and by the prestige which we acquired in the eyes of the natives it gave us a moral ascendency which even when our fortunes were afterwards at their worst was never lost again. Muhammud Ali had himself gained but little in the struggle. He was indeed nominally ruler of the Carnatic, but he had to rely for his position solely on the support of the English bayonets. Indeed the promises of which he had been obliged to be lavish to his native allies to keep them faithful to his cause when that cause seemed all but lost, now came upon him to trouble him, and so precarious was his position that he was obliged to ask the English to leave two hundred English troops and fifteen hundred of their Sepoys to protect the place against Murari Reo and the Rajahs of Mysore and Tanjore.

The fatigues of the expedition had been great, and when the force reached the sea-coast Major Lawrence was forced to retire to Fort St. David to recover his health, while Clive, whose health had now greatly broken down, betook himself to Madras, which had, when the danger of invasion by the French was at an end, become the headquarters of the government of the presidency. There were, however, two French strongholds dangerously near to Madras, Covelong and Chengalpatt. Two hundred recruits had just arrived from England, and five hundred natives had been enlisted as Sepoys. Mr. Saunders begged Clive to take the command of these and reduce the two fortresses. He took with him two twenty-four pounders, and four officers, of whom two were Charlie Marryat and Peters, to both of whom Clive was much attached, owing to their courage, readiness and good humor. Covelong was first attacked. It mounted thirty guns and was garrisoned by fifty French and three hundred Sepoys.

"I don't like the look o' things, Mr. Charles," Tim Kelly said; "there's nothing but boys altogether, white and black. Does it stand to reason that a lot of gossoons who haven't learnt the goose step, and haven't as much as a shred of faith ayther in themselves or their officers, are fit to fight the French?"

"Oh, I don't know, Tim," Charlie said. "Boys are just as plucky as men in their way, and are ready to do all sorts of foolhardy things which men would hesitate to attempt."

"And that is so, Mr. Charles, when they've only other boys to dale with; but as they're growing up they take some time before they're quite sure they're a match for men. That's what it is yer honor, I tell ye, and you will see it soon."

Tim's predictions were speedily verified. The very

morning after they arrived before the fort the garrison made a sally, fell upon the troops, and killed one of their officers. The whole of the new levies took to their heels and fled away from the fight. Clive with his three officers threw himself among them, and for some time in vain attempted to turn the tide. It was not, indeed, until several had been cut down that the rout was arrested, and they were brought back to their duty. A day or two later a shot striking a rock killed or wounded fourteen men, and excited such a panic that it was some time before the rest would venture near the front.

The enemy with a considerable force marched from Chengalpatt to relieve the place. Clive left half his force to continue the siege, and with the rest marched out and offered battle to the relieving force. Daring and confidence as usual prevailed. Had the enemy attacked there is little doubt they would have put Clive's raw levies to flight. They were, however, cowed by his attitude of defiance, and retreated hastily. The governor of Covelong at once lost heart and surrendered the place, which he might have maintained for months against the force before it, and on the fourth day of the siege capitulated. A few hours afterwards the enemy from Chengalpatt, ignorant of the fall of the fort, again advanced, and Clive met them with his whole force. Taken by surprise they suffered heavily. Clive pursued them to the gates of their fort, to which he at once laid siege. Fortunately for the English, the commander of this place, like him of Covelong, was cowardly and incapable. Had it not been so, the fort, which was very strong, well provisioned, and well garrisoned, might have held out for an indefinite time. As it was it surrendered on the fourth day, and Clive took possession on the 31st of August. He returned to Madras, and there, a short time afterwards, married Miss Maskelyne. Finding his health, however, continuing to deteriorate, he sailed for Europe in February, 1753. It was but five years since he had first taken up arms to defend Fort St. David, an unknown clerk without prospects and without fortune, utterly discontented and disheartened. Madras was in the hands of the French. Everywhere their policy was triumphant, and the soil surrounded by the walls of St. David's alone remained to the English in Southern India. In the five years which had elapsed all had changed. The English were masters of the Carnatic. The French were broken and discredited. The English were regarded by the natives throughout the country as the coming power, and of this great change no slight portion was due to the enemy and genius of Clive himself.

CHAPTER XI.

AN IMPORTANT MISSION.

A FEW days after the return of the expedition against Covelong and Chengalpatt, Charlie received a note from Governor Saunders requesting him to call upon him at eleven o'clock. Charlie, of course, attended at Government House at the time named, and found Captain Clive with Mr. Saunders.

"I have sent for you, Mr. Marryat, to ask you if you are ready to undertake a delicate and somewhat dangerous mission. Captain Clive tells me that he is convinced that you will be able to discharge the duties satisfactorily. He has been giving me the highest report of your conduct and courage, and he tells me that you speak the language with some facility."

"I have been working hard, sir," Charlie said, "and have had a moonshee for the last year; and as, except when on duty, I have spoken nothing but the native language with him, I can now speak it almost as fluently as I can English."

"So Captain Clive has been telling me," Mr. Saunders said; "and it is indeed on that ground that I select you for the service. Your friend, Mr. Peters, has equally distinguished himself in the field, Captain Clive tells me, but he is greatly your inferior in his knowledge of the vernacular."

This was indeed the case. Peters had but little

natural aptitude for foreign languages, and after working hard for a time with the moonshee he found that he was making so little progress in comparison with Charlie that he lost heart; and although he had continued his lessons with the moonshee he had done so only to the extent of an hour or so a day, whereas Charlie had devoted his whole leisure time to the work.

"The facts of the case are these, Mr. Marryat. Owing to the failure of Muhammud Ali to fulfil the ridiculously onerous terms extorted from him by some of his native allies during the siege of Trichinopoli, several of them are in a state of discontent, which is likely soon to break out into open hostilities. The Rajahs of Mysore and Tanjore are, I have learned, already in communication with Pondicherry, and will, I believe shortly acknowledge the son of Chunda Sahib, whom Dupleix has declared ruler of the Carnatic. Murari Reo has already openly joined the French. Their influence in the Deccan is now so great that Bussy may be said to rule there. Now, there is a chief named Boorhau Reo, whose territory lies among the hills, and extends from the plain nearly up to the plateau land of the Deccan. His position, like that of many of the other small rajahs, is precarious. In days like the present, when might makes right, and every petty state tries to make profit out of the constant wars at the expense of its neighbor, the position of a chief surrounded by half a dozen others more powerful than himself is by no means pleasant. Boorhau Reo feels that he is in danger of being swallowed by the nizam or by the Marattas, and he earnestly desires to ally himself with us, believing, as he says, that we are destined to be masters here. I have assured him that although gratified at his expressions of friendship, we can enter into no alliance with him. The position of his territory would enable him to be of great assistance to us in any war in which the whole force of the Deccan, controlled as it is at present by Bussy, might be utilized against us in the Carnatic. He would be able to harass convoys, cut communications, and otherwise trouble the enemy's movements. But although we see that his aid would be very useful to us in case of such a war, we do not see how on our part we could give him any protection. We have now, with the greatest difficulty, brought affairs to a successful conclusion in the Carnatic, but Dupleix is active and energetic and well supported at home. Many of the chiefs lately our allies, have, as I have just said, declared against us or are about to do so, and it is out of the question for us to think of supporting a chief so far removed from us as Boorhau. I have, therefore, told him that we greatly desire his friendship, but are at present powerless to protect him should he be attacked by his northern neighbors. He is particularly anxious to train his men after the European fashion, as he sees that our Sepoys are a match for five times their number of the untrained troops of the Indian princes.

"This brings me to the subject before us. I have written to him to say that I will send to him an English officer capable of training and leading his troops, and whose advice may be useful to him upon all occasions; but that, as were it known that he had received a British officer and was employing him to train his troops, it would excite the instant animosity of Bussy and of the Peishwar, I should send one familiar with the language and who may pass as a native. Captain Clive has strongly recommended you for this difficult mission."

"I fear, sir, that I could hardly pass as a native. The moonshee is constantly correcting mistakes which I make in speaking."

"That may be so," Mr. Saunders said: "but there

are a score of dialects in Southern India, and you could be passed upon nineteen of the twenty peoples who speak them as belonging to one of the other."

"If you think, sir, that I shall do," Charlie said, "I shall be glad to undertake the mission."

"Very well, Mr. Marryat, that is understood then. You will receive full instructions in writing, and will understand that your duty is not only to drill the troops of this chief, but to give him such advice as may suit his and our interests, to strengthen his good feeling towards us, and to form as far as possible a compact little force which might at a critical moment be of immense utility. You will, of course, master the geography of the country, of which we are all but absolutely ignorant, find out about the passes, the mountain paths, the defensible positions. All these things may some day be of the highest importance. You will have a few days to make your arrangements and settle as to the character you will adopt. This you had better do in consultation with some one who thoroughly understands the country. It is intended that you shall go down to Trichinopoli with the next convoy, and from there make your way to the stronghold of Boorhau."

"Shall I take any followers with me?"

"Yes," Mr. Saunders said. "As you will go in the character of a military adventurer who has served among our Sepoys long enough to learn European drill, you had better take two, three, or four men, as you like, with you as retainers. You might pick out two or three trusty men from the Sepoys you command."

Charlie left Government House in high spirits. It was certainly an honor to have been selected for such a post. It was quite possible that it would be a dangerous one. It was sure to be altogether different from the ordinary life of a subaltern in the Company's army. Peters was very sorry when he heard from Charlie that they were at last to be separated. It was now nearly two years since they had first met on board the *Lizzie Anderson*, and since that time they had been constantly together, and were greatly attached to each other. Charlie, perhaps, had taken the lead. The fact of his having a stock of fire-arms, and being able to lend them to Peters, had given him perhaps the first slight and almost imperceptible advantage. His feat of jumping overboard to rescue Tim Kelly had been another step in advance, and although Charlie would have denied it himself there was no doubt that he generally took the lead, and that his friend was accustomed to lean upon him and to look to him always for the initiative. It was therefore a severe blow to Peters to find that Charlie was about to be sent on detached service. As for Tim Kelly, he was uproarious in his grief when he heard that he was to be separated from his master.

"Shure, Mr. Charlie, ye'll never have the heart to lave a poor boy that sarved ye be night and day for eighteen months. Tim Kelly would gladly give his life for ye, and ye wouldn't go and lave him behind ye and go all alone among these black thaves of the world."

"But it is impossible that I can take you, Tim," Charlie said. "You know yourself that you cannot speak ten words of the language. How then could you possibly pass undetected, whatever disguise you put on?"

"But I'd never open my mouth at all at all, yer honor, barring for mate and drink."

"It's all very well for you to say so, Tim," Charlie answered; "but I do not think that anything short of a miracle would silence your tongue. But leave us now, Tim, and I will talk the matter over with Mr.

Peters. I should be glad enough to have you with me if we could arrange it."

The moonshee was taken into their counsels, and was asked his opinion as to the disguise which Charlie could adopt with least risk of detection. The moonshee replied that he might pass as a Bheel. These hill tribes speak a dialect quite distinct from that of the people around them, and the moonshee said that if properly attired Charlie would be able to pass anywhere for one of these people, provided always that he did not meet with another of the same race. "You might assert," he said, "that your father had taken service with some rajah on the plain, and that you had there learned to speak the language. In this way you would avoid having to answer any difficult questions regarding your native place; but as to that, you can get up something of the geography before you leave."

"There are several Bheels among our Sepoys," Charlie said. "I can pick out three or four of them who would be just the men for me to take. I believe they are generally very faithful and attached to their officers."

When Tim again entered the room he inquired anxiously if his master hit upon any disguise which would suit him. "What do you say, Mr. Moonshine?" Tim said.

The moonshee shook his head. Between these two a perpetual feud had existed ever since the native had arrived at Arcot to take his place as a member of Charlie's establishment. In obedience to Charlie's stringent orders Tim never was openly rude to him; but he never lost an opportunity of making remarks of a disparaging nature as to the value of Charlie's studies. The moonshee, on his part, generally ignored Tim's existence altogether, addressing him, when obliged to do so, with a ceremonious civility which annoyed Tim more than open abuse would have done. "I think," he said gravely in reply to Tim's demand, "that the very worshipful one would have most chance of escaping detection if he went in rags, throwing dust on his hair and passing for one afflicted."

"And what does he mean by afflicted, Mr. Charles?" the Irishman said wrathfully, as the two young officers laughed.

"He means one who is a born fool, Tim."

Tim looked furiously at the moonshee.

"It would," the latter said sententiously, "be the character which the worshipful one would support with the greatest ease."

"The black thief is making fun of me," Tim muttered; "but I'll be aven with him one of these days or my name isn't Tim Kelly. I was thinking, yer honor, that I might represent one deaf and dumb."

"But you're always talking, Tim, and when you're not talking to others you talk to yourself. It's quite impossible you could go as a dumb man; but you might go, as the moonshee suggests, as a half-witted sort of chap with just sense enough to groom a horse and look after him, but with not enough to understand what's said to you or to answer any questions."

"I could do that asy enough, Mr. Charles."

"And you have to keep from quarrelling, Tim. I hear you quarrelling on an average ten times a day; and as in such a character as we're talking about you would, of course, be exposed to all sorts of slights and unpleasantnesses, you would be in continual hot water."

"Now, yer honor," Tim said reproachfully, "you're too hard on one entirely. I like a bit of a row as well as any man, but it's all for divarsion; and I could go on for a year without quarrelling with a soul. Just try me, Mr. Charles, just try me for a month, and if at the end of that time you find me in your way, or that I don't keep my character, then send me back agin to the regiment."

It was arranged that the moonshee should remain with Peters, who, seeing that Charlie owed his appointment to a post which promised excitement and adventure, to his skill in the native languages, was determined that he would again set to in earnest and try and master its intricacies. The moonshee went down to the bazaar and purchased the clothes which would be necessary for the disguises, and Charlie found in his company four Sepoys who willingly agreed to accompany him in the character of his retainers upon his expedition. As to their costume there was no difficulty. When off duty the Sepoys in the Company's service were accustomed to dress in their native attire. Consequently it needed only the addition of a tulwar or short curved sword, a shield thrown over one shoulder, a long matchlock, and two or three pistols and daggers stuck into a girdle to complete their equipment. Charlie himself was dressed gayly in the garb of a military officer in the service of an Indian rajah. He was to ride, and a horse, saddle, and gay housings were procured. He had at last given in to Tim's entreaties, and that worthy was dressed as a syce or horse-keeper.

Both Charlie and Tim had had those portions of their skin exposed to the air darkened, and both would pass muster at a casual inspection. Charlie in thus concealing his nationality desired only to hide the fact that he was an officer in the Company's service. He believed that it would be impossible for him to continue to pass as a Bheel. This however, would be of no consequence after a time. Many of the native princes had Europeans in their service. Runaway sailors, deserters from the English, French, and Dutch armed forces in their possessions on the sea-coast, adventurers influenced either by a love of a life of

CHARLIE'S MISSION TO RAJAH BOORHAU.

excitement, or whom a desire to escape the consequences of folly or crime committed at home had driven to a roving life—such men might be found in many of the native courts. Once settled, then, in the service of the rajah, Charlie intended to make but little farther pretence or secrecy as to his nationality. Outwardly he would still conform to the language and appearance of the character he had chosen, but he would allow it to be supposed that he was an Englishman, a deserter from the Company's service, and that his comrades were Sepoys in a similar position. His employment, then, at the court of the rajah would have an effect the exact reverse of that which it would have done had he appeared in his proper character. Deserters were of all men the most opposed to their countrymen, to whom they had proved traitors. In battle they could be relied upon to fight desperately, for they fought with ropes round their necks. Therefore, while the appearance of an English officer as instructor of the forces of the rajah would have drawn upon himself the instant hostility of all opposed to the British, the circulation of a report that his troops were being disciplined by some English and native deserters from the Company's forces would excite no suspicion whatever.

To avoid attracting attention Charlie Marryat and his party set out before daylight from Madras. Their appearance, indeed, would have attracted no attention when they once had passed beyond the boundaries of the portion of the town occupied by the whites. In the native quarter the appearance of a small zemindar or landowner attended by four or five armed followers on foot, was of such common occurrence as to attract no attention whatever; and, indeed, numbers of these come in to take service in the Sepoy regiments, the profession of arms being always considered honorable in India.

For a fortnight they travelled by easy stages without question or suspicion being excited that they were not what they seemed. They were now among the hills, and soon arrived at Ambur, the seat of the rajah. The town was a small one, and above it rose the fortress, which stood on a rock rising sheer from the bottom of the valley, and standing boldly out from the hillside. The communication was effected by a shoulder which, starting from a point half-way up the rock, joined the hill behind it. Along this shoulder were walls and gateways. An enemy attacking these would be exposed to the fire from the summit of the rock. From the point where the shoulder joined the rock a zigzag road had been cut with enormous labor, in the face of the rock, to the summit.

"It is a strong place," Charlie said to Tim Kelly, who was walking by his horse's head, "and should be able to hold out against anything but starvation, that is to say, if properly defended."

"It's a powerful place, surely," Tim said; and would puzzle the ould boy himself to take. Even Captain Clive, who is afeard of nothing, would be bothered by it."

As they rode up the valley two horsemen were seen spurring towards them from the town. They drew rein before Charlie, and one bowing said:

"My master, the rajah, sends his greeting to you, and begs to know if you are the illustrious soldier, Nadir Ali, for whom his heart has been longing."

"Will you tell your lord that Nadir Ali is here," Charlie said, "and that he longs to see the face of the rajah."

One of the horsemen at once rode off, and the other took his place by the side of Charlie; and having introduced himself as captain of the rajah's body-guard, rode with him through the town. Had Charlie appeared in his character as English officer the rajah and all his troops would have turned out to do honor to his arrival. As it was, a portion of the garrison only appeared at the gate and lined the walls. Through these the little party passed, and up the sharp zigzags, which were so steep that had it not been that his dignity prevented him from dismounting, Charlie would gladly have got off and proceeded on foot; for it was as much as the animal could do to struggle up the steep incline. At each turn there was a gateway, with little flanking towers on which jingalls or small wall-pieces commanded the road.

"Faith, then, it's no fool that built this place. I shouldn't like to have to attack it wid all the soldiers of the king's army, let alone those of the Company."

"It is tremendously strong, Tim, but it is astonishing what brave men can do."

In the after wars which England waged in India the truth of what Charlie said was over and over again proved. Numerous fortresses, supposed by the natives to be absolutely impregnable, and far exceeding in strength that just described, have been carried by assault by the dash and daring of English troops.

They gained at last the top of the rock. It was uneven in surface, some portions being considerably more elevated than others. Roughly, its extent was about a hundred yards either way. The lower level was covered with buildings occupied by the garrison and storehouses. On the upper level, some forty feet higher, stood the palace of the rajah. It communicated with the courtyard below by a broad flight of steps. These led to an arched gateway, with a wall and battlements, forming an interior line of defence should an assailant gain a footing in the lower portion of the stronghold. Alighting from his horse at the foot of the steps Charlie, followed by his five retainers, mounted to the gateway. Here another guard of honor was drawn up. Passing through these they entered a shady courtyard, on one side of which was a stone pavilion. The flat ceiling was supported by massive columns closely covered with intricate sculpture. The roof was arabesqued with deeply cut patterns picked out in bright colors. A fountain played in the middle. On the farther side the floor, which was of marble, was raised, and two steps led to a wide recess, with windows of lattice stonework giving a view over the town and valley below. In this recess were piles of cushions and carpets, and here reclined the rajah, a spare and active-looking man of some forty years old. He rose as Charlie approached, the soldiers and Sepoys remaining beyond the limits of the pavilion.

"Welcome, brave Nadir Ali," he said courteously; "my heart is glad, indeed, at the presence of one whose wisdom is said to be far beyond his years, and who has learned the arts of war of the infidels from beyond the seas." Then inviting Charlie to take a seat on the divan with him, he questioned him as to his journey, and the events which were taking place in the plains, until the attendants, having handed round refreshments, retired at his signal. "I am glad to see you, Sahib," he said, when they were alone; "though, in truth, I looked for one older than yourself. The great English governor of Madras tells me, however, in a letter which I received four days since, that you are skilled in war, that you fought by the side of that great Captain Clive at Arcot, Arni, Kavaripak, and at Trichinopoli, and that the great warrior himself chose you to come to me. Therefore I doubt neither your valor nor your prudence, and put myself in your hands wholly. The governor has already told you doubtless, of the position in which I am placed here."

"Governor Saunders explained the whole position to me," Charlie said. "You are at present menaced on all sides by powerful neighbors. You believe that the fortunes of the English are on the increase, and as you think the time may come ere long when they will turn the French out of the Deccan and become masters there, as they have already become masters in the Carnatic, you wish to fight by their side, and share their fortunes. In the meantime, you desire to be able to defend yourself against your neighbors, for at present the English are too far away to assist you. To enable you to do this I have been sent to drill and discipline your troops like our Sepoys, and to give you such advice as may be best for the general defence of your country. I have brought with me five soldiers, four Bheels, and one of my countrymen. The latter will be of little use in drilling your troops, for he is ignorant of the language, and has come as my personal attendant. The other four will assist me in my work. Your followers here will, no doubt, discover in a very short time that I am an Englishman. Let it be understood that I am a deserter, that I have been attracted to your court by the promise of high pay, and that I have assumed the character of a Bheel lest my being here might put you on bad terms with the English." Charlie then asked the rajah as to the strength of his military force.

"In times of peace," the rajah said, "I keep three hundred men under arms; in case of taking the field, three thousand. To defend Ambur against an attack of an enemy I could muster ten thousand men."

"You could not call out three thousand men without attracting the attention of your neighbors?" Charlie asked.

"No," the rajah said; "that would bring my neighbors upon me at once."

"I suppose, however, you might assemble another five hundred men without attracting attention."

"Oh, yes," the rajah said; "eight hundred men are not a force which could attract any great attention."

"Then I should propose that we begin with eight hundred," Charlie said. "For a month, however, I will confine myself to the troops you at present have. We must in the first place train some officers. If you will pick out those to whom you intend to give commands and sub-commands I will choose from the men, after drilling them for a few days, forty of the most intelligent as what we call non-commissioned officers. For the first month we will work hard in teaching these officers and sub-officers their duties. Then, when the whole eight hundred assemble, we can divide them into four parties. There will be one of my drill-instructors to each party, ten under officers, and four or five of the officers whom you will appoint. Six week's hard work should make these eight hundred men fairly acquainted with drill. The English Sepoys have often gone out to fight with less. At the end of the six weeks let the five hundred men you have called out, in addition to your body-guard of three hundred, return to their homes, and replace them by an equal number of fresh levies, and so proceed until you have your three thousand fighting men thoroughly trained. In nine months all will have had their six weeks of exercise, and could take their places in the ranks again at a day's notice. Two hundred of your men I will train in artillery; although I do not belong to that branch of the service, I learned the duties at Arcot."

The rajah agreed heartily to Charlie's proposals, well pleased at the thought that he should, before the end of a year, be possessed of a trained force which would enable him to hold his own against his powerful neighbors until an opportunity might occur when, in alliance with the English, he should be able to turn the tables upon them, and to aggrandize himself at their expense.

CHAPTER XII.

A MURDEROUS ATTEMPT.

HANDSOME rooms with a suite of attendants were assigned to Charlie in the rajah's palace, and he was formally appointed commander of his forces. The four Sepoys were appointed to junior ranks, as was also Tim Kelly, who, however insisted on remaining in the position of chief attendant upon his master, being, in fact, a sort of major-domo and valet in one, looking after his comforts when in the palace, and accompanying him as personal guard whenever he rode out.

"You niver know, yer honor, what these natives may be up to. They'll smile with you one day and stab ye the next. They're treacherous varmint, yer honor, if you do but give 'em the chance."

At first Charlie perceived that his position excited some jealousy in the minds of those surrounding the rajah. He therefore did all in his power to show to them that he in no way aspired to interfere in the internal politics or affairs of the little state,—that he was a soldier and nothing more. He urged upon the rajah, who wished to have him always by him, that it was far better that he should appear to hold aloof, and to avoid all appearance of favoritism, or of a desire to obtain dominance in the counsels of the rajah. He wished that the appointments to the posts of officers in the new force should be made by the rajah, who should lend an ear to the advice of his usual councillors; but that once appointed they should be under his absolute command and control, and that he should have power to dismiss those who proved themselves indolent and incapable, to promote active and energetic men, wholly regardless of influence or position.

The next morning Charlie and his four assistants set to work to drill the three hundred men of the garrison, taking them in parties of twenty. They were thus able, in the course of a few days, to pick out the most active and intelligent for the sub-officers, and these with the existing officers of the body and the new ones appointed by the rajah, were at once taken in hand to be taught their duty.

For a month the work went on steadily and without interruption, and from morn till night the courtyard echoed with the words of command. At the end of that time the twenty officers and forty sub-officers had fairly learned their duty. The natives of India are very quick in learning drill, and a regiment of newly raised Sepoys will perform manœuvres and answer to words of command in the course of a fortnight as promptly and regularly as would one of English recruits in three months. A good many changes had taken place during the month's work. Many of the officers became disgusted with hard and continuous work, to which they were unaccustomed, while some of the sub-officers showed a deficiency of the quickness and intelligence needed for the work. Their places, however, were easily filled, and as the days went on all took an increasing degree of interest, as they acquired facility of movement, and saw how quickly, according to the European methods, manœuvres were gone through. At the end of a month, then, the sixty men were able in turn to instruct others, and a body of five hundred men being called out, the work of drilling on a large scale began.

The drill-ground now was a level space in the valley below the town, and the whole population assembled day after day to look on with astonishment at the exercises. The four great companies, or battalions as Charlie called them, were kept entirely separate, each under the command of one of the Sepoys, under whom were a proportion of the officers and sub-officers. Every evening Charlie came down for an hour and put each body through its drill, distributing blame or praise as it was deserved, thus keeping up a spirit of emulation between the battalions. At the end of a fortnight, when the simpler manœuvres had been learned, Charlie, for two hours each day, worked the whole together as one regiment, and was surprised himself to find how rapid was the progress which each day effected. The rajah himself often came down to the drill-ground and took the highest interest in the work. He himself would fain have had regular uniforms, similar to those worn by the Sepoys in the service of the European powers, provided for the men; but Charlie strongly urged him not to do so. He admitted that the troops would look immensely better if clad in regular uniform than as a motley band, each dressed according to his own fancy. He pointed out, however, that while the news that the rajah was having some of his men drilled by European deserters would attract but little attention among his neighbors, the report that he was raising Sepoy battalions would certainly be received by them in a hostile spirit.

"By all means," Charlie said, get the uniforms made for the whole force and keep them by you in store. They can be at once served out in case of war, and the sight of a number of Sepoy battalions where they expected only to meet an irregular force, will have an immense effect upon any force opposed to you."

The rajah saw the force of this argument, and at once ordered five thousand suits of white uniforms, similar to those worn by the Sepoys in the English and French service, to be made and stored up in the magazines. While his lieutenants were drilling the main body Charlie himself took in hand a party of forty picked men, and instructed them in the use of field-guns. The superiority of Europeans in artillery was one of the reasons which gave to them such easy victory in their early battles with the native forces in India. The latter possessed a very powerful artillery in point of numbers, but there was no regular drill nor manner of loading. They were in the habit, too, of allowing each gun to cool after it was fired before being loaded again. It was thought, therefore, good practice if a gun were discharged once in a quarter of an hour. They were then utterly astounded and dismayed at the effects of the European guns, each of which could be loaded and fired twice, or even three times, a minute.

So month passed after month until Rajah Boorhau was in a position to put, if necessary, five battalions of Sepoys, each seven hundred strong, into the field, with thirty guns, served by trained artillerymen. So quietly had the work gone on that it attracted no attention among his neighbors. The mere rumor that the rajah had some European deserters in his service, and that these were drilling four or five hundred men, was considered of so little moment that it passed altogether unheeded.

The accounts of the state of affairs in the Carnatic, which reached Charlie, were not satisfactory. Dupleix, with his usual energy, was aiding the son of Chunda Sahib with men and money in his combat with the British protégé, and most of the native allies of the latter had fallen away from him. Trichinopoli was again besieged, and the fortunes of England, lately so flourishing, were waning again. In the Deccan French influence was supreme. Bussy, with a strong and well-disciplined French force, maintained Salabut Jung, whom the French had placed on the throne, against all opponents. At one time it was the Peishwar, at another the Marattas, against whom Bussy turned his arms, and always with success, and the French had acquired the four districts on the coast known as the Northern Sircas. It was in vain that Charlie endeavored to gain an accurate knowledge of the political position, so quickly and continually did this change. At one time the Peishwar and the Nizam, as the Subadar of the Deccan was now called, would be fighting in alliance against one or other of the Maratta chiefs. At another time they would be in conflict with each other, while the Rajah of Mysore, Murari Reo, and other chiefs were sometimes fighting on one side, sometimes on another.

Proud of his rapidly increasing force, Boorhau Reo would, more than once in the course of the year, have joined in the warfare going on around. Charlie, however, succeeded in restraining him from doing so, pointing out that the victor of one day was the vanquished of the next, and that it was worse than useless to join in a struggle of which the conditions were so uncertain, and the changes of fortune so rapid, that none could count upon others for aid, however great the assistance they might have rendered only a short time before.

"Were you to gain territory, Rajah, which you might, perhaps, largely do, from the efficient aid which you might render to one party or the other, you would be the object of a hostile combination against which you could not hope to struggle."

The rajah yielded at once to Charlie's arguments; but the influence of the latter added to the hostility which the favor shown him by the rajah had provoked among many of the leading men of the state. Where the sides were often so closely balanced as was the case in these intestine struggles, the aid of every rajah, however small his following, was sought by one or other of the combatants, and the counsellors of those able to place a respectable force in the field were heavily bribed by one side or the other. Those around Rajah Boorhau found their efforts completely baffled by the influence of the English commander of his forces, and a fraction of increasing strength and power was formed to overthrow him. The rajah himself had kept his secret well, and one or two only of his advisers knew that the Englishman was a trusted agent of the Company.

The soldiers were much attached to their English leader. They found him always just and firm. Complaints were always listened to, tyranny or ill-treatment by the officers suppressed and punished, merit rewarded. Among the officers the strictness of the discipline alienated many, who contrasted the easy life which they had led before the introduction of the European system, with that which they now endured. So long as they were engaged in mastering the rudiments of drill they felt their disadvantage ; but when this was acquired each thought himself capable of taking the place of the English adventurer and of leading the troops he had organized to victory. Already Charlie had received several anonymous warnings that danger threatened him. The rajah was, he knew, his warm friend, and he, in his delight at seeing the formidable force which had been formed from his irregular levies, had presented him, as a token of his gratitude, with large sums of money.

In those days this was the method by which Indian princes rewarded European officers who rendered them service, and it was considered by no means derogatory to the latter to accept the money. This was, indeed, the universal custom, and Charlie, knowing that Captain Clive had received large presents of this kind, had no hesitation in following his example. The treasures stored up by many of these Indian princes were immense, and a lac of rupees, equivalent to ten thousand pounds, was considered by no means a large present. Charlie, foreseeing that sooner or later the little state would become involved in hostilities, took the precaution of forwarding the money he had received down to Madras, sending it piecemeal, in charge of native merchants and traders. It was by these paid into the Madras treasury, where a large rate of interest for all moneys lent by its employés was given by the Company.

For those at home he felt no uneasiness. It was very seldom that their letters reached him; but he learned that they were still in high favor with his uncle, that his mother continued installed as the head of his house, and that the girls were both at excellent schools.

Charlie mentioned to the rajah the rumors which had reached him of a plot against him. The rajah assured him of his own support under all circumstances, and offered that a strong guard should be placed night and day over the apartments he occupied.

This Charlie declined. "A guard can always be corrupted," he said. "My Irish servant sleeps in my ante-room, my four lieutenants are close at hand, and knowing that the soldiers are, for the most part, attached to me, I do not think that open force will be used. I will, however, cause a large bell to be suspended above my quarters; its ringing will be a signal that I am attacked, in which case I rely upon your highness putting yourself at the head of the guard and coming to my assistance."

Tim Kelly was at once furious and alarmed at the

news that danger threatened his master, and took every precaution that he could imagine to ensure his safety. He took to going down to the town himself to purchase provisions, and so far as possible prepared these himself. He procured two or three monkeys, animals which he held in horror, and offered them a portion of everything that came on the table, before he placed it before his master. Charlie at first protested against this, as his dinner became cold by waiting, but Tim had an oven prepared and ordered dinner half an hour before the time fixed by his master. Each dish as brought in was, after a portion had been given to a monkey, placed in the oven, and thus half an hour was given to allow the poison to work. This was done without Charlie's knowledge, the oven being placed in the ante-room, and the dishes thence brought in in regular order by the body servant, whom even Tim allowed to be devoted to his master.

One day Charlie was just sitting down to his soup when Tim ran in.

"For the love of Heaven, Mr. Charles, don't put that stuff to your mouth. It's pisoned, or at any rate, if it isn't, one of the other dishes is."

"Poisoned, Tim! Nonsense, man; you are always thinking of poisonings and plots."

"And its lucky for your honor that I am," Tim said. "Jist come into the next room and look at the monkeys."

Charlie went in. One of the little creatures was lying upon the ground evidently in a state of great agony. The other was sitting up rocking itself backwards and forward like a human being in pain.

"They look bad, poor little beasts," Charlie said; "but what has that got to do with my soup?"

"Shure, yer honor, isn't that jist what I keep the cratures for, just to give them a taste of everything yer honor has, and I claps it into the oven there to kape it warm till I've had time to see by the monkeys whether it's good."

"It looks very serious," Charlie said gravely. "Do you go quietly out, Tim, call two men from the guard-house and seize the cook, and place one or two men as sentries over the other servants. I will go across to the rajah."

The latter, on hearing what had happened, ordered the cook to be brought before him, together with the various dishes prepared for the dinner.

The man upon being interrogated vehemently denied all knowledge of the affair.

"We shall see," the rajah said. "Eat up that plate of soup."

The man turned pale.

"Your highness will observe," he stammered, "that you have already told me that one of these dishes is poisoned. I cannot say which, and whichever I eat may be the fatal one."

The rajah made a signal to him to obey his orders, but Charlie interposed.

"There is something in what he says, your highness. Whether the man is innocent or guilty he would shrink equally from eating any of them. It is really possible that he may know nothing of it. The poison may have been introduced into the materials beforehand. If the man is taken to a dungeon, I think I could suggest a plan by which we could test him. I believe him to be guilty," he said when the prisoner had been removed.

"Then why not let him be beheaded at once?" the rajah asked.

"I would rather let ten guilty men escape," Charlie replied, "than run the risk of putting one innocent one to death. I propose, sir, that you order the eight dishes of food, which have been prepared for my dinner, to be carefully weighed. Let these be all placed in the cell of the prisoner, and there let him be left. In the course of two or three days he will, if guilty, endeavor to assuage his hunger by eating little bits of food from every dish except that which he knows to be poisoned, but will take such a small portion from each that he will think it will not be detected. If he is innocent, and is really ignorant which dish is poisoned, he will not touch any of them until driven to desperation by hunger. Then he will seize on one or more and devour them to the end, running the chance of death by poison rather than endure the pangs of hunger longer."

"Your plan is a wise one," the rajah said. "It shall be tried. Let the dishes be taken to him every morning and removed every evening. Each evening they shall be weighed."

These orders were carried out, and on the following morning the dishes were placed in the cell of the prisoner. When removed at night they were found to be untouched. The next evening several of the dishes were found to have lost some ounces in weight. The third evening all but one had been tasted.

"Let the prisoner be brought in again," the rajah ordered when informed of this. "Dog," he said, "you have betrayed yourself. Had you been innocent you could not have known in which of the dishes the poison had been placed. You have eaten of all but one. If that one contains poison you are guilty."

Then turning to an attendant he ordered him to take a portion of the untouched food and to throw it to a dog. Pending the experiment the prisoner was removed. Half an hour later the attendant returned with the news that the dog was dead.

"The guilt of the man is confirmed," the rajah said. "Let him be executed."

"Will you give him to me, your highness?" Charlie asked. "His death would not benefit me now, and to save his life he may tell me who is my enemy. It is of no use punishing the instrument and letting the instigator go free."

"You are right," the rajah agreed. "If you can find out who bribed him, justice shall be done though it were the highest in the state."

Charlie returned to his own quarters, assembled his lieutenants and several other of his officers, and had the man brought before him.

"Hossein," he said, "you have taken money to take my life. I looked upon you as my faithful servant. I had done you no wrong. It has been proved that you attempted to poison me. You, when driven by hunger, ate small quantities, which you thought would pass unobserved, of all the dishes but one. That dish has been given to a dog and he has died. You knew then which was the poisoned dish. The rajah has ordered your execution. I offer you life if you will tell me who it was that tempted you."

The prisoner preserved a stolid silence.

"We had better procced to torture him at once," one of the rajah's officers said.

The man turned a little paler. He knew well the horrible tortures which would in such an instance be inflicted to extort the names of those who had bribed him.

"I will say nothing," he said firmly, "though you tear me limb from limb."

"I have no intention of torturing you," Charlie said. "A confession extorted by pain is as likely to be false as true, and even did you tell me one name there might still be a dozen engaged in it who would remain unknown. No, Hossein, you have failed in your duty, you have tried to slay a master who was kind to you and trusted you."

"No, sahib," the man exclaimed passionately. "You did not trust me. The food I sent you was tested and tried. I knew it; but I thought that the poison would not have acted on the monkeys until you had eaten the dish. The fool who sold it me deceived me. Had you trusted me I would never have done it. It was only when I saw that I was suspected and doubted without cause that my heart turned against you, and I took the gold which was offered to me to kill you. I swear it by the Prophet."

Charlie looked at him steadily.

"I believe you," he said. "You were mistaken. I had no suspicions. My servant feared for me and took these precautions without telling me. However, Hossein, I pardon you, and if you will swear to me to be faithful in future I will trust you. You shall again be my cook, and I will eat the food as you prepare it for me."

"I am my lord's slave," the man said in a low tone. "My life is his."

Charlie nodded, and the guard standing on either side of the prisoner stepped back, and without another word he left the room a free man.

Charlie's officers remonstrated with him upon having not only pardoned the man, but restored him to his position of cook.

"I think I have done wisely," Charlie said. "I must have a cook, for Tim Kelly here is not famous that way, and although he might manage for me when alone, he certainly could not turn out a dinner which would be suitable when I have some of the rajah's kinsmen and officers dining with me. Did I get another cook he might be just as open to the offers of my enemies as Hossein has been, and do you not think that, after what has passed, Hossein will be less likely to take bribes than any other man?"

Henceforth the oven was removed from the antechamber, and Charlie took his meals as Hossein prepared them for him. The man said little, but Charlie felt sure from the glances that he cast at him that he could rely upon Hossein now to the death.

Tim Kelly, who felt the strongest doubts as to the prudence of the proceeding, observed that Hossein no longer bought articles from men who brought them up to sell to the soldiers, but that every morning, he went out early and purchased all the supplies he desired from the shopkeepers in the town. Tim mentioned the fact to his master, who said:

"You see, Tim, Hossein has determined that I shall not be poisoned without his knowing it. The little pedlers who come up here with herbs, and spices, and the ingredients for curry might be bribed to sell Hossein poisoned goods. By going down into the town and buying in the open market it is barely possible that the goods could be poisoned. You need have no more anxiety whatever, Tim, as to poison. If the attempt is made again it will probably be by sword or dagger."

"Well, yer honor," said Tim, "anything's better than pison. I've got to sleep almost with one eye open. And you've got sentries outside your windows. What a pity it is that we ain't in a climate where one can fasten the windows and boult the shutters! But now the wet season is over again ye might have yer bed put, as ye did last year, on the roof of your room, with a canopy over it to keep off the dew. Ye would be safe thin, except from any one coming through the room where I sleeps."

Charlie's bedroom was at the angle of a wall, and on two sides he could look down from his windows two hundred feet, sheer into the valley below. The view from the flat terraced roof was a charming one, and, as Tim said, Charlie had, in the fine weather, converted the terrace into a sleeping-room. A broad canopy supported by poles at the corner, stretched over it, and even in the hottest weather the nights were not unpleasant here.

CHAPTER XIII.

AN ATTEMPT AT MURDER.

THE house, of which the bedroom occupied by Charlie formed part, was elsewhere two stories higher, this room jutting out alone into the angle of the wall. The rest of the suite of rooms were in the house itself, but access could be obtained to this room through the window, which looked on to the terrace of the wall. Charlie's lieutenants always took pains to place men upon whom they could thoroughly rely as sentries on this terrace. One night, a fortnight after the events which have been described, Charlie was asleep on his bed on the flats above his room. On one side the house rose straight beside it. On two others was the fall to the valley, on the fourth side was the wall, along which two sentries were pacing to and fro. From time to time, from a door some distance along the side of the house, opening on to the wall, a white figure came out, stretched himself as if unable to sleep, looked for a while over the parapet down into the valley, appeared to listen intently, and then sauntered into the house again. It was the cook, Hossein. It was his custom. Successive sentries had for many nights past seen him do the same, but in a country where the nights are hot, a sleepless servant attracts but little attention. Upon the occasion of one of these visits to the parapet he stood in an attitude of deep attention longer than usual. Then he carelessly sauntered back. It was but a moment later that his face appeared at the window next to that of Charlie's bedroom. He stretched his head out and again listened intently. Then he went to Tim, who was sleeping heavily on a couch placed there, and touched him. He put his hand on his lips as Tim sprang up. "Take arm," he said in Hindostanee. "Bad man coming."

Tim understood the words, and seizing a sword and pistol which lay close to the bedside, followed Hossein, who had glided up the stairs with a drawn tulwar in his hand. At the moment he did so there was a noise of heavy bodies dropping, followed by a sudden shout from Charlie. There was a sound of clashing of arms and the report of a pistol. As Tim's eyes came on a level with the terrace he saw Hossein bound with uplifted blade into the midst of a group of men in the corner. Three times the blade rose and fell, and each time a loud shriek followed. Then he disappeared in the midst. Tim was but a few seconds behind him. Discharging his pistol into the body of one of the men, and running his sword into another, he, too, stood by the side of his master. Charlie, streaming with blood, was half sitting, half lying in the angle of the parapet. Hossein, his turban off, his long hair streaming down his back, was standing over him, fighting furiously against some ten men who still pressed forward, while several others lay upon the ground.

In spite of the arrival of Charlie's two allies they still pressed forward, but the shots of the pistols had been echoed by the muskets of the sentries. Loud shouts were heard, showing that the alarm was sounding through the palace. One more desperate effort the assailants made to beat the two men who opposed them over the parapet, but Hossein and the Irishman stood firm. The weight and numbers of their opponents, however, told upon them, when the first of the sentries appeared upon the platform, followed closely by his comrade, and both with levelled bayonets charged into the fray. The assailants now thought only of escape, but their position was a desperate one. Some rushed to the end of the terrace and tried to climb the ropes by which they had slid down from the upper roof of the house. Others endeavored to rush down the staircase, but Tim with one of the sentries guarded this point, until a rush of feet below told that the guard were coming to their assistance. It was well that help was at hand, for the conspirators, desperate at finding themselves in a trap, gathering themselves together rushed with the fury of wild beasts upon Tim and the sentry. One was impaled upon a bayonet, another cut down by Tim, and then, borne back by the weight of their opponents, they were hurled backwards down the stairs. As the assailants followed them with a rush, the guard sprang through the open window from the terrace below into the room. There was a short and desperate conflict. Then two of the conspirators bounded up the staircase on to the roof, ran to the parapet and leaped over into the valley, two hundred feet below. They were the last of the eighteen men who had lowered themselves from the roof above to attack Charlie.

As soon as Tim picked himself up he hastened to ascend the stairs again, and to run to the side of his master. Charlie was insensible. Leaning against the parapet, too weak to stand, but still holding his sword and ready to throw himself once more before him, stood Hossein, who now, seeing Tim approach, and that all danger was over, dropped his sword and sank upon the ground. A minute or two later the rajah himself, sword in hand, hurried up. He was greatly concerned and excited at the sight which met his eyes. Charlie was at once lifted and carried down to one of the rajah's own rooms, where he was instantly attended

THE FATE OF THE ASSASSINS.

to. A hasty examination showed that only two of the attacking party still breathed. None of those who had fallen above survived, so fierce and deadly had been the blows struck by Hossein and Tim. Charlie himself had cut down one and shot another before he fell, slashed in many places, just as Hossein bounded through his assailants.

The bodies of the dead were by the rajah's orders laid together for identification in the morning. The two who still lived were carried to the guard-room, and their wounds dressed in order that the names of their employers might be obtained from them. In the mean time Charlie's lieutenants had hastily formed a body of their soldiers together, and these at once fell upon a number of men who were crowding up the steps to the palace with shouts of "Death to the Englishman." A few volleys poured among these effectually scattered them, and they broke and hurried down the steep road, through the gates to the town, the sentries on the way offering no opposition, but many falling under the fire from the parapet of the fort. In ten minutes all was over. The gates were again closed and a strong guard placed over them, and the attempted insurrection was at an end.

The native surgeon who attended Charlie pronounced that none of the five wounds he had received, although for the most part severe, were necessarily fatal, and that there was every chance of his recovery. Hossein's wounds, three in number, were pronounced to be more dangerous, one being a deep stab in the body given by a man who had rushed at him as he was guarding the blow of another. Tim's wounds were comparatively slight, and he suffered more from the bruises he had received when hurled backwards down the stone staircase. However, with one arm in a sling and his head bandaged, he was able to take his place by his master's bedside. Having heard from him that it was entirely due to Hossein that Charlie's life had been saved, the rajah directed that every attention should be paid to him, and several times during the night Tim stole away to his bedside to press his hand, and call down blessings upon him. The stanching of his wounds and the application of strong restoratives presently caused Charlie to open his eyes.

"The Lord be praised, Mr. Charles," Tim said, "that you're coming to yourself again. Don't you trouble, sir. We've done for the murdhering rascals, and plase God you'll soon be about again. Jist drink this draught, yer honor, and go off to sleep if you can. In the morning I'll tell you all about it. You're in the rajah's own room," he continued, seeing Charlie's eyes wander wonderingly around him, "and all you've got to do is just to lie still and get well as soon as you can."

It was a fortnight before Charlie, still very weak and feeble, was able to totter from his room to that in which Hossein was lying. He himself knew nothing of what had passed after he fell. The conflict had to him been little more than a dream. Awakened from sleep by the sound of his assailants as they dropped from the ropes, he had leaped up as a rush of figures came towards him, catching up his sword and pistol as he did so. He had shot the first and cut down the next who rushed at him, but at the same moment he had felt a sharp pain and remembered no more. Tim heard from Hossein, when the latter, two days after the fight, was able to speak, that he had suspected that some renewed attempt might be made upon his master's life, and that for many nights he had not slept, contenting himself with such repose as he could snatch in the daytime, between the intervals of preparing meals. A few minutes before the attack he fancied he heard a movement on the roof of the house, and running to Charlie's room he had from the window seen some dark figures sliding down the wall. Then he roused Tim and rushed up to the rescue. Tim eloquently described to his master the manner in which Hossein sprung upon his foes, and cut his way through in time to drive back those who were hacking at him as he lay prostrate, and how he found him standing over him, keeping at bay the whole of his assailants.

Charlie with difficulty made his way to the bedside of the brave Mahommedan. The latter, however, did not know him. He was in the delirium of fever. He was talking rapidly to himself. "He trusted me," he said. "He gave me my life. Should I not give mine for him? Any one else would have had me hung as a dog. I will watch; I will watch; he shall see that Hossein is not ungrateful."

Charlie's eyes filled with tears as he looked at the wasted form of his follower. "Is there any hope for him?" he asked the doctor.

"It is possible, just possible that he may live," the latter said. "Allah only knows."

"Do all you can to save him," Charlie said; "I shall be ever grateful to you if you do."

Tim, now that his master could dispense with his services, transferred his attentions to the bedside of Hossein, and was unremitting in the care and attention with which he kept the bandages on his head cool with fresh water, and wetted his hot lips with refreshing drinks. It was another week before his illness took a turn. Then the fever left him, and he lay weak and helpless as an infant. Strong soups now took the place of the cooling drinks, and in a few days the native doctor was able to say confidently that the danger was passed, and that Hossein would recover.

In the mean time the investigations of the rajah had brought to light the details of the conspiracy. The wounded men had confessed that they were employed by three of the principal persons at the rajah's court, one of them being the rajah's brother. The information, however was scarcely needed, as it was found in the morning that their apartments were empty, they having fled with the men who had attacked the gates of the palace. These consisted partly of soldiers whom they had bribed, and of desperadoes from the town, who had singly entered the fort during the day, and had been concealed in the apartments of the conspirators until the signal for attack was given. The intention of the conspirators was not only to kill the Englishman but to dethrone the rajah, and install his brother in his place. The attack had commenced with the attempt upon Charlie's life, because it was believed that his death would paralyze the troops who were faithful to the rajah.

At the end of six weeks Charlie was able to resume his duties, and his appearance at the parade ground was hailed with enthusiastic shouts by the soldiers. The rajah was more attached to him than ever, and had again made him large presents in token of the regret he felt at the sufferings he had endured in his cause. Drilling was now carried on with redoubled energy, and large numbers of new levies had been summoned to the standard. A storm was gathering over Ambur. The rajah's brother was raising a force to attack him, and had by means of large promises in case of success, persuaded Murari Reo to take up his cause and he had, it was said, also sent messages to the nizam, pointing out that, in case of war with the English, the Rajah of Ambur would be a thorn in his side. He told of the numbers of troops who had been drilled, and how formidable such a force would be if opposed to him at a critical moment, while if he, the claimant, gained power the army of Ambur would be at the disposal of the nizam.

The rajah on his side had also sent messengers to Hyderabad with assurances to the nizam of his fidelity and friendship. He urged that the preparations he had made were intended solely for the defence of his state against marauding bands of Marattas, and especially against those of Murari Reo, who was a scourge to all his neighbors. In the mean time every effort was made to strengthen the defences of Ambur. The walls surrounding the town were repaired, and although these in themselves could have offered but a slight defense to a determined assault, the approaches to the town were all covered by the guns of the fort above. The weak point of the defence was the hill behind the town. This sloped up gradually to a point higher than the level of the projecting rock upon which the castle stood. It then rose in rugged cliffs some two hundred feet higher, and then fell away again steeply to its summit. This was too far back for the fire of guns placed upon it to injure the castle or town. Guns placed, however, at the foot of the rocky wall would dominate the castle and render it at last untenable. Charlie had often looked with an anxious eye at this point, and one morning, accompanied by the rajah, he rode up to examine the position. The highest point of the slope at the foot of the crag was nearly opposite the castle, and it was here that an active enemy, making his way along the slope, would place his guns. Here Charlie determined to establish a battery. News had arrived that the rajah's brother had raised a force of three thousand men, and that with seven thousand Marattas he was about to march. This force Charlie felt certain that he could meet and defeat in the open. But more disquieting news was that Bussy, hearing that the rajah's troops had been trained by an Englishman, had advised the nizam to declare for his rival and to send a considerable force to his assistance, if necessary.

Fresh messengers were sent off with new assurances of the rajah's loyalty to the nizam.

"It may not do much good," Charlie said, "but if we can induce him to remain quiet until we have defeated Murari Reo, it will be so much gained." Charlie himself despatched a messenger to Mr. Saunders begging that assistance might be sent to the rajah. Having decided upon the position for a battery, energetic steps were taken to form it. A space large enough for the construction of the battery, and for the tents and stores of the artillerymen and two hundred infantry, was marked out, and the rajah ordered the whole population of Ambur, men, women and children to assist at the work. The troops, too, were all employed, and under Charlie's superintendence a wondrous change was soon effected. The spot chosen was levelled, a strong earthwork was erected round it, and then the surrounding ground was removed. This was a work of immense labor, the ground consisting first of a layer of soil, then of *débris* which had fallen from the face of the rock above, stones and boulders, to the depth of some fifteen feet, under which was the solid earth.

The slope resembled an ant-hill. The soldiers and able-bodied men broke up the boulders and rock with sledge-hammers, or, when necessary, with powder, and blasted the rock when needed. The women and children carried away the fragments in baskets. The work lasted for a fortnight, at the end of which a position of an almost impregnable nature was formed. At the foot of the earthworks protecting the guns, both at the face and sides, the ground, composed of great boulders and stones, sloped steeply out, forming a bank fifteen feet deep. At its foot, again, the solid rock was blasted away so as to form a deep chasm thirty feet wide and ten feet high round the foot of the fort. For a hundred yards on each side the earth and stones had been entirely removed down to the solid rock. Ten guns were placed in the battery, and the fire of these swept the slopes behind the town and castle, rendering it impossible, until the fort was carried, for an enemy to attack the town on that side, or to operate in any way against the only point at which an attack could be made upon the castle.

The rajah was delighted at this most formidable accession to the defensive power of his fortress, which was now in a position to defy any attack which could be made against it. A store of provisions and ammunition was collected there, and the command given to one of Charlie's Sepoy lieutenants, with a hundred trained artillerymen, and two hundred infantry. Numbers of cattle had been driven into the town and castle, and stores of provisions collected.

It was but two days after the battery was complete that the news arrived that the rajah's brother with Murari Reo had entered the rajah's dominions, and was marching up the valley to the assault. The rajah had in the first place wished to defend a strong gorge through which the enemy would have to pass, this having hitherto been considered the defensible point of his capital against an invasion. Charlie pointed out, however, that although no doubt a successful defence might be made here, it would only be a repulse which would leave the enemy but little weakened for further operations. He argued that it was better to allow them to advance to the point where the valley opened out into a plain, some two miles wide. He had no doubt whatever that the rajah's troops would be able to inflict a crushing defeat upon the invaders, who would be so disheartened thereby that they would be little likely to renew the attack.

Two bodies of troops, each three hundred strong, were sent down to the gorge, with orders to remain in hiding among the heights, to allow the invading army to pass unmolested, and then to inflict the greatest possible loss upon them as they returned. These were under the command of another of Charlie's lieutenants, who received orders from him to erect breastworks of rock on the slopes above the entrance to the gorge, after the enemy had passed on, and to line these with a portion of his men who should pour a heavy fire into the enemy as they came down the valley, while the rest were to line the heights above the gorge and to roll down rocks upon those who passed through the fire of their comrades.

The uniforms were served out to the soldiers, and Charlie surveyed with pride the five battalions of trained troops which with twelve guns marched down into the valley and took up their post beyond it, at a point which he had carefully chosen, where the guns of the castle would be able to play upon an advancing body of troops. A body of trained artillerymen were told off for this service, and the last-raised levies were posted in the castle and on the walls of the town. The position was so chosen that the flanks of the line rested on the slopes on either side. These were broken by inclosures and gardens, into which on either side half a battalion was thrown forward so as to deliver a flanking fire upon an enemy advancing against the centre. Across the valley, two hundred yards in front of the position, the stream which watered it made a sharp turn, running for some distance directly across it, and several small canals for the irrigation of the fields rendered the ground wet and swampy. Across the line occupied by his troops, a breastwork had been thrown up, and in front of this rows of sharp-pointed stakes had been stuck in the ground. Altogether the position was a formidable one.

An hour or two after the position so carefully prepared had been taken up, large bodies of Maratta horse were seen dashing up the valley, and smoke rising from several points showed that they had begun their usual work of plundering and destroying the villages on their way. A few discharges from the field-pieces—those in the castle had been ordered to be silent until the raising of a white flag gave them the signal to open fire—checked the advance of the horsemen, and these waited until their infantry should arrive.

The force of Murari Reo was at that time the most formidable of any purely native army of Southern India. Recruited from desperadoes from all the Maratta tribes, well disciplined by its leader, it had more than once fought without defeat against bodies of Europeans, while it had in all cases obtained easy victories over other native armies.

Presently the horsemen opened, and a compact body of three thousand Maratta infantry, accompanied by an equal number of the irregulars of the rajah's brother, advanced to the attack, while the cavalry at their sides swept down upon the flanks of the rajah's position, and thirty pieces of artillery opened fire. Not a shot was fired in return, Charlie ordering his men to lie down behind the breastworks until they received the word of command to show themselves. The Maratta horsemen, compelled by the bends of the stream to keep near the foot of the slopes, came forward in gallant style, until suddenly from every wall and every clump of bushes on the slopes above them a tremendous fire of musketry broke out, while the twelve field-guns, six of which were posted on either side of Charlie's centre, poured a destructive fire into them. So deadly was the rain of iron and lead that the Maratta horsemen instantly drew bridle, and leaving the ground strewn with their dead, galloped back.

By this time the infantry, covered by the fire of their

artillery, had reached the stream. This was waist deep, and the banks were some two feet above its level. As they scrambled up after crossing it, from the line of embankment in front of them a tremendous fire was opened. Although mowed down in scores the seasoned warriors of the Maratta chief, cheered on by his voice as, recklessly exposing himself, he rode among them, pressed forward. Ever increasing numbers gained a footing across the stream, those in front keeping up a heavy fire at the breastwork, whose face was ploughed by their cannon-shot. As they advanced the guns of the castle opened fire, not upon those in front, for these were too near the line of entrenchment, but upon the struggling mass still crossing the stream, into which a ceaseless fire of musketry was poured from the slopes on their flanks.

Still the Maratta infantry struggled bravely on until within a few yards of the entrenchments. Then, suddenly with a mighty shout the rajah's troops leaped to their feet, poured a volley from the crest of the breastwork into the enemy, and then with fixed bayonets flung themselves upon them. The effect was decisive. The Marattas had at the commencement of the fight scarcely outnumbered the troops of the rajah in front of them, and had derived but little assistance from the levies of their ally, who indeed had contented themselves with keeping up a fire upon the defenders of the slopes. They had already suffered very severely, and the charge made upon them along the whole line was irresistible. Before the bayonets crossed they broke and fled, hotly pursued by the troops of the rajah. These, in accordance with Charlie's orders, did not scatter, but kept in a close line, four deep, which advanced pouring tremendous volleys into their foe. In vain did Murari Reo endeavor to rally his men. His infantry, all order lost, fled at the top of their speed, their flight covered by their cavalry, who sacrificed themselves in two or three brilliant charges right up to the line of pursuers, although suffering terribly from the withering volleys poured into their ranks.

The troops were now formed into heavy columns, and these rapidly marched down the valley after their flying enemy. An hour later the sound of heavy firing was heard in front, and at redoubled speed the troops pressed onward. When they arrived, however, at the gorge they found that the last of the fugitives had passed through. The ground in front was strewn with dead and dying, for as the mass of fugitives had arrived at the gorge, the infantry from above had opened fire upon them. Several times the frightened throng had recoiled, but at last, impelled by the greater fear of their pursuers behind, they had dashed forward through the fire, only to fall in hundreds in the gorge, crushed beneath the rain of rocks showered down upon them from above.

CHAPTER XIV.

THE SIEGE OF AMBUR.

THE victory was a complete and decisive one. A thousand of the best troops of Murari Reo had fallen, besides some hundreds of their irregular allies, whose loss was incurred almost wholly at the gorge in the retreat. The rajah was in the highest state of delight at the splendid result obtained by the European training of his troops, and these, proud of their victory over such formidable opponents, were full of enthusiasm for their young English leader. The rejoicings in Ambur that night were great, and all felt confident that the danger was at an end.

"What think you," the rajah said to Charlie, as, the long feast at an end, they sat together in the divan smoking their narghileys, "will be the result when the news of the defeat of Murari Reo reaches Hyderabad?"

"It is difficult to say," Charlie replied. "It is possible, of course, that it may be considered that it is better to leave you in peace, but upon the other hand it may be that they will consider that you are so formidable a power that it is absolutely necessary to crush you at once, rather than to give you the chance of joining against them in the war which must sooner or later take place between them and the English. In that case it will be a very different affair from that which we have had to-day. Still I should send off a messenger to-morrow to acquaint the nizam with the defeat you inflicted upon the Marattas who have invaded you, to assure him again of your loyalty, and to beg him to lay his authority upon Murari Reo not to renew the attack.

Ten days later a messenger arrived from the nizam ordering the rajah to repair at once to Hyderabad to explain his conduct. The latter sent back a message of humble excuses, saying that his health was so injured by the excitement of recent events that he was unable to travel, but that when he recovered he would journey to Hyderabad to lay his respects at the feet of the nizam. Two or three days later a messenger arrived from Mr. Saunders with a letter to Charlie. In this he expressed his great satisfaction at the defeat Murari Reo had received, a defeat which would for some time keep him quiet, and so relieve the strain upon the English. Affairs had, he said, since the departure of Clive for England been going badly. Dupleix had received large reinforcements, and the English had suffered several reverses. Mr. Saunders begged him to assure the rajah of the respect and friendship of England, and to give him the promise that if he should be driven from his capital he would be received with all honor at Madras, and should be reinstated in his dominions, with much added territory, when the English were again in a position to take the field in force and to settle their long feud with the French.

Ten days later they heard that the army of the nizam, of fifteen thousand troops with eight hundred French under Bussy, were marching against them, and that the horsemen of Murari Reo were devastating the villages near the frontier. A council of war was held. Charlie would fain have fought in the open again, believing that his trained troops, flushed with their recent victory, would be a match even for the army of the nizam. But the rajah and the rest of the council, alarmed at the presence of the French troops, who had hitherto proved invincible against vastly superior forces of natives, shrank from such a course, and it was decided that they should content themselves with the defence of the town and castle. Orders were accordingly issued that the old men, the women and children should at once leave the town, and, under guard of one battalion of troops, take refuge in an almost impregnable hill fort some miles away. One battalion was placed in garrison in the castle. The other three, with the irregulars, took post in the town, whence they could, if necessary, retreat into the castle. The day following the removal of the non-combatants the enemy appeared coming down the valley, having marched over the hills, while the Maratta cavalry again poured up from below.

Charlie had taken the command of the town, as it was against this that the efforts of the enemy would be first directed. It was an imposing sight as the army of the nizam wound down the valley, the great masses of men with their gay flags, the elephants with the gold embroidery of their trappings glistening in the sun, the bands of horsemen careering here and there, the lines of artillery drawn by bullocks, and, less picturesque but far more menacing, the dark body of French infantry who formed the nucleus and heart of the whole. The camp was pitched just out of range of the guns of the fort, and soon line after line of tents, gay with the flags that floated above them, rose across the valley. Charlie had mounted to the castle the better to observe the movements of the enemy, and he presently saw a small body of horsemen ride out of the camp and mount the hillside across the valley. A glass showed that some of these were native officers, while others were in the dark uniform of the French.

"I have no doubt," Charlie said to the rajah, "that is the nizam himself with Bussy gone up to reconnoitre the position. I wonder how he likes the look of it. I wish we could have turfed the battery above and the newly stripped land. We might in that case have given them a pleasant surprise. As it is they are hardly likely to begin by an attack along the slopes in the rear of the town, and you will see that they will commence the attack at the farther face of the town. The battery above cannot aid us in our defence there, and although the castle may help it will only be by a direct fire. If they try to carry the place by a *coup de main* I think we can beat them off, but they must succeed by regular approaches. We must inflict as much loss as we can and then fall back. However, it will be some time before that comes."

The next morning Charlie found that the enemy had during the night erected three batteries on the slopes facing the north wall of the town, that farthest removed from the castle. They at once opened fire, and guns on the walls facing them replied, while those on the castle hurled their shot over the town into the enemy's battery. For three days the artillery fire was kept up without intermission. The guns on the wall were too weak to silence the batteries of the besiegers, although these were much annoyed by the fire from the fort, which dismounted four of their guns and blew up one of their magazines. Several times the town was set on fire by the shell from the French mortars; but Charlie had organized the irregulars into bands with buckets, and these succeeded in extinguishing the flames before they spread. Seeing that the mud wall of the town was crumbling rapidly before the besiegers' fire, Charlie set his troops to work and levelled every house within fifty yards of it, and with the stones and beams formed barricades across the end of the streets beyond. Many of the guns from other portions of the walls were removed and placed on these barricades. The ends of the houses were loopholed, and all was prepared for a desperate defence.

Charlie's experiences at Arcot stood him in good stead and he imitated the measures taken by Clive at that place. When these defences were completed he raised a second line of barricades some distance further back, and here when the assault was expected, he placed one of his battalions, with orders that if the inner line of entrenchments was carried they should allow all the defenders of that post to pass through, and then resist until the town was completely evacuated, when they were to fall back upon the fort. He had, however, little fear that his position would be taken at the first assault.

Upon the evening of the third day the besiegers' fire had done its work, and a gap in the wall some eighty yards' wide was formed. The garrison were ordered to hold themselves in readiness, and a strict watch was set. Towards morning a distant hum in the nizam's camp proclaimed that the troops were mustering for the assault. The besiegers' guns had continued their fire all night, to prevent working parties from placing obstacles in the breach. As the first shades of daylight appeared the fire ceased, and a great column of men poured forward to the assault.

The few remaining guns upon the end wall opened upon them, as did the infantry who lined the parapet, while the guns in the castle at once joined in. The mighty column, however, composed of the troops of the nizam, pressed forward, poured over the fragments of the wall, and entered the clear space behind it. Then from house-top and loophole, and from the walls on either side, a concentrated fire of musketry was poured upon them, while twelve guns, four on each barricade, swept them with grape. The head of the column withered away under the fire, long lines were swept through the crowded mass, and after a minute or two's wild firing at their concealed foes, the troops of the nizam, appalled and shattered by the tremendous fire, broke and fled. The instant they had cleared the breach, the guns of the besiegers again opened furiously upon it, to check any sortie which the besieged might attempt.

An hour later the besiegers hoisted a white flag and requested to be allowed to bury their dead and remove their wounded. This Charlie agreed to, with the proviso that these should be carried by his own men beyond the breach, as he did not wish that the enemy should have an opportunity of examining the internal defences. The task occupied some time, as more than five hundred dead and dying lay scattered in the open space. During the rest of the day the enemy showed no signs of resuming the assault. During the night they could be heard hard at work, and although a brisk fire was kept up to hinder them, Charlie found that they had pushed trenches from the batteries a considerable distance round each corner of the town.

For four days the besiegers worked vigorously, harassed as they were by the guns of the fort and by those of the battery high up on the hillside, which were now able to take in flank the works across the upper angle of the town. At the end of that time they had erected and armed two batteries, which at daylight opened upon the walls which formed the flanks of the clear space behind the breach. Although suffering heavily from the fire of the besieged, and losing many men, these batteries kept up their fire unceasingly night and day, until great gaps had been made in the walls, and Charlie was obliged to withdraw his troops from them behind the line of barricades. During this time the fire of the batteries in front had been unceassing, and had destroyed most of the houses which formed the connecting line between the barricades. Each night, however, the besieged worked to repair damages, and to fill up the gaps thus formed with piles of stones and beams, so that, by the end of the fourth day after the repulse of the first assault, a line of barricades stretched across the line of defence.

The enemy this time prepared to attack by daylight and early in the morning the whole army of the nizam marched to the assault. Heedless of the fire of the castle, they formed up in a long line of heavy masses along the slope. One huge column moved forward against the main breach, two advanced obliquely towards the great gaps in the walls on either side. The latter columns were each headed by bodies of French troops. In vain the guns of the fort, aided by those of the battery on the hill, swept them, the columns advanced without a check until they entered the breaches. Then a line of fire swept along the crest of the barricade from end to end, and the cannon of the besieged roared out. Pressed by the mass from behind, the columns advanced torn and rent by the fire, and at last gained the foot of the barricade. Here those in front strove desperately to climb up the great mound of rubbish, while those behind covered them with a storm of bullets aimed at its summit. More than once the troops of the rajah rushing down the embankment, drove back the struggling masses, but so heavily did they suffer from the fire when they thus exposed themselves, that Charlie forbade them to repeat the attempt. He knew that there was safety behind, and was unwilling that his brave fellows should throw away their lives.

In the centre of the position the native troops, although they several times climbed some distance up the barricade, were yet unable to make way. But the French troops at the flanks were steadily forcing their way up. Many had climbed up by the ruins of the wall, and from its top were firing down on the defenders of the barricade. Inch by inch they won their way up the barricade, already thickly covered with dead, and then Charlie, seeing that his men were beginning to waver, gave the signal.

The long blast of a trumpet was heard even above the tremendous din. In an instant the barricades were deserted, and the defenders rushed into the houses. The partition walls between these on the lower floors had already been knocked down, and without suffering from the heavy fire which the assailants opened as soon as they gained the crest of the barricade, the defenders retreated along these covered ways until in rear of the second line of defence. This was held by the battalion placed there until the whole of the defenders of the town had left it by the gate leading up to the fort. Then Charlie withdrew this battalion also, and the town remained in the hands of the enemy, who had lost, Charlie reckoned, fully fifteen hundred men in the assault. During the fight Tim and the faithful Hossein, now fully recovered and promoted to the rank of an officer, had remained close beside him, and were with him, the last to leave the town.

The instant the evacuation was complete, the guns of the hill battery opened upon the town and a tremendous fire of musketry was poured upon it from every point of the castle which commanded it; while the guns, which from their lofty elevation, could not be depressed sufficiently to bear upon the town, directed their fire upon the bodies of troops still beyond the walls. The enemy had captured the town, indeed, but its possession aided them but little in their assault upon the fort. The only advantage it gave them would have been that it would have enabled them to attack the lower gate of the fort, protected by its outer wall from the fire of the hill battery. Charlie had, however, perceived that this would be the case, and had planted a number of mines under the wall at this point. These were exploded when the defenders of the town entered the fort, and a hundred yards of the wall were thus destroyed, leaving the space across which the enemy must advance to the attack of the gate exposed to the fire of the hill battery, as well as of the numerous guns of the fort bearing upon it.

Two days passed without any further operations on the part of the enemy, and then Bussy, seeing that nothing whatever could be done towards assaulting the fortress so long as the battery remained in the hands of the besieged, determined to make a desperate effort to carry it, ignorant of its immense strength. At night, therefore, he ordered two bodies of men, each fifteen hundred strong, to mount the hillside far to the right and left of the town, to move along at the foot of the wall of rock, and to carry the battery by storm at daybreak. Charlie, believing that such an attempt would be made, had upon the day following the fall of the town taken his post there, and had ordered a most vigilant watch to be kept up each night, placing sentries some hundred yards away on either side to give warning of the approach of an enemy.

Towards daybreak on the third morning a shot upon the left, followed a few seconds later by one on the right, told that the enemy were approaching. A minute or two afterwards the sentries ran in, climbed from the ditch by ladders which had been placed there for the purpose, and, hauling these up after them, were soon in the battery with the news that large bodies of the enemy were approaching on either flank. Scarcely were the garrison at their posts when the French were seen approaching. At once they broke into a run, and, gallantly led, dashed across the space of cleared rock in spite of the heavy fire of musketry and grape. When they came, however, to the edge of the deep gulf in the solid rock they paused. They had had no idea of meeting with such an obstacle as this. It was easy enough to leap down, but impossible to climb up the steep face ten feet high in front of them, and which, in the dim light, could be plainly seen. It was, however, impossible for those in front to pause. Pressed upon by those behind, who did not know what was stopping them, large numbers were compelled to jump into the trench, where they found themselves unable either to advance or retreat.

By this time every gun on the upper side of the castle had opened on the assailing columns, taking them in flank, while the fire of the battery was continued without a moment's intermission. Bussy himself, who was commanding one of the columns, pushed his way through his struggling soldiers to the edge of the trench, when, seeing the impossibility of scaling the sides, unprovided as he was with scaling-ladders, he gave the orders to retreat; and the columns, harassed by the flanking fire of the guns of the castle and pursued by that of the battery, retreated, having lost some hundreds of their number, besides a hundred and fifty of their best men prisoners in the deep trench around the battery. These were summoned to surrender, and resistance being impossible they at once laid down their arms. Ladders were lowered to them and they were marched as prisoners to the fort.

The next morning when the defenders of the fortress looked over the valley, the great camp was gone. The nizam and Bussy, despairing of the possibility of carrying the position at once so enormously strong by nature and so gallantly defended, had raised the siege, which had cost them over two thousand of their best soldiers, including two hundred French—killed and prisoners, and retreated to the plateau of the Deccan.

The exultation of the rajah and his troops was

unbounded. They felt that now and henceforth they were safe from another invasion, and the rajah saw that in the future he should be able to gain greatly increased territory as the ally of the English. His gratitude to Charlie was unbounded, and he literally loaded him with costly presents.

Three weeks later a letter was received by the latter from Mr. Saunders, congratulating him upon the inestimable service which he had rendered, and appointing him to the rank of captain in the Company's service. Now that the rajah would be able to protect himself should any future assault be made upon him—an event most unlikely to happen, as Bussy and the nizam would be unwilling to risk a repetition of a defeat which had already so greatly injured their prestige—he had better return to Madras, where, as Mr. Saunders said, the services of so capable an officer were greatly needed. He warned him, however, to be careful in the extreme how he made his way back, as the country was in a most disturbed state, the Maratta bands being everywhere out plundering and burning. Subsequent information that the Marattas were swarming in the plains below, determined Charlie to accept an offer which the rajah made him, that he should, under a strong escort, cross the mountains and make his way to a port on the west coast in the state of a friendly rajah, where he would be able to take ship and coast round to Madras. The rajah promised to send Charlie's horses and other presents down to Madras when an opportunity should offer and Charlie, accompanied by the four Sepoys, all of whom had been promoted to the rank of officers, by Tim Kelly and Hossein, who would not separate himself a moment from his side, started from Ambur with an escort of thirty horsemen.

The rajah was quite affected at the parting, and the army which he had formed and organized paraded before him for the last time and then shouted their farewell. Charlie himself, although glad to return among his countrymen, from whom he had been nearly two years separated, was yet sorry to leave the many friends he had made. His position was now a very different one from that which he held when he left Madras. Then he was a newly made lieutenant, who had distinguished himself, indeed, under Clive, but who was as yet unknown save to his commander, and who was as poor as when he had landed eighteen months before in India. Now he had gained a name for himself, and his successful defence of Ambur had been of immense service to the Company. He was, too, a wealthy man, for the presents in money alone of the rajah had amounted to over twenty-five thousand pounds, a sum which in these days may appear extraordinary, but which was small to that frequently bestowed by wealthy native princes upon British officers who had done them a good service. Clive himself after his short campaign had returned to England with a far larger sum.

For several days the party rode through the hills without incident, and on the fifth day they saw stretched at their feet a rich flat country dotted with villages, beyond which extended the long blue line of the sea. The distance was greater than Charlie imagined, and 'twas only after two days long ride that he reached Calicut, where he was received with great honor by the rajah, to whom the leader of the escort brought letters of introduction from the Rajah of Ambur. For four days Charlie remained as his guest, and then took a passage in a large native vessel bound for Ceylon, whence he would have no difficulty in obtaining passage to Madras.

These native ships are very high out of water, rising considerably towards the stem and stern, and in form they somewhat resemble the Chinese junk, but are without the superabundance of grotesque painting, carving, and gilding which distinguish the latter. The rajah accompanied Charlie to the shore, and a salute was fired by his followers in honor of the departure of the guest.

The weather was lovely, and the clumsy craft with all sail set was soon running down the coast. When they had sailed some hours from Calicut, from behind a headland four vessels suddenly made their appearance. They were lower in the water and much less clumsy in appearance than the ordinary native craft, and were propelled not only by their sails but by a number of oars on each side. No sooner did the captain and crew of the ship behold these vessels than they raised a cry of terror and despair. The captain, who was part owner of the craft, ran up and down the deck like one possessed, and the sailors seemed scarcely less terrified.

"What on earth is the matter?" Charlie exclaimed. "What vessels are those, and why are you afraid of them?"

"Tulagi Angria! Tulagi Angria!" the captain cried, and the crew took up the refrain. The name that they uttered fully accounted for their terror.

CHAPTER XV.

THE PIRATES' HOLD.

SIVAGI, the founder of the Maratta Empire, had, in 1662, seized and fortified Vijiyadrug, or, as the English call it, Gheriah, a town at the mouth of the river Kanui, one hundred and seventy miles south of Bombay, and also the island of Suwarndrug, about half way between Gheriah and Bombay. Here he established a piratical fleet. Fifty years later Kanhagi Angria, the commander of the Maratta fleet, broke off this connection with the successors of Sivagi, and set up as a pirate on his own account. Kanhagi not only plundered the native vessels, but boldly preyed upon the commerce of the European settlements. The ships of the East India Company, the French Company, and the Dutch, were frequently captured by these pirates. Tulagi Angria, who succeeded his father, was even bolder and more successful, and when the man-of-war brig the *Restoration*, with twenty guns and two hundred men, was fitted out to attack him, he defeated and captured her. After this he attacked and captured the French man-of-war *Jupitre*, with forty guns, and had even the insolence to assail an English convoy, guarded by two men-of-war, the *Vigilant*, of sixty-four guns, and the *Ruby*, of fifty. The Dutch, in 1735, sent a fleet of seven ships of war, two bomb-vessels, and a strong body of troops against Gheriah. The attack was, however, repulsed with considerable loss. From that date the pirates grew bolder and bolder, and were a perfect scourge to the commerce of Western India. Charlie Marryat had of course, frequently heard of the doings of these noted pirates, and the cry of Tulagi Angria at once explained to him the terror of the master and crew.

"What is it, Mr. Charles, what on earth is the botheration about? Is it the little ships they're afeered of?"

"Those ships belong to a pirate called Tulagi Angria," Charlie said, "and I am very much afraid, Tim, that we are likely to see the inside of his fortress."

"But shure, yer honor, we're not afeered of those four little boats."

"We are, Tim, and very much afraid, too. Each of those boats, as you call them, carries four or five times as many men as this ship. They are well armed, while we have only those two little guns, which are useless except for show. If the crew were Englishmen we might attempt a defence, although even then the odds would be terribly against us; but with these natives it is hopeless to think of it, and the attempt would only ensure our throats being cut."

It was clear that the idea of resistance did never even enter the minds of the crew of the trader. Some ran to and fro with gesticulations and cries of despair, some threw themselves upon the deck of the vessel, tore their hair, and rolled as if in convulsions. Some sat down quietly with the air of apathetic resignation, with which the natives of India are used to meet what they consider the inevitable. Hossein, who at the first alarm had bounded to his feet with his hand on his knife, subsided into an attitude of indifference when he saw that Charlie did not intend making any defence.

"It's mighty lucky," Tim said, "that yer honor left all your presents to be forwarded to Madras. I thought you were wrong, Mr. Charles, when you advised me to send them thousand rupees the rajah gave me along with your money. A hundred pounds wasn't a sum that Tim Kelly was likely to handle again in a hurry, and it went agin the grain with me to part with them out of my hands; sure and it's well I took yer honor's advice."

The four Sepoy officers also exchanged a few words with Charlie. They, too, would have resisted had he given the word, hopeless though the effort would have been. But they acquiesced at once in his decision. They had little to lose, but the thought of a prolonged captivity, and of being obliged, perhaps, to enter the service of the Maratta freebooters just when about to return to their wives and families at Madras, was a terrible blow for them.

"Keep up your spirits," Charlie said. "It is a bad business, but we must hope for the best. If we bide our time we may see some chance of escape. You had better lay down your arms in a pile here. Then we will sit down quietly and await their coming on board. They will be here in a minute now."

Scarcely had the seven passengers taken their seats in a group on the poop, when the freebooters ranged alongside and swarmed over the sides on to the deck. Beyond bestowing a few kicks upon the crew, they paid no attention whatever to them, but tore off the hatches and at once proceeded to investigate the contents of the hold. The greater portion of this consisted of native grains, but there were several bales of merchandise consigned by traders at Calicut for Ceylon. The cargo was, in fact, rather more valuable than that generally found in a native coaster, and the pirates were satisfied. The leader of the party, leaving to his followers the task of examining the hold, walked towards the group on the poop. They rose at his approach.

"Who are you?" the Maratta asked.

"I am an officer in the English Company's service," Charlie said, "as are these five natives. The other Englishman is a soldier under my orders."

"Good," the Maratta said emphatically. "Tulagi Angria will be glad to have you. When your people capture any of our men, which is not often, they hang them. Tulagi is glad to have people he can hang too."

After being stripped of any small valuables on their persons the captives were taking on board one of the pirate boats. A score of the Marattas remained in charge of the trader. Her head was turned north, and, accompanied by the four Maratta boats, she proceeded up the coast again. Another trader was captured on the way, but two others evaded the pirates by running into the port of Calicut. The trader was a slow sailer, and they were eight days before they approached Gheriah. Early in the morning a heavy cannonade was heard in the distance, causing the greatest excitement among the Marattas. Every sail was hoisted, the sweeps got out, and leaving the trader to jog along in their rear, the four light craft made their way rapidly along the coast. The firing became heavier and heavier, and as it became light three large ships could be seen about two miles ahead, surrounded by a host of smaller crafts.

"That's a big fight, Mr. Charles," Tim exclaimed. "It reminds me of three big bulls in a meadow attacked by a host of little curs."

"It does, Tim; but the curs can bite. What a fire they are keeping up. But those war-ships ought to thrash any number of them. Count the ports, I can see them now."

"The biggest one," Tim said, "has got twenty five."

"Yes; and the others eighteen and nine. They are

two frigates, one of fifty and the other of thirty-six guns, and a sloop of eighteen. I can't make out the colors, but I don't think they're English."

"They're not English, yer honor," Tim said confidently, "or they would soon make an end of them varmint that's tormenting them."

The scene as the boats approached was very exciting. The three ships were pouring their broadsides without intermission into the pirate fleet. This consisted of vessels of all sizes, from the *Jupitre* and *Restoration* down to large rowing galleys. Although many were sunk, and more greatly damaged by the fire of the Dutch they swarmed round the great ships with wonderful tenacity, and while the larger vessels fought their guns against those of the men-of-war, the smaller ones kept close to them, avoiding as much as possible their formidable broadsides, but keeping up a perpetual musketry fire at their bulwarks and tops, throwing stink-pots, and shooting burning arrows through the ports and getting alongside under the muzzles of the guns and trying to climb up into the ports.

The four newly arrived craft joined in the fray.

"This is mighty unpleasant, yer honor," Tim said, as a shot from one of the Dutch men-of-war struck the craft they were in, crashing a hole through her bulwarks, and laying five or six of her crew upon the deck, killed or wounded by the splinters. "Here we are in the middle of a fight in which we've no consarn whatever, and which is carried on without asking our will or pleasure; and we are as likely to be killed by a Christian shot as these haythen niggers. Hear them yell, yer honor. A faction fight's nothing to it. Look, yer honor, look! There's smoke curling up from a hatchway of the big ship. If they haven't set her afire!"

It was as Tim said. A cloud of black smoke was

rising from the Dutch fifty-gun frigate. A wild yell of triumph broke from the Marattas. The fire of their guns upon her redoubled, while that from the man-of-war died away as the crew were called off to assist in extinguishing the flames. Now the smaller boats pressed still more closely round her, and a rain of missiles was poured through the open ports. Several times the Marattas climbed on board, but each time were driven out again. The smoke rose thicker and thicker, and tongues of flame could be seen shooting up.

"She is doomed," Charlie exclaimed. "Even if unmolested the crew could not extinguish the fire now. It has got too much hold. Ah! the other frigate is on fire too."

Fresh yells of triumph rose from the Marattas. On board the sloop every sail was hoisted in spite of the continued fire of muskets and arrows, which killed many of the sailors employed. The *Jupitre*, however, ran alongside her and grappled with her, and a furious combat could be seen proceeding on the decks. Meanwhile the flames mounted higher and higher on board the twc frigates. The crew now could be seen leaping overboard from the ports, choosing any death rather than that by fire. It was but a choice. Many were drowned, the rest cut or shot down by the Marattas. Down came the Dutch flag, fluttering from the masthead of the sloop, and the wild Maratta yell proclaimed that the victory was everywhere complete. The frigates were now a sheet of flames, and the Maratta craft drew away from them, until with two tremendous explosions their magazines blew up and they sank beneath the waters.

"I should scarcely have believed it possible," Charlie said, "that three fine ships of war, mounting a hundred and four guns, could be destroyed by a fleet of pirates, however numerous. Well, Tim, there is no doubt that these natives can fight when well led. It is just as well, you see, that we did not attempt to offer any resistance in that clumsy craft we were on board."

"You're right there, yer honor. They would have aten us up in five minutes. It makes my heart bleed to think of the sailors of those two fine ships, I don't believe that a soul has escaped: but in the small one some may have been taken prisoners."

When the fight was over the craft in which were the captives ran alongside the flagship of the pirate leader, and the captain reported to him the capture he had made. Fortunately, Tulagi Angria was in a high state of delight at the victory he had just won, and instead of ordering them to be instantly executed, he told the captain to take them on to Suwarndrug and to imprison them there until his arrival. He himself with the rest of his fleet, and the captured Dutch sloop, sailed into Gheriah, and the craft in which Charlie and his companions were imprisoned continued her course to the island stronghold of the pirates.

Suwarndrug was built on a rocky island. It lay within gunshot of the shore. Here, when Kanhagi Angria had first revolted from the authority of the Maratta kingdom, the ruler of the Deccan had caused three strong forts to be built in order to reduce the island fort. The pirates, however, had taken the initiative and had captured these forts as well as the whole line of sea-coast, a hundred and twenty miles in length, and the country behind, twenty or thirty miles broad, extending to the foot of the mountains.

On their arrival at Suwarndrug the prisoners were handed over to the governor, and were imprisoned in one of the casemates of the fort. The next day they were taken out and ordered to work, and for weeks they labored at the fortifications with which the pirates were strengthening their already naturally strong position. The labor was very severe, but it was a consolation to the captives that they were kept together. By Charlie's advice they exerted themselves to the utmost, and thus succeeded in pleasing their masters and in escaping with but a small share of the blows which were liberally distributed among other prisoners, native and European, employed upon the work. Charlie, indeed, was appointed as a sort of overseer, having under him not only his own party but thirty others, of whom twenty were natives, and ten English sailors, who had been captured in a merchantman. Although closely watched he was able to cheer these men by giving them a hope that a chance of escape from their captivity might shortly arrive. All expressed their readiness to run any risk to regain their liberty.

From what he heard the pirates say, Charlie learned that they were expecting an attack from an expedition which was preparing at Bombay. The English sailors were confined in a casemate adjoining that occupied by Charlie and his companions. The guard kept over them was but nominal, as it was considered impossible that they could escape from the island, off which lay a large fleet of the pirate vessels. One morning upon starting to work they perceived by the stir in the fortress that something unusual was taking place, and presently, on reaching the rampart, they saw in the distance a small squadron approaching. They could make out that it consisted of a ship of forty-four guns, one of sixteen, and two bomb vessels, together with a fleet of native craft.

The pirate fleet were all getting up sail.

"It's a bold thing, Tim, to attack this fortress with only two ships, when the pirates have lately beaten a Dutch squadron mounting double the number of guns."

"Ah, yer honor, but thin there is the Union Jack

floating at the masthead. Do you think the creeturs don't know the differ?"

"But the Dutchmen are good sailors and fought well, Tim. I think the difference is that in the last case they attacked the Dutch, while in the present we are attacking them. It makes all the difference in the world with Indians. Let them attack you and they'll fight bravely enough. Go right at them and they're done for. Look, the pirate fleet are already sailing away."

"And do you think the English will take the fort, yer honor?"

"I don't know, Tim. The place is tremendously strong, and built on a rock. There are guns which bear right down on the ships if they venture in close, while theirs will do but little damage to these solidly built walls. Suwarndrug ought to resist a fleet ten times as strong as that before us."

"Shure thin, yer honor, and will we have to remain here all our lives, do ye think?"

"No, Tim, I hope not. Besides I think that we ought to be able to render some assistance to them."

"And how will we do it, yer honor? You have but to spake the word and Tim Kelly is ready to go through fire and water, and so is Hossein; ye may be shure of that."

Seeing that the pirates were now mustering round their guns, and that the ships were ranging up for action, Charlie thought it prudent to retire. Hitherto no attention had been paid to them, but 'twas probable enough that when the pirates' blood became heated by the fight, they would vent their fury upon their captives. He, therefore advised not only the native officers but the sailors to retire to their casemates, which, as the guns placed in them did not command the position taken up by the ships were at present untenanted by any of the garrison. Presently the noise of guns proclaimed that the engagement had begun. The boom of the cannon of the ships was answered by an incessant fire from the far more numerous artillery of the fortress, while now and then a heavy explosion close at hand told of the bursting of the bombs from the mortar vessels, in the fortress.

Charlie had been thinking of the best measures to be taken to aid his friends ever since the squadron came in sight, and after sitting quietly for half an hour he called his officers around him.

"I am convinced," he said, "that if unaided from within, the ships will have no chance whatever of taking this fortress; but I think that we may help them. The upper fort, which contains the magazine, commands the whole of the interior. But its guns do not bear upon the ships where they are anchored. Probably the place at present is almost deserted. As no one pays any attention to us, I propose, with Tim Kelly and the ten English sailors, to seize it. We can close the gate and discharge the guns upon the defenders of the sea face. We could not, of course, defend it for five minutes if they attacked us; but we would threaten to blow up the magazine if they did so. I propose that to-morrow morning you four and Hossein shall strip to your loin-clothes, and just before it becomes light go along the walls, and stop up, with pieces of wood, the touch-holes of as many of the cannon as you can. It would not do to use nails, even if we had them. No one will notice in the dark that you are not Marattas, and if you scatter about you may each manage to close up four or five guns at least. It is, I know a desperate service, and, if discovered you will be instantly killed. But if it succeeds the pirates, scared by discovering, just as our ships open fire, that a number of their guns are disabled, while we take them in the rear from the fort behind, may not improbably surrender at once. At any rate it's worth trying, and I for one would rather run the risk of being killed, than be condemned to pass my life the slave of these pirates, who may at any moment cut our throats in case of any reverse happening to them."

The four native officers at once stated their willingness to join in the plan. Hossein did not consider any reply necessary. With him it was a matter of course to do whatever Charlie suggested. The latter then went into the next casemate and unfolded his plan to the sailors, who heartily agreed to make an effort for their liberty.

The fire continued all day unabated, and at nightfall when a man as usual brought the captives food, he exultingly told them that no damage whatever had been effected by the guns of the fleet. In the evening the party cut a number of pieces of wood; these, measuring by the cannon in the casemate, they made of just sufficient size and length to push down with a slight effort through the touch-hole. When pushed down to their full length they touched the interior of the cannon below, and were just level with the top of the touch-hole. Thus it would be next to impossible to extricate them in a hurry. They might, indeed, be broken and forced in by a solid punch of the same size as the touch-hole, but this would take time, and would not be likely to occur on the moment to the pirates. The skewers, for this is what they resembled, were very strong and tough, being made of slips of bamboo. The prisoners had all knives which they used for cutting their food. With these the work was accomplished.

Towards morning the five natives, with the skewers hidden away in their loin-clothes and their turbans twisted in Maratta fashion, stole out from the casemate. Charlie had ordered, that in case they should see that the ships had drawn off from the position they occupied on the preceding day, they should return without attempting to carry out their task. He himself, with Tim, joined the sailors, and, first ascending the ramparts and seeing that the ships were still at anchor abreast of the fort, he and his comrades strolled across the interior of the fort in the direction of the magazine. They did not keep together, nor did all move directly towards the position which they wished to gain.

The place was already astir. Large numbers of the pirates thronged the interior. Groups were squatted round fires, busy in cooking their breakfasts, numbers were coming from the magazines with powder to fill up the small magazines on the walls, others again were carrying shot from the pyramids of missiles piled up here and there in the courtyard. None paid any attention to the English prisoners. Presently a dull boom was heard. There was a whistling sound, and with a thud, followed by a loud explosion, a bomb fell and burst in the open space.

This was the signal for action.

The pirates in a moment hurried down to the bastions overlooking the sea, and the Englishmen gathered in a group near the entrance to the magazine. Besides their knives they had no arms, but each had picked up two or three heavy stones. A minute after the explosion of the shell the cannonade of the ships broke out. It was answered by only a few guns from the fortress, and yells of astonishment and rage were heard to arise. A moment later five natives ran up to the group of Englishmen. Their work had been well done, and more than three-fourths of the guns on the sea face had been rendered temporarily useless.

Charlie gave the word, and with a rush they entered the upper fort. There were but two or three men there, who were just hurrying out with their bags of powder. These, before they realized the position, were instantly knocked down and bound. The gate

"IF YOU ATTACK US, WE WILL BLOW UP THE MAGAZINE."

of the fort was then shut and barred, and the party ran up to the bastion above. Not a single pirate was to be seen there. The six guns which stood there were at once loaded with grape, and a heavy discharge was poured into the crowded masses of pirates upon the bastions on the sea face. These, already greatly disturbed at finding that most of their guns had in some way been rendered useless, were panic-stricken at this sudden and unexpected attack from the rear. Many of them broke from their guns and fled to shelter, others endeavored to turn their cannon to bear upon the magazine.

The wildest confusion raged. At last some of their leaders rallied the men, and with yells of fury a rush was made towards the magazine. They were received with another discharge of grape, which took terrible effect. Many recoiled, but their leaders, shouting to them that the guns were discharged, and there were but a dozen men there, led them on again.

Charlie leaped upon the edge of the parapet and shouted:

"If you attack us we will blow up the magazine. I have but to lift my hand and the magazine will be fired."

The boldest of the assailants were paralyzed by the threat. Confusion reigned throughout the fortress.

The fleet kept up their fire with great vigor, judging by the feebleness of the reply that something unusual must be happening within the walls. The gunners, disheartened by finding their pieces useless, and unable to extract the wooden plugs, while Charlie's men continued to ply them with grape, left their guns and with the greater portion of the garrison, disorganized and panic-stricken, retired into shelter. A shell from the ships falling on to a thatched building set it on fire. The flames rapidly spread, and soon all the small huts occupied by the garrison were in flames.

The explosion of a magazine added to the terror of the garrison, and the greater portion of them, with the women and children, ran down to the water, and taking boats attempted to cross to Fort Goa, on the mainland. They were, however, cut off by the English boats and captured. Commodore James, who commanded the squadron, now directed his fire at Fort Goa, which was being feebly attacked on the land side by a Maratta force, which had been landed from the Maratta fleet accompanying the English ships, a few miles down the coast. The fort shortly surrendered; but while the Marratas were marching to take possession, the governor, with some of his best men, took boat and crossed over to the island, of which, although the fire had ceased after the explosion of the magazine, the English had not taken possession.

The fire from its guns again opened, and as Commodore James thought it probable that the pirates would in the night endeavor to throw in large reinforcements, he determined to carry it by storm. The ships opened fire upon the walls, and under cover of this half the seamen were landed; these ran up to the gate and thundered at it with their axes. Charlie and his companions aided the movement by again opening a heavy fire of grape upon the guns which bore upon the sally-port, and when the gates were forced the garrison, utterly dispirited by the cross-fire to which they were subjected, at once laid down their arms.

CHAPTER XVI.

A TIGER HUNT.

COMMODORE JAMES was greatly astonished at the easy success which he had gained. The extraordinary cessation of fire from the sea face and the sound of artillery within the walls had convinced him that a mutiny among the garrison must have taken place; but, upon entering the fort he was surprised indeed at being received with a hearty English cheer from a little body of men on the summit of an interior work. The gate of this was at once thrown open, and Charlie, followed by his party, advanced towards the commodore.

"I am Captain Marryat, sir, of the Company's service in Madras, and was captured three months ago by these pirates. When you attacked the place yesterday I arranged to effect a small diversion, and with the assistance of these five native officers, of my soldier servant here, and these ten men of the merchant service, we have, I hope been able to do so. The native officers disabled the greater portion of the guns during the night, and when you opened fire this morning we seized this inner work, which is also the magazine, and opened fire upon the rear of the sea defences. By dint of our guns and of menaces to blow up the place if they assaulted it, we kept them at bay until their flag was hauled down."

"Then, sir," Commodore James said warmly; "I

have to thank you most heartily for the assistance you have given. In fact it is you who have captured the fortress. I was by no means prepared to find it so strong, and, indeed, had come to the conclusion last night that the force at my command was wholly insufficient for its capture. Fortunately, I determined to try the effect of another day's fire. But had it not been for you this would assuredly have been as ineffectual as the first. You have, indeed, performed a most gallant action, and I shall have great pleasure in reporting your conduct to the authorities at home."

The sailors had now landed in considerable force. The garrison were disarmed and taken as prisoners on board the ships. Very large quantities of powder were found stored up, and strong parties at once began to form mines for the blowing up of the fortifications. This was a labor of some days; when they were completed and charged a series of tremendous explosions took place. Many of the bastions were completely blown to pieces; in others the walls were shattered. The prisoners were again landed and set to work, aided by the sailors. The great stones which composed the walls were toppled over the steep faces of the rock on which the fort stood, and at the end of a fortnight the pirate hold of Suwarndrug, which had so long been the terror of the Indian seas, had disappeared.

The fleet returned to Bombay, for it was evidently wholly insufficient to attempt an assault on Gheriah, defended as that place would be by the whole pirate fleet, which had, even without the assistance of its guns, proved itself a match for a squadron double the strength of that under the command of Commodore James. The rejoicings at Bombay were immense, for enormous damage had been inflicted on the commerce of that place by this pirate hold, situated but eighty miles from the port. Commodore James and his officers were fêted, and Charlie Marryat had his full share of honor; the gallant sailor everywhere assigning to him the credit of its capture.

Charlie would now have sailed at once for Madras, but the authorities wished him to remain, as Clive was shortly expected to arrive with a considerable force which was destined to act against the French at Hyderabad. The influence of Bussy with the nizam rendered this important province little better than a French possession, and the territory of our rivals upon the sea-coast had been immensely increased by the grant of the five districts known as the Northern Sirdars to Bussy. It was all that the English could do to hold their own around Madras, and it was out of the question for them to think of attempting single-handed to dislodge Bussy from Hyderabad. Between the nizam, however, and the Peishwar of the Deccan there was a long standing feud, and the Company had proposed to this prince to aid him with a strong English force in an attack upon Hyderabad.

Colonel Scott had in the first place been sent out to command this expedition; but when Clive, wearied with two years' life of inactivity in England, applied to be appointed to active service, the directors at once appointed him governor of Fort St. David, and obtained for him the rank of lieutenant-colonel in the royal army. They directed him to sail at once for Bombay with three companies of the Royal Artillery, each a hundred strong, and three hundred infantry recruits. Upon his arrival there he was to give Colonel Scott any assistance he required. That officer, however, had died before Clive arrived.

Upon reaching Bombay Clive found that events had occurred in the south which would prevent the intended expedition from taking place. The French government had suddenly recalled Dupleix, the great man whose talent and statesmanship had sustained their cause. On his return to France, instead of treating him with honor for the work he had done for them, they even refused to repay him the large sums which he had advanced from his private fortune to carry on the struggle against the English, and Dupleix died in poverty and obscurity. In his place the French governor had sent out a man by the name of Godchen, who was weak and wholly destitute of ability. At the time of his arrival the English were hardly pressed, and a strong French fleet and force were expected on the coast. When, however, Mr. Saunders proposed to him a treaty of neutrality between the Indian possessions of the two powers he at once accepted it, and thus threw away all the advantages which Dupleix had struggled so hard to obtain. The result of this treaty, however was that the English were unable to carry out their proposed alliance with the peishwar against the nizam and Bussy.

Upon Clive's arrival Charlie at once reported himself to him. For a time, however, no active duty was assigned to him, as it was uncertain what steps would now be taken. Finally it was resolved that, taking advantage of the presence of Clive and his troops, and of a squadron which had arrived under Admiral Watson, the work commenced by Commodore James should be completed by the capture of Gheriah and the entire destruction of the pirate power.

The peishwar had already asked them to aid him in his attack upon Angria, and Commodore James was now sent with the *Protector* and two other ships to reconnoitre Gheriah, which no Englishman then living had seen. The natives described it as of enormous strength, and it was believed that it was an Eastern Gibraltar. Commodore James found the enemy's fleet at anchor in the harbor. Notwithstanding this he sailed in until within cannon-shot, and so completely were the enemy cowed and demoralized by the loss of Suwarndrug that they did not venture out to attack him.

After ascertaining the position and character of the defences, he returned, at the end of December, to Bombay, and reported that while exceedingly strong the place was by no means impregnable. The Maratta army under the command of Ramajee Punt marched to blockade the place on the land side; and on the 11th of February, 1756, the fleet, consisting of four ships of the line, of seventy, sixty-four, sixty, and fifty guns, a frigate of forty-four and three of twenty, a native ship called a grab, of twelve guns, and five mortar ships, arrived before the place. Besides the seamen the fleet had on board a battalion of eight hundred Europeans and a thousand Sepoys.

The fortress of Gheriah was situated on a promontory of rock a mile and a quarter broad, lying about a mile up a large harbor forming the mouth of a river. The promontory projects to the southwest on the right of the harbor on entering, and rises sheer from the water in perpendicular rocks fifty feet high. On this stood the fortifications. These consisted of two lines of walls, with round towers, the inner wall rising several feet above the outer. The promontory was joined to the land by a sandy slip, beyond which the town stood. On this neck of land between the promontory and the town were the docks and slips on which the pirate vessels were built or repaired, and ten of these, among which was the *Derby*, which they had captured from the Company, lay moored side by side close by the docks when the fleet arrived off the place.

Charlie Marryat had been sent by Clive as commissioner with the Maratta army. A party of Maratta horsemen came down to Bombay to escort him to Chaule, at which place the Maratta army were assembled for their march. He was accompanied by Tim and Hossein, who were, of course, like him, on horseback. A long day's ride took them to their first halting place, a few miles from the foot of a splendid range of hills which rise like a wall, from the low land, for a vast distance along the coast. At the top of these hills—called in India, ghauts—lay the plateau of the Deccan, sloping gradually away to the Ganges, hundreds of miles to the east.

"Are we going to climb up to the top of them mountains, your honor?"

"No, Tim, fortunately for our horses. We shall skirt their foot for a hundred and fifty miles, till we get behind Gheriah."

"You wouldn't think that a horse could climb them," Tim said. "They look as steep as the side of a house."

"In many places they are, Tim, but you see there are breaks in them. At some points, either from the force of streams or from the weather, the rocks have crumbled away, and the great slopes, which everywhere extend half-way up, reach the top. Zigzag paths are cut in these which can be travelled by horses and pack animals. There must be quantities of game," Charlie said to the leader of the escort, "on the mountain sides."

"Quantities," the Maratta said. "Tigers and bears swarm there, and are such a scourge that there are no villages within miles of the foot of the hills. Even on the plateau above, the villages are few and scarce near the edge so great is the damage done by wild beasts. But that is not all. There are numerous bands of Dacoits, who set the authority of the peishwar at defiance, plunder travellers and merchants going up and down, make raids into the Deccan, and plunder the low land nearly up to the gates of Bombay. Numerous expeditions have been sent against them, but the Dacoits know every foot of the hills. They have numerous impregnable strongholds on the rocks, which you can see rising sheer up hundreds of feet from among the woods on the slopes, and can, if pressed, shift their quarters and move fifty miles away among the trees, while the troops are in vain searching for them."

"I suppose there is no chance of their attacking us," Charlie said.

"The Dacoit never fights if he can help it, and then only when driven into a corner, or when there appears a chance of very large plunder. He will always leave a strong party of armed men, from whom nothing but hard blows is to be got, in peace."

The journey occupied five days and was most enjoyable. The officer of the escort, as the peishwar's agent, would have requisitioned provisions at each of the villages, but Charlie insisted, under one pretence or another, on buying a couple of sheep or kids at each halting place, for the use of his own party and the escort. For a few copper coins an abundant supply of fruit and vegetables was obtainable; and, as each night they spread their rugs under the shade of some overhanging tree and smoked their pipes lazily after the very excellent meal which Hossein always prepared, Charlie and Tim agreed that they had spent no pleasanter time in India than that occupied by their journey.

Charlie was received with much honor by Ramajee Punt, and was assigned a gorgeous tent next to his own.

"People in England, Mister Charles," said Tim that evening, "turn up their noses at the thought of living in tents, but what do they know of them? The military tent is an uncomfortable thing, and as for the gypsy tent a dacent pig wouldn't look at it. Now this is like a palace, with its carpet under foot and its sides covered with silk hangings, and its furniture fit for a palace. Father Murphy wouldn't believe me if I told him about it on oath. If this is making war, yer honor, I shall be in no hurry for pace."

The Maratta force took up its position beleaguering the town on the land side some weeks before the arrival of the fleet, Commodore James with his two ships blockading it at sea. There was little to do, and Charlie accepted with eagerness an offer of Ramajee Punt that they should go out for two or three days' tiger hunting at the foot of the hills.

"Well, Mr. Charles," Tim said when he heard of the intention, "if you want to go tiger hunting, Tim Kelly is not the boy to stay behind. But, shure, yer honor, if the creeturs will lave ye alone why should you meddle with them? I saw one in a cage at Arcot, and it's a baste I shouldn't wish to see on a lone road on a dark night. It had a way of wagging its tail that made you feel uncomfortable like to the sole of yer boots, and after looking at me for some time, the baste opened its mouth and gave a roar that shook the whole establishment. It's a baste safer to let alone than to meddle with."

"But we shall be up on top of an elephant. We shall be safe enough there, you know."

"Maybe, yer honor," Tim said doubtfully; "but I mind me that when I was a boy me and my brother Peter was throwing sods at an old tom-cat of my mother's who had stolen our dinners, and it ran up a wall ten feet high. Well, yer honor, the tiger is as big as a hundred tom-cats, and by the same token he ought to able to run up a wall—"

"A thousand feet high, Tim? He can't do that; indeed, I question whether he could run up much higher than a cat. We are to start this evening and shall be there by midnight. The elephants have gone on ahead."

At sunset the party started. It consisted of Ramajee Punt, one of his favorite officers, and a score of soldiers. An officer had already gone on to enlist the services of the men of two or three villages as beaters. A small but comfortable tent had been erected for the party and supper prepared. The native shikari or sportsman of the neighborhood had brought in the news that tigers were plentiful, and that one of unusual size had been committing great depredations, and had only the day before carried off a bullock into the thickets a mile from the spot at which they were encamped.

"The saints preserve us!" Tim said when he heard the news; "a cat big enough to carry off a mouse in her mouth as big as a bullock."

"It seems almost impossible, Tim, but it is a fact that tigers can carry in their mouths full-sized bullocks for considerable distances, and that they can kill them with one stroke of their paw. However, they are not as formidable as you would imagine, as you will see to-morrow."

In the morning the elephants were brought out. Charlie took his place in the front of a howdah with Tim behind him. Three rifles were placed in the seat, and these Tim was to hand to his master as he discharged them. Ramajee Punt and his officer were also mounted on elephants, and the party started for their destination.

"It's as bad as being at sea, Mr. Charles," Tim said.

"It does roll about, Tim. You must let your body go with the motion just as on board ship. You will soon get accustomed to it."

On reaching the spot, which was a narrow valley with steep sides running up into the hill, the elephants came to a stand. The mouth of the valley was some fifty yards wide, and the animal might break from the trees at any point. The ground was covered with high coarse grass. Ramajee Punt placed himself in the centre, assigning to Charlie the position on his right, telling him that it was the best post, as it was on this side the tiger had been seen to enter. Soon after they had taken their places, a tremendous clamor arose near the head of the valley. Drums were beaten, horns blown, and scores of men joined in with shouts and howls.

"What on arth are they up to, Mr. Charles?"

"They are driving the tiger this way, Tim. Now, sit quiet and keep a sharp lookout, and be ready to hand me a rifle the instant I have fired."

The noise increased and was plainly approaching. The elephant fidgeted uneasily.

"That baste has more sinse than we have," said Tim; "and would be off if that little black chap, astraddle of his neck, didn't keep on patting his head."

Presently the mahout pointed silently to the bushes ahead, and Charlie caught sight for a moment of some yellow fur. Apparently the tiger had heard or scented the elephants, for it again turned and made up the valley. Presently a redoubled yelling, with the firing of guns, showed that it had been seen by the beaters. Ramajee Punt held up his hand to Charlie as a signal that next time the tiger might be expected. Suddenly there was a movement among the bushes, a tiger sprang out about half-way between Charlie's elephant and that of Ramajee Punt. It paused for a moment on seeing them, and then, as it was about to spring forward, two balls struck it. It sprang a short distance, however, and then fell, rolling over and over. One ball had broken a foreleg, the other had struck it on the head. Another ball from Ramajee Punt struck it as it rolled over and over, and it lay immovable.

"Why didn't you hand me the next rifle, Tim?" Charlie said sharply.

"It went clane out of my head altogether. To think, now, and you kilt it in a moment. The tiger is a poor baste anyhow. I've seen a cat make ten times as strong a fight for its life. Holy Moses!"

The last exclamation was called from Tim's lips by a sudden jerk. A huge tiger, far larger than that which had fallen, had sprung up from the brushwood and leaped upon the elephant. With one fore-paw he grasped the howdah, with the other clung to the elephant's shoulder an inch or two only behind the leg of the mahout. Charlie snatched the rifle from Tim's hand and thrust the muzzle into the tiger's mouth, just as the elephant swerved round with sudden fright and pain. At the same moment the weight of the tiger on the howdah caused the girths to give way, and Charlie, Tim, and the tiger fell together on the ground. Charlie had pulled his trigger just as he felt himself going, and at the same moment he heard the crack of Ramajee Punt's rifle. The instant they touched the ground Tim and Charlie cast themselves over and over two or three times and then leaped to their feet, Charlie grasping his rifle to make the best defence he could if the tiger sprang upon him. The creature lay, however, immovable.

"It is dead, Tim," Charlie exclaimed; "you needn't be afraid."

"And no wonder, yer honor, when I pitched head first smack on to his stomach. It would have killed a horse."

It might have done, Tim, but I don't think it would have killed a tiger. Look there."

Charlie's gun had gone off at the moment when the howdah turned round, and had nearly blown off a portion of the tiger's head, while almost at the same instant the ball of Ramajee Punt had struck it in the back breaking the spine. Death had, fortunately for Tim, been instantaneous. The tiger last killed was the great male which had done so much damage, the first, a female. The natives tied the legs together, placed long bamboos between them, and carried the animals off in triumph to the camp. The elephant on which Charlie had ridden ran some distance before the mahout could stop him. He was, indeed, so terrified by the onslaught of the tiger that it was not considered advisable to endeavor to get him to face another that day. Ramajee Punt, therefore, invited Charlie to take his seat with him on his elephant, an arrangement which greatly satisfied Tim, whose services were soon dispensed with.

"I'd rather walk on my own feet, Mister Charles, than ride any more on those great bastes. They're uncomfortable anyhow. It's a long way to fall if the saddle goes round, and next time one might not find a tiger handy to light on."

Two more tigers were killed that afternoon, and, well pleased with his day's sport, Charlie returned to the hunting camp. The next day Hossein begged that he might be allowed to accompany Charlie in Tim's place, and as the Irishman was perfectly willing to surrender it, the change was agreed upon. The march was a longer one than it had been on the previous morning. A notorious man-eating tiger was known to have taken up his abode in a large patch of jungle at the foot of an almost perpendicular wall of rock about ten miles from the place where the camp was pitched. The patch of jungle stood upon a steep terrace whose slopes were formed of boulders, the patch being some fifty or sixty yards long and thirty deep.

"It is a nasty place," Ramajee Punt said, "to get him from. The beaters cannot get behind to drive him out, and the jungle is too thick to penetrate."

"How do you intend to proceed?" Charlie asked.

"We will send a party to the top of the hill and they will throw down crackers. We have brought some rockets, too, which we will send in from the other side. We will take our places on our elephants at the foot of the terrace."

The three elephants took their posts at the foot of the boulder-covered rise. As soon as they had done so the men at the top of the rock began to throw down numbers of lighted crackers, while from either side parties sent rockets whizzing into the jungle. For some time the tiger showed no signs of his presence, and Charlie began to doubt whether he could be really there. The shikaris, however, declared that he was certainly in the jungle. He had on the day before carried off a woman from a neighboring village, and had been traced to the jungle, round which a watch had been kept all night. Suddenly, uttering a mighty roar, the tiger bounded from the jungle and stood at the edge of the terrace. Startled at his sudden appearance the elephants recoiled, shaking the aim of their riders. Three shots were, however, fired almost at the same moment, and the tiger with another roar bounded back into the jungle.

"I think," the rajah said, "that he is badly hit. Listen to his roarings."

The tiger for a time roared loudly at intervals. Then the sounds became lower and less frequent, and at last ceased altogether. In vain did the natives above shower down crackers. In vain were the rockets discharged into the jungle. An hour passed since he had last been heard.

"I expect that he's dead," Charlie said.

"I think so too, Ramajee Punt replied; "but one can never be certain. Let us draw off a little and take our luncheon. After that we can try the fireworks again. If he will not move then we must leave him."

"But surely," Charlie said, "we might go in and see whether he's dead or not."

"A wounded tiger is a terrible foe," the Ramajee answered. "Better leave him alone."

Charlie, however, was anxious to get the skin to send home, with those of the others he had shot, to his mother and sisters. It might be very long before he had an opportunity of joining in another tiger hunt, and he resolved that if the tiger gave no signs of life when the bombardment of the jungle with fireworks recommenced, he would go in and look for his body.

CHAPTER XVII.

THE CAPTURE OF GHERIAH.

AFTER having sat for an hour under the shade of some trees, and partaken of luncheon, the party again moved forward on their elephants to the jungle. The watchers declared that no sound whatever had been heard during their absence, nor did the discharge of fireworks, which at once recommenced, elicit the slightest response. After this had gone on for half an hour, Charlie, convinced that the animal was dead, dismounted from his elephant. He had with him a heavy double barrelled rifle of the rajah's, and Hossein, carrying a similiar weapon and a curved tulwar which was sharpened almost to a razor edge, prepared to follow immediately behind him. Three or four of the most courageous shikaris, with cocked guns, followed in Hossein's steps.

Holding his gun advanced before him, in readiness to fire instantly, Charlie entered the jungle at the point where the tiger had retreated into it. Drops of blood spotted the grass, and the bent and twisted brushwood showed the path that the tiger had taken. Charlie moved as noiselessly as possible. The path led straight forward towards the rocks behind, but it was not until within four or five yards of this that any sign of the tiger could be seen. Then the bushes were burst asunder, and the great yellow body hurled itself forward upon Charlie. The attack was so sudden and instantaneous that the latter had not even time to raise his rifle to his shoulder. Almost instinctively, however, he discharged both of the barrels, but was at the same moment hurled to the ground, where he lay crushed down by the weight of the tiger, whose hot breath he could feel on his face. He closed his eyes only to open them again at the sound of a heavy blow, while a deluge of hot blood flowed over him. He heard Hossein's voice, and then became insensible. When he recovered he found himself lying with his head supported by Hossein outside the jungle.

"Is he dead?" he asked faintly.

"He is dead, Sahib," Hossein replied. "Let the Sahib drink some brandy and he will be strong again."

Charlie drank some brandy and water which Hossein held to his lips. Then the latter raised him to his feet. Charlie felt his limbs and his ribs. He was bruised all over, but otherwise unhurt, the blood which covered him having flowed from the tiger.

One of the balls which he had fired had entered the tiger's neck, the other had broken one of its forelegs, and Charlie had been knocked down by the weight of the animal, not by the blow of its formidable paw. Hossein had sprung forward on the instant, and with one blow of his sharp tulwar, had shorn clear through skin and muscle and bone, and had almost severed the tiger's head from its body. It was the weight upon him which had crushed Charlie into a state of insensibility. Here he had lain for four or five minutes before Hossein could get the frightened natives to return and assist him to lift the great carcass from his master's body. Upon examination it was found that two of the three bullets first fired had taken effect. One had broken the tiger's shoulder and lodged in his body, the other had struck him fairly on the chest and had gassed within an inch or two of his heart.

"I thought," Ramajee Punt said, as he viewed the body, "that one of his legs must have been rendered useless. That was why he lay quiet so long in spite of our efforts to turn him out."

Charlie was too much hurt to walk, and a litter was speedily formed and he was carried back to the camp, where his arrival in that state excited the most lively lamentations on the part of Tim.

The next morning he was much recovered, and was able in the cool of the evening to take his place in a howdah, and to return to the camp before Gheriah.

A few days later the fleet made its appearance off the town, and the same evening Tulagi Angria rode up to Ramajee Punt's camp. Charlie was present at the interview, at which Angria endeavored to prevail on Ramajee Punt and Charlie to accept a large ransom for his fort, offering them each great presents if they would do their utmost to prevail on Admiral Watson and Colonel Clive to agree to accept it. Charlie said at once that he was sure it was useless, that the English had now made a great effort to put a stop to the ravages which he and his father before him had, for so many years, inflicted upon their commerce, and that he was sure that nothing short of the total destruction of the fort and fleet would satisfy them. The meeting then broke up, and Charlie, supposing that Angria would immediately return, went back to his tent, where he directed Hossein at once to mingle with the men who had accompanied Angria, and to find out anything that he could concerning the state of things in the fort. Hossein returned an hour later.

"Sahib," he said, "Ramajee Punt is thinking of cheating the English. He is keeping Angria a prisoner. He says that he came into his camp without asking for a safe conduct, and that therefore he shall detain him. But this is not all. Angria has left his brother in command of the fort, and Ramajee, by threatening

Angria with instant execution, has induced him to send an order to deliver the fort at once to him. Ramajee wants, you see, Sahib, to get all the plunder of the fort for himself and his Marattas."

"This is very serious," Charlie said, "and I must let the admiral know at once what is taking place."

When it became dark Charlie, with Tim and Hossein, made his way through the Maratta camp down to the shore of the river. Here were numbers of boats hauled up on the sand. One of the lightest of these was soon got into the water and rowed gently out into the force of the stream. Then the oars were shipped and they lay down perfectly quiet in the boat, and drifted past the fort without being observed. When they once gained the open sea the oars were placed in the row-locks, and half an hour's rowing brought them along-side the fleet. Charlie was soon on board the flagship, and informed the admiral and Colonel Clive what Hossein had heard. It was at once resolved to attack upon the following day. The two officers did not think it was likely that the pirates would, even in obedience to their chief's orders, surrender the place until it had been battered by the fleet.

The next morning the fort was summoned to surrender. No answer was received, and as soon as the sea breeze set in, in the afternoon the fleet weighed anchor and proceeded towards the mouth of the river. The men-of-war were in line on the side nearest to the fort to protect the mortar vessels and smaller ships from its fire. Passing the point of the promontory they stood into the river, and anchored at a distance of fifty yards from the north face of the fort. A gun from the admiral's ship gave the signal, and a hundred and fifty pieces of cannon at once opened fire, while the mortar vessels threw shell into the fort and town. In ten minutes after the fire began a shell fell into one of Angria's large ships and set her on fire. The flames soon spread to the others fastened together on either side of her, and in less than an hour this fleet, which had for fifty years been the terror of the Malabar coast, was utterly destroyed.

In the mean time the fleet kept up their fire with the greatest vigor upon the enemy's works, and before nightfall the enemy's fire was completely silenced. No white flag, however, was hung up, and the admiral had little doubt that it was intended to surrender the place to the Marattas. As soon, therefore, as it became quite dark, Colonel Clive landed with the troops, and took up a position between the Marattas and the fort, where, to his great disappointment and disgust Ramajee Punt found him in the morning. The admiral again summoned the fort, declaring that he would renew the attack and give no quarter unless it was surrendered immediately. The governor sent back to beg the admiral to cease from hostilities until next day, as he was only waiting for orders from Angria to surrender. Angria declared that he had already sent the orders.

At four in the afternoon, therefore, the bombardment was renewed and in less than half an hour a white flag appeared above the wall. As, however, the garrison made no further sign of surrender, and refused to admit Colonel Clive with his troops when he advanced to take possession, the bombardment was again renewed more vigorously than ever. The enemy were unable to support the violence of the fire, and soon shouted over the walls to Clive that they surrendered, and he might enter and take possession. He at once marched in, and the pirates laid down their arms and surrendered themselves prisoners. It was found that a great part of the fortifications had been destroyed by the fire, but a resolute garrison might have held the fort itself against a long siege. Two hundred guns fell into the hands of the captors, together with great quantities of ammunition and stores of all kinds. The money and effects amounted to a hundred and twenty thousand pounds, which was divided among the captors. The rest of Angria's fleet, among them two large ships on the stocks, was destroyed. Ramajee Punt sent parties of his troops to attack the other forts held by the pirates. These, however, surrendered without resistance, and thus the whole country which the pirates had held for seventy years fell again into the hands of the Marattas, from whom they had wrested it.

Admiral Watson and the fleet then returned to Bombay in order to repair the damages which had been inflicted upon them during the bombardment. There were great rejoicings upon their arrival there, the joy of the inhabitants, both European and native, being immense at the destruction of the formidable pirate colonies which had so long ravaged the seas.

After the repairs were completed, the fleet with the troops which had formed the expedition were to sail for Madras. Charlie, however, did not wait for this, but, finding that one of the Company's ships would sail in the course of a few days after their return to Bombay, he obtained leave from Colonel Clive to take a passage in her and to proceed immediately to Madras. Tim and Hossein of course accompanied him, and the voyage down the west coast of India and round Ceylon was performed without any marked incident.

When within but a few hours of Madras the barometer fell rapidly. Great clouds rose up upon the horizon, and the captain ordered all hands aloft to reduce sail.

"We are in," he said, "for a furious tempest. It is the breaking up of the monsoon. It is a fortnight earlier than usual. I had hoped that we should have got safely up the Hoogly before it began."

Half an hour later the hurricane struck them, and for the next three days the tempest was terrible. Great waves swept over the ship, and every time that the captain attempted to show a rag of canvas it was blown from the bolt ropes. The ship, however, was a stout one and weathered the gale. Upon the fourth morning the passengers, who had, during the tempest, been battened below, came on deck. The sky was bright and clear, and the waves were fast going down. A good deal of sail was already set, and the hands were at work to repair damages.

"Well, captain," Charlie said to that officer, "I congratulate you on the behavior of the ship. It has been a tremendous gale, and she has weathered it stoutly."

"Yes, Captain Marryat, she has done well. I have only once or twice been out in so severe a storm since I came to sea."

"And where are we now?" Charlie asked, looking round the horizon. "When shall we be at Madras?"

"Well," the captain said with a smile, "I am afraid that you must give up all idea of seeing Madras just at present. We have been blown right up the bay, and are only a few hours sail from the mouth of the Hoogly. I have a far larger cargo for that place than for Madras, and it would be a pure waste of time for me to put back now. I intend, therefore, to go to Calcutta first, discharge and fill up there, and then touch at Madras on my way back. I suppose it makes no great difference to you."

"No, indeed," Charlie said. "And I am by no means sorry of the opportunity of getting a glimpse of Calcutta, which I might never otherwise have done. I believe things are pretty quiet at Madras at present, and I have been so long away now that a month or two sooner or later will make but little difference."

A few hours later Charlie noticed a change in the

color of the sea, the mud-stained waters of the Hoogly discoloring the Bay of Bengal far out from its mouth. The voyage up was a tedious one. At times the wind fell altogether, and, unable to stem the stream, the ship lay for days at anchor, the yellow tide running swiftly by it.

"The saints presarve us, Mr. Charles! did you ever see the like?" Tim Kelly exclaimed. "There's another dead body floating down towards us, and that is the eighth I've seen this morning. Are the poor hathen craturs all committing suicide together?"

"Not at all, Tim," Charlie said, "the Hoogly is one of the sacred rivers of India, and the people on its banks, instead of burying their dead, put them into the river and let them drift away."

"I calls it a bastly custom, yer honor, and I wonder it is allowed. One got athwart the cable this morning, and it frightened me nigh out of my sinses, when I happened to look over the bow, and saw the thing bobbing up and down in the water. This is tadious work, yer honor, and I'll be glad when we're at the end of the voyage."

"I shall be glad too, Tim. We have been a fortnight in the river already, but I think there is a breeze getting up, and there is the captain on deck giving orders."

In a few minutes the ship was under way again and the same night dropped her anchor in the stream abreast of Calcutta. Charlie shortly after landed, and, proceeding to the Company's offices, reported his arrival and that of the four Sepoy officers. Hossein, who was not in the Company's service, was with him merely in the character of a servant.

As the news of the share Charlie had had in the capture of Suwarndrug had reached Calcutta he was well received, and one of the leading merchants of the town, Mr. Haines, who happened to be present when

Charlie called upon the governor, at once invited him warmly to take up his residence with him during his stay. Hospitality in India was profuse and general. Hotels were unknown, and a stranger was always treated as an honored guest. Charlie, therefore, had no hesitation whatever in accepting the offer. The four native officers were quartered in the barracks, and, returning on board ship, Charlie, followed by Tim and Hossein, and by some coolies bearing his luggage, was soon on his way to the bungalow of Mr. Haines. On his way he was surprised at the number and size of the dwellings of the merchants and officials which offered a very strong contrast to the quiet and unpretending buildings round the fort of Madras. The house of Mr. Haines was a large one, and stood in a large and carefully kept garden. Mr. Haines received him at the door, and at once led him to his room, which was spacious, cool, and airy. Outside was a wide verandah, upon which, in accordance with the customs of the country, servants would sleep.

"Here is your bath-room," Mr. Haines said, pointing to an adjoining room; "I think you will find everything ready. We dine in half an hour."

Charlie was soon in his bath, a luxury which in India every European indulges in at least twice a day. Then in his cool white suit, which at that time formed the regular evening dress, he found his way to the drawing-room. Here he was introduced to the merchant's wife, and to his daughter, a girl of some thirteen years old, as well as to several guests who had arrived for dinner.

The meal was a pleasant one, and Charlie, after being cooped up for some weeks on board ship, enjoyed it much. A dinner in India is to one unaccustomed to it a striking sight. The punkah waving slowly to and fro overhead drives the cool air which comes in through the open windows down upon the table. Each guest brings his own servant, who, either in white or colored robes, and in turbans of many different hues and shapes, according to the wearer's caste, stands behind his master's chair. The light is always a soft one, and the table richly garnished with bright-colored tropical flowers.

Charlie was the hero of the hour, and was asked many questions concerning the capture of Suwarndrug, and also about the defence of Ambur, which, though now an old story, had excited the greatest interest through India. Presently, however, the conversation turned to local topics, and Charlie learned from the anxious looks and earnest tones of the speakers that the situation was considered a very serious one. He asked but few questions then; but after the guests had retired and Mr. Haines proposed to him to smoke one more quiet cigar in the cool of the verandah before retiring to bed, he took the opportunity of asking his host to explain to him the situation, with which he had no previous acquaintance.

"Up to the death of Ali Kerdy, the old viceroy of Bengal, on the 9th of April, we were on good terms with our native neighbors. Calcutta has not been, like Madras, threatened by the rivalry of a European neighbor. The French and Dutch, indeed, have both trading stations like our own, but none of us have taken part in native affairs. Ali Kerdy has been all powerful, there have been no native troubles, and therefore no reason for our interference. We have just gone on as for many years previously as a purely trading company. At his death he was succeeded in the government by Suraja Dowlah, his grandson. I suppose in all India there is no prince with a worse reputation than this young scoundrel has already gained for himself for profligacy and cruelty. He is constantly drunk, and is surrounded by a crew of reprobates as wicked as himself. At the death of Ali Kerdy, Sokut Jung, another grandson of Ali, set up in opposition to him, and the new viceroy raised a large force to march against him. As the reputation of Sokut Jung was as infamous as that of his cousin it would have made little difference to us which of the two obtained the mastery; within the last few days, however, circumstances have occurred which have completely altered the situation.

"The town of Dacca was about a year ago placed under the governorship of Rajah Ragbullub, a Hindoo officer in high favor with Ali Kerdy. His predecessor had been assassinated and plundered by order of Suraja Dowlah, and when he heard of the accession of that prince he determined at once to fly, as he knew that his great wealth would speedily cause him to be marked out as a victim. He therefore obtained a letter of recommendation from Mr. Watts, the agent of the Company at their factory at Cossimbazar, and sent his son Kissendas with a large retinue, his family and treasures, to Calcutta. Two or three days after his accession Suraja Dowlah despatched a letter to Mr. Drake, our governor, ordering him to surrender Kissendas and the treasures immediately. The man whom he sent down arrived in a small boat without any state or retinue, and Mr. Drake, believing that he was an impostor, paid no attention to the demand, but expelled him from the settlement. Two days ago a letter came from the viceroy, or, as we generally call him, the nabob, to Mr. Drake, ordering him instantly to demolish all the fortifications which he understood he had been erecting. Mr. Drake has sent word back assuring the nabob that he is erecting no new fortifications, but simply executing some repairs in the ramparts facing the river, in view of the expected war between England and France. That is all that has been done at present; but seeing the passionate and overbearing disposition of this young scoundrel there is no saying what will come of it."

"But how do we stand here?" Charlie asked. "What are the means of defence, supposing he should take it into his head to march with the army which he has raised to fight against his cousin to the attack of Calcutta?"

"Nothing could be worse than our position," Mr. Haines said. "Ever since the capture of Madras, nine years ago, the directors have been sending out orders that this place should be put in a state of defence. During the fifty years which have passed peacefully here, the fortifications have been entirely neglected. Instead of the space round them being kept clear, warehouses have been built close against them, and the fort is wholly unable to resist any attack. The authorities of the Company here have done absolutely nothing to carry out the orders from home. They think, I am sorry to say, only of making money with their own trading ventures; and although several petitions have been presented to them by the merchants here urging upon them the dangers which might arise at the death of Ali, they have taken no steps whatever, and indeed have treated all warnings with scorn and derision.

"What force have we here?" Charlie asked.

"Only a hundred and seventy-four men, of whom the greater portion are natives."

"What sort of man is your commander?"

"We have no means of knowing," Mr. Haines said. "His name is Minchin. He is a great friend of the governor's, and has certainly done nothing to counteract the apathy of the authorities. Altogether to my mind things look as bad as they possibly can."

A week later, on the 15th of June, a messenger arrived with the news that the nabob with fifty thousand men was advancing against the town, and that in two days he would appear before it. All was confusion and alarm. Charlie at once proceeded to the fort, and placed his services at the disposal of Captain Minchin. He found that officer fussy and alarmed.

"If I might be permitted to advise," Charlie said, "every available man in the town should be set to work at once pulling down all the buildings around the walls. It would be clearly impossible to defend the place when the ramparts are on all sides commanded by the musketry fire of surrounding buildings."

"I know what my duty is, sir," Captain Minchin said, "and do not require to be taught it by so very young an officer as yourself."

"Very well, sir," Charlie replied calmly. "I have seen a great deal of service, and have taken part in the defence of two besieged towns; while you, I believe, have never seen a shot fired. However, as you're in command you will, of course, take what steps you think fit; but I warn you that unless those buildings are destroyed the fort cannot resist an assault for twenty-four hours."

Then, bowing quietly he retired, and returned to Mr. Haines' house. That gentleman was absent having gone to the governor's. He did not come back until late in the evening. Charlie passed the time in endeavoring to cheer up Mrs. Haines and her daughter, assuring them that if the worst came to the worst there could be no difficulty in their getting on board ship. Mrs. Haines was a woman of much common sense and presence of mind, and under the influence of Charlie's quiet chat she speedily recovered her tranquillity. Her daughter Ada, who was a very bright and pretty girl, was even sooner at her ease, and they were laughing and chatting brightly when Mr. Haines arrived. He looked fagged and dispirited.

"Drake is a fool," he said. "Just as hitherto he has scoffed at all thought of danger, now he is prostrated at the news that danger is at hand. He can decide on nothing. At one moment he talks of sending messengers to Suraja Dowlah, to offer to pay any sum he may demand in order to induce him to retire; the next he talks of defending the fort to the last. We can get him to give no orders, to decide on nothing, and the other officials are equally impotent and imbecile."

On the 18th the army of the nabob approached. Captain Minchin took his guns and troops a considerable distance beyond the walls, and opened fire upon the enemy. Charlie, enraged and disgusted at the folly of conduct which could only lead to defeat, marched with them as a simple volunteer. The result was what he had anticipated. The enemy opened fire with an immensely superior force of artillery. His infantry advanced and clouds of horsemen swept round the flanks and menaced the retreat. In a very few minutes Captain Minchin gave the order to retire, and abandoning their guns the English force retreated in all haste to the town.

Charlie had, on setting out, told Mr. Haines what was certain to occur, and had implored him to send all his valuables at once on board ship, and to retire instantly into the fort. Upon the arrival of the troops at the gate they found it almost blocked with the throng of frightened Europeans and natives flying from their houses beyond it to its protection. Scarcely were all the fugitives within and the gates closed when the guns of Suraja Dowlah opened upon the fort, and his infantry, taking possession of the houses around it, began a galling musketry fire upon the ramparts. Captain Minchin remained closeted with the governor, and Charlie, finding the troops bewildered and dismayed, without leading or orders, assumed the command, placed them upon the walls, and kept up a vigorous musketry fire in reply to that of the enemy.

Within all was confusion and dismay. In every spot sheltered from the enemy's fire Europeans and natives were huddled together. There was neither head nor direction. With nightfall the fire ceased, but still Mr. Drake and Captain Minchin were undecided what steps to take. At two o'clock in the morning they summoned a council of war, at which Charlie was present, and it was decided that the women and children should at once be sent on board. There should have been no difficulty in carrying this into effect. A large number of merchantmen were lying in the stream opposite the fort, capable of conveying away in safety the whole of the occupants. Two of the members of the council had early in the evening been despatched on board ship to make arrangements for the boats being sent on shore; but these cowardly wretches instead of doing so, ordered the ships to raise their anchors and drop two miles farther down the stream. The boats, however, were sent up the river to the fort. The same helpless imbecility which had characterized every movement again showed itself. There was no attempt whatever at establishing anything like order or method. The water-gate was open, and a wild rush of men, women, and children took place down to the boats.

Charlie was on duty on the walls. He had already said good-bye to Mrs. Haines and her daughter, and though he heard shouts and screams coming from the water-gate he had no idea what had taken place until Mr. Haines joined him.

"Have you seen them safely off?" Charlie asked.

"My wife has gone," Mr. Haines said; "my daughter is still here. There has been a horrible scene of confusion. Although the boats were amply sufficient to carry all, no steps whatever had been taken to secure order. The consequence was, there was a wild rush; women and children were knocked down and trampled upon. They leaped into the boats in such wild haste that several of these were capsized and numbers of people drowned. I kept close to my wife and child till we reached the side of the stream. I managed to get my wife into a boat, and then a rush of people separated me from my daughter, and before I could find her again the remaining boats had all pushed off. Many of the men have gone with them, and among them I am ashamed to say, several of the officers. However, I trust the boats will come up again to-morrow and take away the rest. Two have remained, a guard having been placed over them, and I hope to get Ada off to her mother in the morning."

Towards morning Mr. Haines again joined Charlie. "What do you think?" he said. "Those cowardly villains, Drake and Minchin, have taken the two boats and gone off on board ship!"

"Impossible!" Charlie exclaimed.

"It is too true," Mr. Haines said. "The names of these cowards should be held as infamous as long as the English nation exists. Come, now, we are just assembling to choose a commander. Mr. Peeks is the senior agent; but I think we shall elect Mr. Holwell, who is an energetic and vigorous man."

It was as Mr. Haines had expected. Mr. Holwell was elected, and at once took the lead. He immediately assigned to Charlie the command of the troops. Little was done at the council beyond speaker after speaker rising to express his execration of the conduct of the governor and Captain Minchin. With daybreak the enemy's fire recommenced. All day long Charlie hurried from post to post encouraging his men and aiding in working the guns. Two or three times when the enemy showed in masses, as if intending to assault, the fire of the artillery drove them back, and up to nightfall they had gained but little success. The civilians as well as the soldiers had done their duty nobly but the loss had been heavy from the fire of the enemy's sharpshooters in the surrounding buildings, and it was evident that however gallant the defence the fort could not much longer resist. All day long signals had been kept flying for the fleet, two miles below, to come up to the fort; but although these could be plainly seen, not a ship weighed anchor.

CHAPTER XVIII.

THE "BLACK HOLE" OF CALCUTTA.

AT nightfall, when the fire of the enemy slackened, Charlie went to Mr. Holwell.

"It is impossible, sir," he said, "that the fort can hold out, for in another three or four days the whole of the garrison will be killed. The only hope of safety is for the ships to come up and remove the garrison, which they can do without the slightest danger to themselves. If you will allow me, sir, I will swim down to the ships and represent our situation. Cowardly and inhuman as Mr. Drake has proved himself, he can hardly refuse to give orders for the fleet to move up."

"I don't know," said Mr. Holwell; "after the way in which he has behaved there are no depths of infamy of which I believe him incapable. But you are my right hand here. Supposing Mr. Drake refuses, you could not return."

"I will come back, sir," Charlie answered. "I will, if there be no other way, make my way along by the river bank. It is comparatively free of the enemy, as our guns command it. If you will place Mr. Haines at the corner bastion with a rope, he will recognize my voice, and I can regain the fort."

Mr. Holwell consented, and as soon as it was perfectly dark Charlie issued out at the water-gate, took off his coat, waistcoat, and boots, and entered the stream.

The current was slack; but he had no difficulty in keeping himself afloat until he saw close ahead of him the lights of the ships. He hailed that nearest him. A rope was thrown and he was soon on board. Upon stating who he was a boat was at once lowered, and he was taken to the ship upon which Mr. Drake and Captain Minchin had taken refuge. Upon saying that was the bearer of a message from the gentleman now commanding the fort he was conducted to the cabin, where Mr. Drake and Captain Minchin, having finished their dinner, were sitting comfortably over their wine with Captain Young, the senior captain of the Company's ships there.

"I have come, sir," Charlie said to Mr. Drake, "from Mr. Holwell, who has, in your absence, been elected to the command of the fort. He bids me tell you that our losses have been already very heavy, and that it is impossible that the fort can hold out for more than twenty-four hours longer. He begs you, therefore, to order up the ships to-night, in order that the garrison may embark."

"It is quite out of the question," Mr. Drake said coldly—"quite. It would be extremely dangerous. You agree with me, Captain Young, that it would be most dangerous?"

"I consider that it would be dangerous," Captain Young said.

"And you call yourself," Charlie exclaimed indignantly, "a British sailor! You talk of danger, and would desert a thousand men, women, and children, including two hundred of your own countrymen, and leave them at the mercy of an enemy!"

"You forget whom you are speaking to, sir," Mr. Drake said angrily.

"I forget nothing, sir," Charlie replied, trying to speak calmly. "Then, sir, Mr. Holwell has charged me that if—which, however, he could not believe for a moment to be possible—you refuse to move up the ships to receive the garrison on board, that you would at least order all the boats up, as these would be amply sufficient to carry them away. Even in the daytime there would be no danger for the ships, and at night, at least boats might come up without being exposed to any risk whatever."

"I shall certainly do nothing of the sort," Mr. Drake said. "The danger is even greater for the boats than for the ships."

"And am I, sir, to return to the garrison of that fort with the news that you utterly desert them, that you intend to remain quietly here while they are sacrificed before your eyes? Is it possible that you are capable of such infamy as this?"

"Infamy!" exclaimed the three men, rising to their feet.

"I place you in arrest at once, for your insolence," Mr. Drake said.

"I despise your arrest as I do yourself. I did not believe it possible," Charlie said, at last giving vent to his anger and scorn; "and England will not believe that three Englishmen so cowardly, so infamous as yourselves, are to be found. As for you, Captain Minchin, if ever after this I come across you, I will flog you publicly first, and shoot you afterwards like a dog if you dare to meet me. As for you, Mr. Drake—as for you, Captain Young—you will be doomed to infamy by the contempt and loathing which Englishmen will feel when this deed is known. Cowards, base, infamous cowards!"

Charlie stepped back to go.

"Seize him!" Mr. Drake said, himself rushing forward.

Charlie drew back a step, and then with all his strength smote the governor between the eyes, and he

HOW CHARLIE DEALT WITH HIS SUPERIOR OFFICERS.

fell in a heap beneath the table. Then Charlie grasped a decanter.

"Now," he said, "if either of you hounds move a finger I'll brain you."

The two officers stood paralyzed. Charlie walked to the door and sprang up the cabin stairs, and as he did so, heard shouts for assistance from behind. He gained the deck, walked quietly to the bulwark, and placing his hand upon it, sprang over the side into the river. He swam to shore, and, climbing up the bank made his way along it back to the fort, where he arrived without any misadventure. A fury of indignation seized all in the fort when the result of Charlie's mission became known.

With daybreak the attack recommenced, but the garrison all day bravely repulsed every attempt of the enemy to gain a footing. The fire from the houses was, however, so severe, that by nightfall nearly half the garrison were killed or wounded. All day the signals to the fleet were kept flying, but not a ship moved. All night an anxious watch was kept in hopes that at the last moment some returning feeling of shame might induce the recreants to send up the boats of the ships. But the night passed without a movement on the river, and in the morning the fleet was seen still lying at anchor.

The enemy recommenced the attack even more vigorously than before. The men fell fast, and, to Charlie's great grief, his friend, Mr. Haines, was shot by a bullet as he was standing next to him. Charlie anxiously knelt beside him.

"It is all over with me," he murmured. "Poor little Ada. Do all you can for her, Marryat. God knows what fate is in store for her."

"I will protect her with my life, sir," Charlie said earnestly.

Mr. Haines pressed his hand feebly in token of

gratitude, and two or three minutes later breathed his last.

By mid-day the loss had been so heavy that the men would no longer stand to their guns. Many of the European soldiers broke open the spirit stores, and soon drank to intoxication. After a consultation with his officers Mr. Holwell agreed that further resistance was hopeless. The flag of truce was therefore hoisted, and one of the officers at once started for the nabob's camp, with instructions to make the best terms he could for the garrison. When the gates were opened the enemy, seizing the opportunity, rushed in in great numbers, and as resistance was impossible the garrison laid down their arms. Charlie at once hurried to the spot where Ada and the only other European lady who had not escaped, were anxiously awaiting news. Both were exhausted with weeping.

"Where is papa, Captain Marryat?" Ada asked.

Charlie knew that the poor girl would need all her strength for what she might have to undergo, and at once resolved that, for the present at least, it would be better that she should be in ignorance of the fate of her father. He therefore said that for the present Mr. Haines was unable to come, and had asked him to look after her. It was not until five o'clock that the nabob entered the fort. He was furious at hearing that only five lacs of rupees had been found in the treasury, as he had expected to become possessed of a vastly larger sum. Kissendas, the first cause of the present calamities, was brought before him; but the capricious tyrant, contrary to expectation, received him courteously, and told him he might return to Dacca. The whole of the Eurasions, or half-castes, and natives found in the fort were also allowed to return to their homes. Mr. Holwell was then sent for and after the nabob had expressed his resentment at the small amount found in the treasury he was dismissed, the nabob assuring him of his protection. Mr. Holwell returned to his English companions, who, one hundred and forty-six in number, including the two ladies, were drawn up under the verandah in front of the prison. The nabob then returned to his camp.

Some native officers went in search of some building where the prisoners could be confined, but every room in the fort had already been taken possession of by the nabob's soldiers and officers. At eight o'clock they returned with the news that they could find no place vacant, and the officer in command at once ordered the prisoners into a small room, used as a guard room for insubordinate soldiers, eighteen feet square. In vain they protested that it was impossible the room could contain them, in vain implored the officer to allow some of them to be confined in an adjoining cell. The wretch was deaf to their entreaties. He ordered his soldiers to charge the prisoners, and these, with blows of the butt-ends of the muskets and prods of the bayonets, were driven into the narrow cell. Tim Kelly had kept close to his master during the preceding days. The whole of the four native officers who had so distinguished themselves under Charlie were killed during the siege. Hossein, who would fain have shared his master's fortunes, was forcibly torn from him when the English prisoners were separated from the natives.

The day had been unusually hot. The night was close and sultry, and the arched verandah outside further hindered the circulation of the air. This was still heavy with the fumes of powder, creating an intolerable thirst. Scarcely were the prisoners driven into their narrow cell, where even standing wedged closely together there was barely room for them, than cries for water were raised.

"Tim, my boy," Charlie said to his companion, "we may say good-bye to each other now, for I doubt if one will be alive when the door is opened in the morning."

On entering, Charlie, always keeping Ada Haines by his side, had taken his place against the wall farthest from the window, which was closed with iron bars.

"I think, yer honor," Tim said, "that if we could get nearer to the window we might breathe a little more easily."

"Ay, Tim; but there will be a fight for life round that window before long. You and I might hold our own if we could get there, though it would be no easy matter where all are struggling for life, but this poor little girl would be crushed to death. Besides, I believe that what chance there is, faint as it may be, is greater for us here than there. The rush towards the window, which is beginning already as you see, will grow greater and greater; and the more men struggle and strive, the more air they require. Let us remain where we are. Strip off your coat and waistcoat, and breathe as quietly and easily as you can. Every hour the crowd will thin, and we may yet hold on till morning."

This conversation had been held in a low voice. Charlie then turned to the girl.

"How are you feeling, Ada?" he asked cheerfully. "It's hot, isn't it?"

"It is dreadful," the girl panted, "and I seem choking from want of air; and oh, Captain Marryat, I am so thirsty!"

"It is hot, my dear, terribly hot, but we must make the best of it; and I hope in a few days you will join your mamma on board ship. That will be pleasant won't it?"

"Where is papa?" the girl wailed.

"I don't know where he is now, my child. At any rate we must feel very glad that he's not shut up here with us. Now take your bonnet off and your shawl, and undo the hooks of your dress, and loosen everything you can. We must be as quiet and cheerful as possible. I'm afraid, Ada, we have a bad time before us to-night. But try to keep cheerful and quiet, and, above all, dear, pray God to give you strength to carry you through it, and to restore you safe to your mamma in a few days."

As time went on the scene in the dungeon became terrible. Shouts, oaths, cries of all kinds, rose in the air. Round the window men fought like wild beasts. tearing each other down, or clinging to the bars for dear life, for a breath of the air without. Panting, struggling, crying, men sank exhausted upon the floor, and the last remnants of life were trodden out of them by those who surged forward to get near the window. In vain Mr. Holwell implored them to keep quiet for their own sakes. His voice was lost in the terrible din. Men, a few hours ago rich and respected merchants, now fought like maddened beasts for a breath of fresh air. In vain those at the window screamed to the guards without, imploring them to bring water. Their prayers and entreaties were replied to only with brutal scoffs.

Several times Charlie and Tim, standing together against the wall behind, where there was now room to move, lifted Ada between them, and sat her on their shoulders in order that, raised above the crowd, she might breathe more freely. Each time, after sitting there for a while, the poor girl begged to come down again, the sight of the terrible struggle ever going on at the window being too much for her, and when released, leaning against Charlie, supported by his arm, with her head against his shoulder, and her hands over her ears to shut out the dreadful sounds which filled the cell. Hour passed after hour. There was more room now, for already half the inmates of the place had succumbed. The noises, too, had lessened, for no longer could the parched lips and throats utter articulate sounds. Charlie and Tim, strong men as they were leaned utterly exhausted against the wall, bathed in perspiration, gasping for air.

"Half the night must be gone, Tim," Charlie said, "and I think, with God's help, we shall live through it. The numbers are lessening fast, and every one who goes leaves more air for the rest of us. Cheer up, Ada dear, 'twill not be very long till morning."

"I think I shall die soon," the girl gasped. "I shall never see papa or mamma again. You have been very kind, Captain Marryat, but it is no use."

"Oh, but it is of use," Charlie said cheerfully. "I don't mean to let you die at all, but to hand you over to mamma safe and sound. There, lay your head against me, dear, and say your prayers, and try and go off to sleep."

Presently, however, Ada's figure drooped more and more, until her whole weight leaned upon Charlie's arm.

"She has fainted, Tim," he said. "Help me to raise her well in my arms, and lay her head on my shoulder. That's right. Now you'll find her shawl somewhere under my feet; hold it up and make a fan of it. Now try to send some air into her face."

By this time not more than fifty out of the hundred and forty-six who entered the cell were alive. Suddenly a scream of joy from those near the window proclaimed that a native was approaching with some water. The struggle at the window was fiercer than ever. The bowl was too wide to pass through the bars, and the water was being spilt in vain; each man who strove to get his face far enough through to touch the bowl being torn back by his eager comrades behind.

"Tim," Charlie said, "you are now much stronger

than most of them. They are faint from the struggles. Make a charge to the window. Take that little shawl and dip it into the bowl or whatever they have there, and then fight your way back with it."

"I will do it, yer honor," said Tim, and he rushed into the struggling group. Weak as he was from exhaustion and thirst, he was as a giant to most of the poor wretches who had been struggling and crying all night, and in spite of their cries and curses he broke through them and forced his way to the window.

The man with the bowl was on the point of turning away, the water being spilt in the vain attempts of those within to obtain it. By the light of the fire which the guard had lit without, Tim saw his face.

"Hossein," he exclaimed, "more water, for God's sake! The master's alive yet."

Hossein at once withdrew, but soon again approached with the bowl. The officer in charge angrily ordered him to draw back.

"Let the infidel dogs howl," he said. "They shall have no more."

Regardless of the order, Hossein ran to the window, and Tim thrust the shawl into the water at that moment when the officer, rushing forward, struck Hossein to the ground: a cry of anguish rising from the prisoners as they saw the water dashed from their lips. Tim made his way back to the side of his master. Had those who still remained alive been aware of the supply of water which he carried in the shawl they would have torn it from him; but none save those just at the window had noticed the act, and inside it was still entirely dark.

"Thank God, yer honor, here it is," Tim said; "and who should have brought it but Hossein. Shure, yer honor, we both owe our lives to him this time, for I'm sure I should have been choked by thirst before morning."

Ada was now lowered to the ground, and forcing her teeth asunder a corner of the folded shawl was placed between her lips, and the water allowed to trickle down. With a gasping sigh she presently recovered.

"That is delicious," she murmured. "That is delicious."

Raising her to her feet, Charlie and Tim both sucked the dripping shawl, until the first agonies of thirst were relieved. Then tearing off a portion in case Ada should again require it, Charlie passed the shawl to Mr. Holwell, who, after sucking it for a moment, again passed it on to several standing round, and in this way many of those who would otherwise have succumbed were enabled to hold on until morning.

Presently the first dawn of daylight appeared, giving fresh hopes to the few survivors. There were now only some six or eight standing by the window, and a few standing or leaning against the walls around. The room itself was heaped high with the dead.

It was not until two hours later that the doors were opened and the guard entered, and it was found that of the hundred and forty-six Englishmen inclosed there the night before, but twenty-three still breathed. Of these very few retained strength to stagger out through the door. The rest were carried out and laid in the verandah. When the nabob came into the fort in the morning he ordered Mr. Holwell to be brought before him. He was unable to walk, but was carried to his presence. The brutal nabob expressed no regret for what had happened, but loaded him with abuse on account of the paucity of the treasure, and ordered him to be placed in confinement.

The other prisoners were also confined in a cell. Ada, the only English female who had survived the siege, was torn, weeping, from Charlie's arms, and conveyed to the zenana, or ladies' apartments, of one of the nabob's generals.

A few days later the English captives were all conveyed to Moorshedabad, where the rajah also returned after having extorted large sums from the French and Dutch, and confiscated the whole of the property of the English in Bengal.

The prospect was a gloomy one for the captives. That the English would in time return and extort a heavy reckoning from the nabob, they did not doubt for a moment. But nothing was more likely than that at the news of the first disaster which befell his troops the nabob would order his captives to be put to death. Upon the march up the country Charlie had, by his cheerfulness and good temper, gained the good-will of the officer commanding the guard, and upon arriving at their destination he recommended him so strongly to the commander of the prison that the latter, instead of placing him in the apartment allotted to the remainder of the prisoners, assigned a separate room to him, permitting Tim, at his request, to occupy it with him. It was a room of fair size, in a tower on one of the angles of the walls. It had bars, but these did not prevent those behind them looking out at the country which stretched around. The governor of the prison, finding that Charlie spoke the language fluently, often came up to sit with him, conversing with him on the affairs of that unknown country, England. Altogether they were fairly treated. Their food was plentiful, and beyond their captivity they had little to complain of. Over and over again they talked about the possibilities of effecting an escape, but on entering the prison they had noticed how good was the watch, how many and strong the doors through which they had passed. They had meditated upon making a rope and escaping from the window; but they slept on the divan, each with a rug to cover them, and these torn into strips and twisted would not reach a quarter of the way from their window to the ground, and there was no other material of which a rope could possibly have been formed.

"Our only hope," Charlie said one day, "is in Hossein. I am sure he will follow us to the death, and if he did but know where we are confined he would not, I am certain, rest night or day till he had opened a communication with us. See, Tim, there is my regimental cap, with its gold lace. Let us fasten it outside the bars with a thread from that rug. Of course we must remove it when we hear any one coming."

This was speedily done, and for the next few days one or other remained constantly at the window.

"Mr. Charles!" Tim exclaimed in great excitement one day; "there is a man I've been watching for the last half hour. He seems to be picking up sticks, but all the while he keeps getting nearer and nearer, and two or three times it seems to me that he has looked up in this direction.

Charlie joined Tim at the window.

"Yes, Tim, you are right. That's Hossein, I'm pretty sure."

The man had now approached within two or three hundred yards of the corner of the wall. He was apparently collecting pieces of dried brushwood for firing. Presently he glanced in the direction of the window. Charlie thrust his arm through the bar and waved his hand. The man threw up his arm with a gesture which, to a casual observer, would have appeared accidental, but which the watchers had no doubt whatever was intended for them. He was still too far off from them to be able to distinguish his features, but they had not the least doubt that it was Hossein.

CHAPTER XIX.

A DARING ESCAPE.

"AND what's to be done next, Mister Charles? That's Hossein, sure enough, but it don't bring us much nearer to getting out."

"The first thing is to communicate with him in some way, Tim."

"If he'd come up to the side of the moat, yer honor might spake to him."

"That would never do, Tim. There are sure to be sentries on the walls of the prison. We must trust to him. He can see the sentries and will know best what he can do."

It was evident that Hossein did not intend doing anything at present, for still stooping and gathering brush-wood he gradually withdrew farther and farther from the wall. Then they saw him make his sticks into a bundle, put them on his shoulder, and walk away. During the rest of the day they saw no more of Hossein.

"I will write," Charlie said—"fortunately I have a pencil—telling him that we can lower a light string down to the moat if he can manage to get underneath with a cord which we can hoist up, and that he must have two disguises in readiness."

"I don't think Hossein can read," Tim said, "any more than I can myself."

"I dare say not, Tim, but he will probably have

friends in the town. There are men who were employed in the English factory at Kossimbazar hard by. These will be out of employment and will regret the expulsion of the English. We can trust Hossein. At any rate I will get it ready. Now the first thing we have to do is to loosen one of these bars. I wish we had thought of doing it before. However, the stonework is pretty rotten and we shall have no difficulty about that. The first thing is to get a tool of some sort."

They looked around the room and for some time saw nothing which could in any way serve. The walls, floor, and wide bench running round upon which the cushions which served as their beds were laid, were all stone. There was no other furniture of any kind.

"Divil a bit of iron do I see in the place, Mister Charles," Tim said. "They don't even give us a knife for dinner, but stew all their meats up into a smash."

"There is something, Tim," Charlie said, looking at the door. "Look at those long hinges."

The hinges were of ornamented iron-work, extending half across the door. Upon one of the scrolls of this iron-work they set to work. Chipping a small piece of stone off an angle of the wall outside the window, with great difficulty they thrust this under the end of the scroll as a wedge. Another piece, slightly larger, was then pushed under it. The gain was almost imperceptible, but at last the piece of iron was raised from the woodwork sufficiently to allow them to get a hold of it with their thumbs. Then little by little they bent it upwards until at last they could obtain a firm hold of it. The rest was comparatively easy. The iron was tough and strong, but by bending it up and down they succeeded at last in breaking it off. It was the lower hinge of the door upon which they had operated, as the loss of a piece of iron there would be less likely to catch the eye of any one coming in. They collected some dust from the corner of the room, moistened it and rubbed it on to the wood so as to take away its freshness of appearance; and they then set to work with the piece of iron, which was of a curved shape, about three inches long, an inch wide, and an eighth of an inch thick. Taking it by turns they ground away the stone around the bottom of one of the bars. For the first inch the stone yielded readily to the iron, but below that it became harder and their progress was slow. They filled the hole which they had made with water to soften the stone and worked steadily away till night, when, to their great joy, they found that they had reached the bottom of the bar. They then enlarged the hole inwards in order that the bar might be pulled back. Fortunately it was much decayed by age, and they had no doubt that by exerting all their strength together they could bend it sufficiently to enable them to get through. At the hour when their dinner was brought they had ceased their work, filled up the hole with dust collected from the floor, put some dust of the stone over it and smoothed it down, so that it would not have been noticed by any one casually looking from the window.

It was late at night before they finished their work. Their hands were sore and bleeding, and they were completely worn out with fatigue. They had saved from their dinner a good-sized piece of bread. They folded up into a small compass the leaf from his pocket-book upon which Charlie had written in Hindustanee his letter to Hossein, and thrust this into the centre of the piece of bread. Then Charlie told Tim to lie down and rest for three hours while he kept watch, as they must take it in turns all night to listen in case Hossein should come outside. The lamp was kept burning.

Just as Charlie's watch was over he thought he heard a very faint splash in the water below. Two or three minutes later he again thought he heard the sound. He peered out of the window anxiously, but the night was dark and he could see nothing. Listening intently, it seemed to him several times that he heard the same faint sound. Presently something whizzed by him, and looking round, to his delight he saw a small arrow with a piece of very thin string attached. The arrow was made of very light wood. Round the iron point was a thick wrapping of cotton which would entirely deaden its sound as it struck a wall. It was soaked in water, and Charlie had no doubt that the sound he heard was caused by its fall into the moat after ineffectual trials to shoot through the window. Round the centre of the arrow a piece of greased silk was wrapped. Charlie took this off, and found beneath it a piece of paper on which was written in Hindustanee: "If you have a bar loosed, pull the string and haul up a rope, if not, throw the arrow down. I will come again to-morrow night."

Tim had by this time joined Charlie, and they speedily began to pull in the string. Presently a thicker string came up into their hands. They continued to pull, and soon the end of a stout rope, in which knots were tied every two feet came up to them. They fastened this to one of the bars and then took hold of that which they had loosened, and putting their feet against the wall, exerted themselves to the utmost. The iron was tougher than they had expected, but they were striving for liberty, and with desperate exertions they bent it inwards, until at last there was room enough for them to creep through.

"Can you swim, Tim?"

"Not a stroke, yer honor. Shure you should know that when you fished me out of the water."

"Very well, Tim; as I kept you up then 'twill be

easy enough for me now to take you across the moat. I will go first, and when I get into the water will keep hold of the rope till you come down. Take off your boots, for they would be heard scraping against the wall. Be sure you make as little noise as possible, and lower yourself quietly into the water."

Charlie then removed his own boots, squeezed himself through the bars, and grasping the rope tightly began to descend. He found the knots of immense assistance, for had it not been for them, unaccustomed as he was to the work, he would have been unable to prevent himself from sliding down too rapidly. The window was fully sixty feet above the moat and he was very thankful when at last he felt the water touch his feet. Lowering himself quietly into it, he shook the rope to let Tim know that he could begin his descent. Before Tim was half-way down Charlie could hear his hard breathing and muttered ejaculations to himself:

"Shure I'll never get to the bottom at all, my arms are fairly breaking. I shall squash Mr. Charles if I fall on him."

"Hold your tongne, Tim," Charlie said in a loud whisper.

Tim was silent, but the panting and puffing increased, and Charlie swam a stroke or two away expecting every moment that Tim would fall. The Irishman, however, held on, but let himself into the water with a splash which aroused the attention of the sentry above, who instantly challenged. Tim and Charlie remained perfectly quiet. Again the sentry challenged. Then there was a long silence. The sentry probably was unwilling to rouse the place by a false alarm, and the splash might have been caused by the fall of a piece of decayed stone from the face of the wall.

"Tim, you clumsy fellow," whispered Charlie, "you nearly spoiled all."

"Shure, yer honor, I was kilt entirely, and my arms were pulled out of my sockets. Holy Mother, who'd have thought 'twould be so difficult to come down a rope! The sailors are great men entirely."

"Now, Tim, lie quiet, I will turn you on your back and swim across with you."

The moat was some twenty yards wide. Charlie swam across towing Tim after him, and taking the greatest pains to avoid making the slightest splash. The opposite side was of stonework and rose six feet above the water. As soon as they touched the wall a stout rope was lowered to them. "Now, Tim, you climb up first."

"Is it climb up, yer honor? I couldn't do it if it was to save my sowl. My arms are gone altogether, and I'm as weak as a child. You go, Mister Charles, I'll hould on by the rope till morning. They can but shoot me."

"Nonsense, Tim! Here, I will fasten the rope round your body. Then I will climb up and we will pull you up after me."

In another minute Charlie stood on the bank and grasped the hand of his faithful follower. Hossein threw himself on his knees and pressed his master to him. Then he rose, and at a word from Charlie they hauled Tim to the top. The rope was taken off him, and noiselessly they made their way across the country. Not a word was spoken till they were at a considerable distance from the fort.

"Where are you taking us, Hossein?" Charlie asked at last.

"I have two peasants' dresses in a deserted cottage a quarter of a mile away." Not another word was spoken until they reached the hut, which stood at the end of a small village. When they had entered this

Charlie first thanked in the warmest terms his follower for having rescued them.

"My life is my lord's," Hossein answered simply; "he gave it me. It is his again whenever it is useful to him."

"No, Hossein, the balance is all on your side now. You saved my life that night at Ambur; you saved it that night at Calcutta, for, without the water you brought us, I question whether we could have lived till morning. Now you have procured our freedom. The debt is all on my side now, my friend."

"Hossein is glad that his lord is content," the Mahommedan murmured; "now what will my lord do?"

"Have you any place in the town to which we could go, Hossein?"

"Yes, Sahib, I hired a little house. I was dressed as a trader. I have been here for two months, but I could not find where you were confined, although I have tried all means, until I saw your cap."

"It was foolish of me not to have thought of it before," Charlie said. "Well, Hossein, for a little time we had better take refuge in your house. They will not think of searching in the city, and as Calcutta is in their hands there is nowhere we could go. Besides, I must discover, if possible, where Miss Haines is kept a prisoner, and rescue her if it can be done."

"The white girl is in the zenana of Rajah Dulab Ram," Hossein replied.

"Where is the rajah's palace?"

"He has one in the city, one at Ajervam, twenty miles from here. I do not know at which she is lodged."

"We must find that out presently," Charlie said. "It is something to know she is in one of two houses. Now, about getting back into the town."

"I have thought of that," Hossein said. "I have bought a quantity of plantains and two large baskets.

After the gates are opened you will go boldly in with the baskets on your head. No questions are asked of the country people who go in and out. I have some stain here which will darken your skins. I will go in first in my merchant's dress which I have here. I will stop a little way inside the gate, and when I see you coming will walk on. Do you follow me a little behind, My house is in a quiet street. When I reach the door, do you come up and offer to sell me plantains. If there are people about I shall bargain with you until I see that no one is noticing us. Then you can enter. If none are about you can follow me straight in."

Hossein now set about the disguises. A light was struck, and both Tim and Charlie were shaved up to the line which the turban would cover. Charlie's whiskers, which were somewhat faint, as he was still under twenty-one years old, gave but little trouble. Tim, however, grumbled at parting with his much more bushy appendages. The shaven part of the heads, necks, and faces were then rubbed with a dark fluid, as were the arms and legs. They were next wrapped in dark blue clothes in peasant fashion and turbans wound round their heads. Hossein then, examining them critically, announced that they would pass muster anywhere.

"I feel mighty quare," Tim exclaimed; "and it seems to me downright ondacent to be walking about with my naked legs."

Charlie laughed. "Why, Tim, you are accustomed to see thousands of men every day with nothing on but a loin-cloth."

"Yes, yer honor, but then they're hathens, and it seems natural for them to do so; but for a dacent boy to go walking about in the streets with a thing on which covers no more than his shirt, is onnatural altogether. Mother of Moses, what a shindy there would be in the streets of Cork if I were to show myself in such a state!"

Charlie now lay down for a sleep till morning, while Tim, who had had three hours' repose, settled himself for a comfortable chat with Hossein, to whom sleep appeared altogether unnecessary. Between Hossein and Tim there was a sort of brotherly attachment, arising from their mutual love of their master. During the two years which Tim had spent apart from all Europeans save Charlie, he had contrived to pick up enough of the language to make himself fairly intelligible; and since the day when Hossein had saved Charlie's life at Ambur the warmest friendship had sprung up between the good-humored and warm-hearted Irishman and the silent and devoted Mahommedan. Tim's friendship even extended so far as to induce a toleration of Hossein's religion. He had come to the conclusion that a man who at stated times in the day would leave his employment, whatever it might be, spread his carpet, and be for some minutes lost in prayer, could not be altogether a hathen, especially when he learned from Charlie that the Mahommedans, like ourselves, worship one God. For the sake of his friend, then, he now generally excluded the Mahommedans from the general designation of heathen, which he still applied to the Hindoos.

He learned from Hossein that the latter, having observed from a distance the Europeans driven into the cell at Calcutta, perceived at once how fatal the consequences would be. He had, an hour or two after they were confined there, approached with some water, but the officer on guard had refused to let him give it. He had then gone into the native town, but being unable to find any fruit there, had walked out to the gardens and had picked a large basketful. This he had brought as an offering to the officer, and the latter had then consented to his giving one bowl of water to the prisoners, among whom, as he had told him, was his master. For bringing a second bowl contrary to his orders, Hossein had, as Tim saw, been struck down, but had the satisfaction of believing that his master and Tim had derived some benefit from his effort. On the following morning, to his delight, he saw them issue among the few survivors from the dungeon, and had, when they were taken up the country, followed close behind them, arriving at the town on the same day as themselves. He had ever since been wandering round the prison. He had taken a house so close to it that he could keep a watch on all the windows facing the town, and had day after day kept his eyes fixed upon these without success. He had at last found out from one of the soldiers that the white prisoners were confined on the other side of the prison, but until he saw Charlie's cap he had been unable to discover the room in which they were confined.

In the morning they started for the town. Groups of peasants were already making their way towards the gate with fruit and grain, and keeping near one of these parties, while sufficiently distant to prevent the chance of their being addressed, Charlie and Tim made their way to the gate, the latter suffering acutely in his mind from the impropriety of his attire. No questions were asked as they passed the guard. They at once perceived Hossein standing a little way off, and followed him through the busy streets. They soon turned off into a quieter quarter, and stopped at a house in a street in which scarcely any one was stirring. Hossein glanced round, as he opened the door, and beckoned to them to enter at once. This they did, and were glad, indeed, to set down the heavy baskets of plantains.

"My lord's room is upstairs," Hossein said, and led the way to a comfortably furnished apartment. "I think that you might stay here for months unsuspected. A sweeper comes every day to do my rooms down-stairs. He believes the rest of the house to be untenanted, and you must remain perfectly quiet during the half hour he is here. Otherwise, no one enters the house but myself."

Hossein soon set to work and prepared an excellent breakfast. Then he left them, saying that he would now devote himself to finding out whether the young white lady was in the town palace of the rajah. He returned in the afternoon.

"She is here, Sahib," he said. "I got into conversation with one of the retainers of the rajah, and by giving him some wonderful bargains in Delhi jewelry succeeded in opening his lips. I dare not question him too closely, but I am to meet him to-morrow to show him some more silver bracelets."

"It is fortunate, Hossein, that you have some money, for neither Tim nor I have a rupee."

"Thanks to the generosity of my lord," Hossein said, "I am well supplied."

The next day Hossein discovered that the windows of the zenana were at the back of the palace, looking into the large garden. "I hear, however," he said, "that the ladies of the zenana are next week going to the rajah's other palace. The ladies will, of course, travel in palanquins; but upon the road I might get to talk with one of the waiting-women, and might bribe her to pass a note into the hands of the white lady."

"I suppose they will have a guard with them, Hossein?"

"Surely, a strong guard," Hossein answered.

The time passed until the day came for the departure of the rajah's zenana. Charlie wrote a note as follows:—"My dear Ada, I am free and am on the lookout for an opportunity to rescue you. Contrive to put a little bit of your handkerchief through the lattice-work of the window of your room, as a signal to us which it is. On the second night after your arrival we will be under it with a ladder. If others, as is probable, sleep in your room, lie down without undressing more than you can help. When they are asleep get up and go to the window and open the lattice. If any of them wake, say you are hot and cannot sleep, and wait quietly till they are off again. Then stretch out your arm and we shall know you are ready. Then we will put up the ladder, and you must get out and come to us as quickly as possible. Once with us you will be safe."

This note was wrapped up very small and put into a quill. As soon as the gates were open Hossein and his companions left the town and proceeded as far as a grove half-way between the town and the rajah's country palace.

"They are sure to stop here for a rest," Hossein said. "I will remain here and try to enter into conversation with one of them. It will be better for you to go on for some distance and then turn aside from the road. When they have all passed, come back into the road again and I will join you."

After waiting two hours Hossein saw two carts full of women approaching, and had no doubt that these were the servants of the zenana. As he had expected, the drivers halted their cattle in the shade of the trees, and the women, delighted to enjoy their liberty, alighted from the carts and scattered in the grove. Presently one of them, a middle-aged woman, approached the spot where Hossein had seated himself. Hossein drew out a large and beautiful silver bracelet of Delhi workmanship.

"Would you like to buy this?" he asked.

"How should I buy it?" she said; "I am only a servant. It is very beautiful;" and she looked at it with longing eyes.

"I have two of them," he said, "and they will both be yours if you will do me a service."

"What is it?" she asked.

"They will be yours if you will give this quill to the little white girl who is in the zenana."

The woman hesitated. "It is dangerous," she said.

"Not at all," Hossein replied. "It only gives her news of a friend whom she thought was dead. It will cheer her heart and will be a kind action. None can ever know it."

"Give them to me," the woman said, holding out her hand; "I will do it."

"No," Hossein replied. "I will give you one now, the other when I know that the note is delivered. I shall be watching to-morrow. If she places her handkerchief in her lattice, I shall know that she has got it. When she does this I will bury the other bracelet a few inches in the ground just under that window. You can dig it up when you will."

"I understand," the woman said; "you can trust me. We all like the white girl. She is very gentle, but very sad. I would gladly give her pleasure."

Hossein handed to her the bracelet and the quill. She hid them in her dress and sauntered away.

Hossein lay back as if taking a sleep, and so remained until, half an hour later, he heard the shouts of the drivers to the women to take their places in the carts. Then the sound of retreating wheels was heard. Hossein was about to rise when he heard the clatter of horses' hoofs. Looking round he saw eight elephants, each carrying a closed pavilion, moving along the road escorted by a troop of horsemen. In the pavilions, as he knew, were the ladies of the rajah's zenana.

CHAPTER XX.

THE RESCUE OF THE WHITE CAPTIVE.

AFTER the cavalcade had passed, Hossein rose to his feet and followed them, allowing them to go some distance ahead. Presently he was joined by Charlie and Tim, and the three walked quietly along the road until within sight of the rajah's palace. In front stood a great court-yard; behind, also surrounded by a high wall, was the garden. As this was always devoted to the zenana they had little doubt that the rooms of the ladies were on this side, and two hours later they were delighted at seeing a small piece of white stuff thrust through one of the lattices. The woman had been faithful to her trust. Ada had received the letter. They then retired to a distance from the palace, and at once set to work on the fabrication of a ladder. Hossein, followed by Charlie, who better enacted the part than Tim, went into a village and purchased four long bamboo poles, saying he wanted them for the carrying of burdens. Charlie placed these on his shoulder and followed Hossein.

When they arrived at the grove they set to work, having brought with them all the necessary materials. The bamboos were spliced together two and two, and while Charlie and Tim set to to bore holes in these, Hossein chopped down a young tree, and cutting it into lengths prepared the rungs. It took them all that

"I AM HERE, DEAR," HE SAID IN A WHISPER.

evening and the greater part of the next day before they had satisfactorily accomplished their work. They had then a ladder thirty feet long, the height which they judged the window to be above the terrace below. It was strong and at the same time light. They waited until darkness had completely fallen, and then taking their ladder went round to the back of the garden. They mounted the wall, and sitting on the top dragged the ladder after them and lowered it on the other side. It was of equal thickness the whole length, and could therefore be used indifferently either way. They waited patiently until they saw the lights in the zenana windows extinguished. Then they crept quietly up and placed the ladder under the window at which the signal had been shown, and found that their calculations were correct, and that it reached to a few inches below the sill.

Half an hour later the lattice above opened. They heard a murmur of voices, and then all was quiet again. After a few minutes Charlie climbed noiselessly up the ladder, and just as he reached the top an arm was stretched out above him, and a moment afterwards Ada's face appeared.

"I am here, dear," he said in a whisper; "lean out and I will take you."

The girl stretched out over the window. Charlie took her in his arms and lifted her lightly out, and then slowly descended the ladder. No sooner did he touch the ground than they hurried away, Ada sobbing with excitement and pleasure on Charlie's shoulder, Tim and Hossein bearing the ladder; Hossein having already carried out his promise of concealing the second bracelet under the window. In a few minutes they had safely surmounted the wall, and hurried across the country with all speed.

Before leaving the town Hossein had purchased a cart with two bullocks, and had hired a man, who was recommended to him by one of his co-religionists there as one upon whose fidelity he could rely. This cart was awaiting them at a grove. Paying them the amount stipulated, Hossein took the ox-goad and started the bullocks, Tim walking beside him, while Charlie and Ada took their places in the cart. They were sure that a hot pursuit would be set up. The rage of the nabob at the escape of Charlie and his servant had been extreme, and the whole country had been scoured by parties of horsemen, and they were sure that the rajah would use every possible means to discover Ada before he ventured to report to the nabob that the prisoner committed to his charge had escaped.

"Of course I can't see you very well," Ada said, "but I should not have known you in the least."

"No, I am got up like a peasant," Charlie answered. "We shall have to dress you so before morning. We have got things here for you."

"Oh how delighted I was," Ada exclaimed, "when I got your note! I found it so difficult to keep on looking sad and hopeless when I could have sung for joy. I had been so miserable. There seemed no hope, and they said some day I should be sent to the nabob's zenana—wretches! How poor mamma will be grieving for me, and papa!—Ah, Captain Marryat, he is dead, is he not?"

"Yes, my dear," Charlie said gently; "he was killed by my side that afternoon. With his last breath he asked me to take care of you."

"I thought so," Ada said, crying quietly. "I did not think of it at the time; everything was so strange and so dreadful that I scarcely thought at all. But afterwards on the way here, when I turned it all over it seemed to me that it must be so. He did not come to me at all that afternoon. He was not shut up with us in that dreadful place, and everyone else was there.

So it seemed to me that he must have been killed, but that you did not like to tell me."

"It was better for him, dear, than to have died in that terrible cell. Thank God your mamma is safe, and some day you will join her again. We have news that the English are coming up to attack Calcutta. A party are already in the Hoogly, and the nabob is going to start in a few days to his army there. I hope in a very short time you will be safe among your friends."

After travelling for several hours they stopped. Charlie gave Ada some native clothes and ornaments, and told her to stain her face, arms, and legs, to put on the bangles and bracelets, and then to rejoin them. Half an hour later Ada took her seat in the cart, this time transformed into a Hindoo girl, and the party again proceeded. They felt sure that Ada's flight would not be discovered until daybreak. It would be some little time before horsemen could be sent off in all directions in pursuit, and they could not be overtaken until between eleven and twelve. The wagon was filled with grain, on the top of which Charlie and Ada were seated. When daylight came Charlie alighted and walked by the cart. Unquestioned they passed through several villages.

At eleven o'clock Hossein pointed to a large grove at some little distance from the road. "Go in there," he said, "and stay till nightfall. Do you then come out and follow me. I shall go into the next village and remain there till after dark. I shall then start and wait for you half a mile beyond the village."

An hour after the wagon had disappeared from sight the party in the grove saw ten or twelve horsemen galloping rapidly along the road. An hour passed and the same party returned at an equal speed. They saw no more of them, and after it became dark they continued their way, passed through the village, which was three miles ahead, and found Hossein waiting a short distance beyond. Ada climbed into the cart and they again went forward.

"Did you put the rajah's men on the wrong track, Hossein? We guessed that you had done so when we saw them going back."

"Yes," Hossein said. "I had unyoked the bullocks and had lain down the caravanserai when they arrived. They came in, and their leader asked who I was. I said that I was taking down a load of grain for the use of the army at Calcutta. He asked where were the two men and the woman who were with me. I replied that I knew nothing of them. I had overtaken them on the road, and they had asked leave for the woman to ride in the cart. They said they were going to visit their mother, who was sick. He asked if I was sure they were natives, and I counterfeited surprise and said that certainly they were, for which lie Allah will, I trust, be merciful, since it was told to an enemy. I said that they had left me just when we had passed the last village and had turned off by the road to the right, saying they had many miles to go. They talked together and decided that as you were the only people who had been seen along the road they must follow and find you, and so started at once, and I dare say they're searching for you now miles away."

Their journey continued without any adventure until within a few miles of Calcutta. Hossein then advised them to take up their abode in a ruined mud hut at a distance from the road. He had bought at the last village a supply of provisions sufficient to last them for some days.

"I shall now," he said, "go into the town, sell my grain, bullocks, and cart, and find out where the soldiers are."

As soon as the news of the nabob's advance against Calcutta reached Madras, Mr. Pigot, who was now governor there, despatched a force of two hundred and thirty men under the orders of Major Kilpatrick. The party reached Falta on the Hoogly on the 2d of August, and there heard of the capture of Calcutta. By detachments who came down from some of the Company's minor posts the force was increased to nearly four hundred. But sickness broke out among them, and finding himself unable to advance against so powerful an army as that of the nabob, Major Kilpatrick sent to Madras for further assistance. When the news reached that place Clive had recently arrived with a strong force, which was destined to operate against the French at Hyderabad.

The news, however, of the catastrophe at Calcutta at once altered the destination of the force, and on the 16th of October the expedition sailed for Calcutta. The force consisted of two hundred and fifty men of the 39th Foot, the first regiment of the regular English army which had been sent out to India; five hundred and seventy men of the Madras European force; eighty artillerymen; and twelve hundred Sepoys. Of the nine hundred Europeans only six hundred arrived at that time at the mouth of the Hoogly, the largest ship, the *Cumberland*, with three hundred men on board, having grounded on the way. The remainder of the fleet, consisting of three ships of war, five transports, and a fire-ship, reached Falta between the 11th and 20th of December.

Hossein had returned from Calcutta with the news that the party commanded by Major Kilpatrick had been for some weeks at Falta, and the party at once set off towards that place, which was but forty miles distant. Travelling by night and sleeping by day in the woods, they reached Falta without difficulty, and learning that the force was still on board ship they took possession of a boat moored by the bank some miles higher up and rowed down.

Great was their happiness indeed at finding themselves once more among friends. Here were assembled many of the ships which had been at Calcutta at the time it was taken, and to Ada's delight she learned that her mother was on board one of these. They were soon rowed there in a boat from the ship which they had first boarded, and Ada on gaining the deck saw her mother sitting among some other ladies, fugitives like herself. With a scream of joy she rushed forward, and with a cry of, "Mamma, mamma!" threw herself into her mother's arms. It was a moment or two before Mrs. Haines could realize that this dark-skinned Hindoo girl was her child, and then her joy equalled that of her daughter. It was some time before any coherent conversation could take place, and then Ada, running back to Charlie, drew him forward to her mother and presented him to her as her preserver, the Captain Marryat who had stayed with them at Calcutta. Mrs. Haines' gratitude was extreme, and Charlie was soon surrounded and congratulated by the officers on board, to many of whom, belonging as they did to the Madras army, he was well known. Foremost among them, and loudest in his expressions of delight, was his friend Peters.

"You know, Charlie, I suppose," he said presently, "that you are a major now?"

"No, indeed," Charlie said. "How is that?"

"When the directors at home received the report of Commodore James that the fort of Suwarndrug had been captured entirely through you, they at once sent out your appointment as major. You are lucky, old fellow. Here are you a major, while I'm a lieutenant still. However, don't think I'm jealous, for I'm not a bit, and you thoroughly deserve all, and more than you've got."

"And this is Tim," Charlie said; "he has shared all my adventures with me."

Tim was standing disconsolately by the bulwark, shifting uneasily from foot to foot with the feeling of the extreme shortness of his garments stronger upon him than ever.

Peters seized him heartily by the hand. I am glad to see you, Tim, very glad. And so you've been with Major Marryat ever since?"

"For the Lord's sake, Mr. Peters," Tim said in an earnest whisper, "git me a pair of trousers. I'm that ashamed of myself in the presence of the ladies that I'm like to drop."

"Come along below, Tim; come along, Charlie. There are lots of poor fellows have gone done and uniforms are plentiful. We'll soon rig you out again."

"There is one more introduction, Peters. This is my man Hossein. He calls himself my servant; I call him my friend. He has saved my life twice, and has been of inestimable service. Had it not been for him I should still be in prison at Moorshedabad."

Peters said a few hearty words to Hossein and they then went below, returning on deck in half an hour, Charlie in the undress uniform of an officer, Tim in that of a private in the Madras infantry.

Mrs. Haines and Ada had gone below, where they could chat unrestrained by the presence of others, and where an attempt could be made to restore Ada to her former appearance. Mrs. Haines had heard of her husband's death on the day after the capture of Calcutta, Mr. Holwell having been permitted to send on board the ships a list of those who had fallen. She had learned that Ada had survived the terrible night in the dungeon, and that she had been sent up country a captive. She almost despaired of ever hearing of her again, but had resolved to wait to see the issue of the approaching campaign. Now that Ada was restored to her she determined to leave for England in a vessel which was to sail in the course of a week with a large number of fugitives. Mr. Haines was a very wealthy man, and had intended retiring altogether in the course of a few months, and she would therefore be in the enjoyment of an ample fortune in England.

Among those on board the ships at Falta was Mr. Drake, who at once, upon hearing of Charlie's arrival, ordered him to be arrested. Major Kilpatrick, however, firmly refused to allow the order to be carried out, saying, that as Charlie was under his orders as an officer in the Madras army, Mr. Drake had no control or authority over him. He could, however, upon Clive's arrival lay the case before him.

A week later Mrs. Haines and Ada sailed for England, the latter weeping bitterly at parting from Charlie, who promised them that when he came home to England on leave he would pay them a visit. He gave them his mother's address; and Mrs. Haines promised to call upon her as soon as she reached England, and give her full news of him, adding that she hoped that his sisters, the youngest of whom was little older than Ada, would be great friends with her.

Very slowly and wearily the time passed at Falta. The mists from the river were deadly, and of the two hundred and thirty men whom Kilpatrick brought with him from Madras in July only about thirty remained alive, and of these but ten were fit for duty when Clive at last arrived. The fleet left Falta on the 27th of December and anchored off Moiapur on the following day. The fort of Baj-baj, near this place, was the first object of attack, and it was arranged that while Admiral Watson should bombard with the fleet, Clive should attack it on the land side.

Clive, who now held the rank of lieutenant-colonel in the army, had manifested great pleasure at again meeting the young officer who had served under him at Arcot, and who had in his absence obtained a fame scarcely inferior to his own by the defence of Ambur and the capture of Suwarndrug. A few hours after Clive's arrival Mr. Drake had made a formal complaint of the assault which Charlie had committed; but after hearing from Charlie an account of the circumstances Clive sent a contemptuous message to Mr. Drake, to the effect that Charlie had only acted as he should himself have done under the same circumstances, and that at the present time he should not think of depriving himself of the services of one gallant soldier, even if he had maltreated a dozen civilians.

As Clive had been given paramount authority in Bengal, and as Mr. Drake had every reason to suppose that he himself would be recalled as soon as the circumstances attending the capture of Calcutta were known in England, he was unable to do anything further in the matter, and Charlie landed with Clive on the 28th. The force consisted of two hundred and fifty Europeans, and twelve hundred Sepoys, who were forced to drag with them, having no draft animals, two field-pieces and a wagon of ammunition. The march was an excessively fatiguing one. The country was swampy in the extreme, and intersected with water-courses, and after a terribly fatiguing night march and fifteen hours of unintermittent labor, they arrived at eight o'clock in the morning at the hollow bed of a lake, now perfectly dry. It lay some ten feet below the surrounding country, and was bordered with jungle. In the wet season it was full of water. On the eastern and southern banks lay an abandoned village, and it was situated about a mile and a half from the fort of Baj-baj.

Clive was ill, and unable to see after matters himself; indeed, accustomed only to the feeble forces of Southern India, who had never stood for a moment against him in battle, he had no thought of danger.

Upon the other hand the troops of the nabob, who had had no experience whatever of the superior fighting powers of the Europeans, and who had effected so easy a conquest at Calcutta, flushed with victory regarded their European foes with contempt, and were preparing to annihilate them at a blow. Manak Chand, the general commanding the nabob's forces, informed by spies of the movements of the English troops, moved out with fifteen hundred horse and two thousand foot. So worn out were the British upon their arrival at the dried bed of the lake, that after detaching a small body to occupy a village near the enemy's fort, from which alone danger was expected, while another took up the post in some jungles by the side of the main road, the rest threw themselves down to sleep. Some lay in the village, some in the shade of the bushes along the sides of the hollow. Their arms were all piled in a heap sixty yards from the eastern bank. The two field-pieces stood deserted on the north side of the village. Not a single sentry was posted. Manak Chand, knowing that after marching all night they would be exhausted now stole upon them and surrounded the tank on three sides. Happily he did not perceive that their arms were piled at a distance of sixty yards from the nearest man. Had he done so the English would have been helpless in his hands. After waiting an hour, to be sure that the last of the English were sound asleep, he ordered a tremendous fire to be opened on the hollow and village.

Astounded at this sudden attack the men sprang up from their deep sleep, and a rush was instantly made to their arms. Clive, ever coolest in danger, shouted to them to be steady, and his officers well seconded his attempts. Unfortunately the artillerymen in their sudden surprise, instead of rushing to their cannon, joined the rest of the troops as they ran back to their arms, and the guns at once fell into the hands of the enemy. These had now climbed the eastern bank, and a fire from all sides was poured upon the troops huddled together in a mass.

"Major Marryat," Clive said, "if we fall back now, fatigued as the men are and shaken by this surprise, we are lost. Do you take a wing of the Sepoy battalion and clear the right bank. I will advance with the main body directly on the village."

"Come on, my lads," Charlie shouted in Hindustanee; "show them how the men of Madras can fight."

The Sepoys replied with a cheer, advanced with a rush against the bank, drove the defenders at once from the point where they charged, and then swept round the tank towards the village, which Clive had already attacked in front. The loss of Charlie's battalion was small, but the main body, exposed to the concentrated fire, suffered more heavily. They would not, however, be denied. Reaching the bank they poured a volley into the village and charged with the bayonet, just as Charlie's men dashed in at the side. The enemy fled from the village, and taking shelter in the jungles around opened fire. The shouts of their officers could be heard urging them again to sally out and fall upon the British; but at this moment the party which had been sent forward along the road hearing the fray, came hurrying up and poured their fire into the jungle. Surprised at this reinforcement the enemy paused as they were issuing from the wood, and then fell back upon their cavalry. The British artillerymen ran out and seized the guns and opened with them upon the retiring infantry. Clive now formed up his troops in line and advanced against the enemy's cavalry, behind which their infantry had massed for shelter. Manak Chand ordered his cavalry to charge, but just as he did so a cannon-ball from one of Clive's field-pieces passed close to his head. The sensation was so unpleasant that he at once changed his mind. The order for retreat was given, and the beaten army fell back in disorder to Calcutta.

CHAPTER XXI.

THE BATTLE OUTSIDE CALCUTTA.

AFTER the defeat of the enemy, who had surprised and so nearly annihilated him, Clive marched at once towards the fort of Baj-baj. On the way he met Major Kilpatrick, who was advancing, with a force which had been landed from the ships when the sound of firing was heard, to his assistance.

The fleet had at daybreak opened a heavy fire upon the ramparts, and by the afternoon effected a breach. As his men were greatly fatigued and had had but an hour's sleep, Clive determined upon delaying the attack until the morning, and a party of two hundred and fifty sailors with two guns were landed to take part in the storming.

Many of these sailors had drunk freely before landing, and as night fell some of them strolled towards the fort. One of the number named Strahan moved along, unobserved by the enemy, to the foot of the breach, climbed up it, and came suddenly upon a party of its defenders sitting round a fire smoking. Strahan immediately fired his pistol among them with a shout of, "The fort is mine!" and then gave three rousing cheers. The enemy leaped to their feet and ran off for a little way. Then seeing Strahan was alone they rushed back and attacked him, firing as they came. Strahan, drawing his cutlass, defended himself vigorously for some time, but his weapon broke off at the hilt just as a number of Sepoys and men of the 39th, who had been awaked from their sleep by the shouting and firing, came running up. Reinforcements of the garrison also joined their friends, but these were dispirited by the sudden and unexpected attack, and as the troops continued to stream up the breach the garrison were pressed, and, losing heart, fled through the opposite gate of the fort. The only casualty on the British side was that Captain Campbell, marching up at the head of the Sepoys, was mistaken for an enemy by the sailors and shot dead. Strahan was in the morning severely reprimanded by the admiral for his breach of discipline, and retiring from the cabin said to his comrades:

"Well, if I am flogged for this here action, I will never take another fort by myself as long as I live."

Manak Chand was so alarmed at the fighting powers shown by the English in these two affairs, that, leaving only a garrison of five hundred men at Calcutta, he retired with his army to join the nabob at Moorshedabad. When the fleet arrived before the town the enemy surrendered the fort at the first shot, and it was again taking possession of by the English. Major Kilpatrick was at once sent up with five ships and a few hundred men to capture the town of Hoogly, twenty miles farther up. The defences of the place were strong. It was held by two thousand men, and three thousand horsemen lay around it. The ships, however, at once opened a cannonade upon it, and effected a breach before night, and at daybreak the place was taken by storm.

Two days after the capture of Calcutta the news arrived that war had again been declared between England and France. It was fortunate that this was not known a little earlier; for had the French forces been joined to those under Manak Chand the reconquest of Calcutta would not have been so easily achieved. The nabob, furious at the loss of Calcutta and the capture and sack of Hoogly, at once despatched a messenger to the governor of the French colony of Chandranagore, to join him in crushing the English. The governor, however, had received orders that in the event of war being declared between England and France he was, if possible, to arrange with the English that neutrality should be observed between them; he therefore refused the nabob's request, and then sent messengers to Calcutta to treat.

THE TERRITORY OF CALCUTTA in 1757.

The nabob had gathered an army of ten thousand foot and fifteen thousand horse, and advanced against Calcutta, arriving before the town on the 2d February, 1757. Clive's force had now, owing to the arrival of some reinforcements from Europe and the enlisting of fresh Sepoys, been raised to seven hundred European infantry, a hundred artillerymen, and fifteen hundred Sepoys, with fourteen light field-pieces.

The whole of the town of Calcutta was surrounded by a deep cut, with a bank behind, called the Maratta Ditch. A mile beyond this was a large salt-water lake, so that an enemy advancing from the north would have to pass within a short distance of Clive's intrenched position outside the town, affording him great opportunities for a flank attack. On the day of their arrival Clive marched out, but the enemy opened a heavy fire, and he retired.

Clive determined to attack the enemy next morning. Admiral Watson, at his request, at once landed five hundred and sixty sailors, under the command of Captain Warwick of the *Thunderer*. A considerable portion of the enemy had crossed the Maratta Ditch and encamped within it. The nabob himself pitched his tent in the garden of Omichund (a native Calcutta merchant, who, though in the nabob's camp from motives of policy, sympathized entirely with the English), which occupied an advanced bastion within the Maratta Ditch. The rest of the army were encamped between the ditch and the salt-water lake.

Clive's intentions were to march first against the battery which had played on him so effectually the day before, and having carried this, to march directly against the garden in which the nabob was encamped. The force with which he started at three o'clock in the morning of the 3d consisted of the five hundred and sixty sailors, who drew with them six guns; six hundred and fifty European infantry, a hundred European artillery, and eight hundred Sepoys. Half the Sepoys led the advance, the remainder covered the rear. Soon after daybreak the Sepoys came in contact with the enemy's advanced guard, placed in ditches along a road leading from the head of the lake to the Maratta Ditch. These discharged their muskets and some rockets and took to flight. One of the rockets caused a serious disaster. The Sepoys had their ammunition pouches open, and the contents of one of these was fired by the rocket. The flash of the flame communicated the fire to the pouch of the next Sepoy, and so the flame ran along the line, killing, wounding, and scorching many, and causing the greatest confusion. Fortunately the enemy were not near, and Captain Eyre Coote, who led the British infantry behind them, aided Charlie, who led the advance, in restoring order, and the forward movement again went on.

A new obstacle had, however, arisen. With the morning a dense fog had set in, rendering it impossible for the troops to see even a few yards in advance of them. Still they pushed on, and, unopposed, reached a point opposite Omichund's garden, but divided from it by the Maratta Ditch. Presently they heard the thunder of a great body of approaching cavalry. They waited quietly until the unseen horse had approached within a few yards of them, and then poured a mighty volley into the fog. The noise ceased abruptly, and was followed by that of the enemy's cavalry in retreat. The fog was now so dense that it was impossible even to judge of the directions in which the troops were moving. Clive knew, however, that the Maratta Ditch was on his right, and moving a portion of his troops till they touched this, he again advanced, his object being to gain a causeway, which, raised several feet above the country, led from Calcutta across the Maratta Ditch into the country beyond. Towards this Clive now advanced, his troops firing as they marched, into the fog ahead of them, and the guns firing from the flanks obliquely to the right and left.

Without experiencing any opposition Clive reached the causeway, and the Sepoys, turning to their right, advanced along this towards the ditch. As they crossed this, however, they came in the line of fire of their own guns, the officer commanding them being ignorant of what was taking place in front, and unable to see a foot before him. Charlie closely accompanied always by Tim, was at the head of his troops when the iron hail of the English guns struck the head of the column, mowing down numbers of men. A panic ensued, and the Sepoys, terror-stricken at this discharge from a direction in which they considered themselves secure, leaped from the causeway into the dry ditch and sheltered themselves there. Charlie and his companion were saved by the fact that they were a few paces ahead of the column.

"Run back, Tim," Charlie said. "Find Colonel Clive, and tell him that we are being mowed down by our own artillery. If you can't find him, hurry back to the guns and tell the officer what he is doing."

Charlie then leaped down into the ditch and endeavored to rally the Sepoys. A few minutes later Clive himself arrived, and the Sepoys were induced to leave the ditch, and to form again by the side of the causeway, along which the British troops were now marching.

Suddenly, however, from the fog burst out the discharge of two heavy guns which the enemy had mounted on a bastion flanking the ditch. The shouts of the officers and the firing of the men indicated precisely the position of the column. The grape-shot tore through it, and twenty-two of the English troops fell dead and wounded. Immediately afterwards another discharge followed, and the column broken and confused, bewildered by the dense fog, and dismayed by the fire of these unseen guns, fell back.

Clive now determined to push on to the main road, which he knew crossed the fields half a mile in front of him. The country was, however, here laid out in rice-fields, each inclosed by banks and ditches. Over these banks it was impossible to drag the guns, and the sailors could only get them along by descending into the ditches and using these as roads. The labor was prodigious, and the men, fatigued and harassed by this battle in darkness, and by the fire from the unseen guns which the enemy continued to pour in their direction from either flank, began to lose heart. Happily, however, the fog began to lift. The flanks of the columns were covered by bodies of troops thrown out on either side, and after more than an hour's hard work, and abandoning two of the guns which had broken down, Clive reached the main road, again formed his men in columns, and advanced towards the city.

The odds were overwhelmingly against him. There were guns, infantry and cavalry, both in front and behind them. The column pressed on in spite of the heavy fire, crossed the ditch, and attacked a strong body of the enemy drawn up on the opposite side. While it did so, a great force of the nabob's cavalry swept down on the rear, and for a moment captured the guns. Ensign Yorke, of the 39th Foot, faced the rear company about, and made a gallant charge upon the horsemen, drove them back, and recaptured the guns.

Clive's whole army was now across the ditch, and it was open to him either to carry out his original plan of attacking Omichund's garden, or of marching forward into the fort of Calcutta. Seeing that his men were fatigued and worn out with six hours of labor and marching under the most difficult circumstances, he took the latter alternative, entered Calcutta, and then, following the stream, marched back to the camp which he had left in the morning. His loss amounted to thirty-nine Europeans killed and eighteen Sepoys, eighty-two Europeans wounded and thirty-five Sepoys; the casualties being caused almost entirely by the enemy's cannon.

The expedition, from a military point of view, had been an entire failure. He had carried neither the battery nor Omichund's garden. Had it not been for the fog he might have succeeded in both these objects; but, upon the other hand, the enemy were as much disconcerted by the fog as he was, and were unable to use their forces with any effect. Military critics have decided that the whole operation was a mistake; but although a mistake and a failure its consequences were no less decisive.

The nabob, struck with astonishment at the daring and dash of the English in venturing with so small a force to attack him, and to march through the very heart of his camp, was seized with terror. He had lost thirteen hundred men in the fight, among whom were twenty-four rajahs and lesser chiefs, and the next morning he sent in a proposal for peace.

A less determined man than Clive would, no doubt, have accepted the proposal. Calcutta was still besieged by a vastly superior force, supplies of all kinds were running short, the attack of the previous day had been a failure. He knew, however, the character of Asiatics, and determined to play the game of bounce. The very offer of the nabob showed him that the latter was alarmed. He therefore wrote to him, saying that he had simply marched his troops through his highness' camp to show him of what British soldiers were capable; but that he had been careful to avoid hurting any one except those who actually opposed his progress. He concluded by expressing his willingness to accede to the nabob's proposal and to negotiate.

The nabob took it all in. If all this destruction and confusion had been wrought by a simple march through his camp, what would be the result if Clive were to take it into his head to attack him in earnest. He therefore at once withdrew his army three miles to the rear, and opened negotiations. He granted all that the English asked, that all the property and privileges of the Company should be restored, that all their goods should pass into the country free of tax, that all the Company's factories, and all moneys and properties belonging to it or its servants, should be restored or made good, and that permission should be given to them to fortify Calcutta as they pleased.

Having agreed to these conditions, the nabob, upon the 11th of February, retired with his army to his capital, leaving Omichund with a commission to propose to the English a treaty of alliance, offensive and defensive, against all enemies. This proposal was a most acceptable one, and Clive determined to seize the opportunity to crush the French. His previous experiences around Madras had taught him that the French were the most formidable rivals of England in India. He knew that large reinforcements were on their way to Pondicherry, and he feared that the nabob, when he recovered from his panic, might regret the conditions which he had granted, and might ally himself with the French in an effort again to expel the English.

He therefore determined at once to attack the French. The deputies sent by Monsieur Renault, the governor of Chandranagore, had been kept waiting from day to day under one pretence or another, and they now wrote to the governor that they believed that there was no real intention on the part of the English to sign an agreement of neutrality with him, and that they would be the objects of attack. M. Renault immediately sent messengers to the nabob, urging upon him that if the English were allowed to annihilate the French they would be more dangerous enemies than ever, and Suraja-u-Dowlah, having now recovered from his terror, wrote at once to Calcutta, peremptorily forbidding any hostilities against the French. To show his determination he despatched fifteen hundred men to Hoogly, which the English had abandoned after capturing it, with instructions to help the French if attacked, and he sent a lac of rupees to M. Renault to aid him in preparing for his defence.

Clive unwilling to face a coalition between the French and the nabob, was in favor of acceding to the nabob's orders. The treaty of neutrality with the French was drawn up, and would have been signed had it not been for the obstinate refusal of Admiral Watson to agree to it. Between that officer and Clive there had never been any cordial feeling, and from the time of their first connection, at the siege of Gheriah, differences of opinion, frequently leading to angry disputes, had taken place between them. Nor was it strange that this should be so; both were brave and gallant men; but while Watson had the punctilious sense of honor which naturally belongs to an English gentleman, Clive was wholly unscrupulous as to the means which he employed to gain his ends.

Between two such men it is not singular that disagreements arose. Admiral Watson, impelled by feelings of personal dislike to Clive, often allowed himself to be carried to unwarrantable lengths. On the occasion of the capture of Calcutta he ordered Captain Eyre Coote, who first entered it, to hold it in the king's name, and to disobey Clive's orders, although the latter had been granted a commission in the royal army as lieutenant-colonel, and was, moreover, the chief authority of the Company in all affairs on land. Upon Clive's asserting himself Admiral Watson absolutely threatened to open fire upon his troops. Apparently from a sheer feeling of opposition he now opposed the signing of the treaty with the French, and several days were spent in stormy altercations.

Circumstances occurred during this time which strengthened the view he took and changed those of Clive and his colleagues of the council. Just then the news reached Suraja-u-Dowlah that Delhi had been captured by the Afghans, and, terrified at the thought that the victorious northern enemy might next turn their arms against him, he wrote to Clive, begging him to march to his assistance, and offering a lac of rupees a month towards the expense of his army. On the same day that Clive received the letter he heard that Commodore James and three ships, with reinforcements from Bombay, had arrived at the mouth of the Hoogly, and that the *Cumberland*, with three hundred troops, which had grounded on her way from Madras, was now coming up the river.

Almost at the same moment he heard from Omichund, who had accompanied the nabob to Moorshedabad, that he had bribed the governor of Hoogly to offer no opposition to the passage of the troops up the river. Clive was now ready to agree to Admiral Watson's views, and to advance at once against Chandranagore; but the admiral again veered round and refused to agree to the measure unless the consent of the nabob was obtained. He wrote, however, himself, a threatening, and indeed violent, letter to the nabob, ordering him to give his consent. The nabob, still under the influence of his fears from the Afghans, replied in terms which amounted to consent, but the very next day, having received news which calmed his fears as to the Afghans, he wrote peremptorily forbidding the expedition against the French. This letter, however, was disregarded and the expedition prepared to start. It consisted of seven hundred Europeans and fifteen hundred native infantry, who started by land, a hundred and fifty artillery proceeding in boats, escorted by three ships of war and several smaller vessels under Admiral Watson.

The French garrison consisted only of a hundred and forty-six French and three hundred Sepoys. Besides these were three hundred of the European population and sailors of the merchant ships in port, who had been hastily formed into a militia. The governor, indignant at the duplicity with which he had been treated, had worked vigorously at his defences. The settlement extended along the river banks for two miles. In the centre stood the fort, which was a hundred and twenty yards square, mounting ten thirty-two pounder guns on each of its four bastions. Twenty-four pounder guns were placed on the ramparts, facing the river on the south. On an outlying work commanding the water-gate eight thirty-two pounders were mounted. M. Renault set to work to demolish all the houses within a hundred yards of the fort, and to erect batteries commanding the approaches. He ordered an officer to sink several ships in the only navigable channel, about a hundred and fifty yards to the south of the fort, at a point commanded by the guns of one of the batteries. The officer was a traitor. He purposely sank the ships in such a position as to leave a channel through which the English ships might pass and then, seizing his opportunity, deserted to them.

On approaching the town Clive, knowing that Charlie could speak the native language fluently, asked him whether he would undertake to reconnoitre the position of the enemy, with which he was entirely unacquainted. Charlie willingly agreed. When, on the night of the 13th of March, the army halted a few miles from the town, Charlie, disguising himself in a native dress and accompanied by Hossein, left the camp and made his way to the town. This he had no difficulty in entering. It extended a mile and a half back from the river, and consisted of houses standing in large gardens and inclosures. The whole of the Europeans were laboring at the erection of the batteries and the destruction of the houses surrounding them and Charlie and his companion, approaching closely to one of these, were pounced upon by the French officer in command of a working party, and set to work with a number of natives in demolishing the houses. Charlie, with his usual energy, threw himself into the work, and would speedily have called attention to himself by the strength and activity which he displayed, had not Hossein begged him to moderate his efforts.

"Native man never work like that, sahib. Not when he's paid ever so much. Work still less, no pay. The French would soon notice the sahib if he labored like that."

Thus admonished Charlie adapted his actions to those of his companions, and after working until dawn approached he managed, with Hossein, to evade the attention of the officer, and, drawing off, hurried away to rejoin Clive. The latter was moving from the west by a road leading to the northern face of the fort. It was at the battery which Renault was erecting upon this road that Charlie had been laboring. The latter informed Clive of the exact position of the work, and also, that although strong by itself, it was commanded by many adjoining houses, which the French, in spite of their efforts, had not time to destroy. This news decided Clive to advance immediately without giving the enemy further time to complete their operations.

CHAPTER XXII.

PLASSEY.

AS the English troops advanced they were met on the outskirts of the settlement by the enemy, who contested bravely every garden and inclosure with them. The British force was, however, too strong to be resisted, and gradually the French were driven back until they formed in rear of the battery. Clive at once took possession of the houses surrounding it, and from them kept up all day a heavy fire upon the defenders, until at nightfall these fell back upon the fort after spiking their guns. The loss of this position compelled the French to abandon the other outlying batteries, from which, during the night, they withdrew their guns into the fort. The next four days Clive spent in bringing up the guns landed from the fleet and establishing batteries round the fort, and on the 19th he opened fire against it. On the same day the three men-of-war, the *Kent* of sixty-four guns, the *Tiger* of sixty, and the *Salisbury* of fifty, anchored just below the channel which the governor believed he had blocked up. The next four days were spent by the fleet in sounding, to discover whether the statements of the French deserter were correct. During this time a heavy cannonade was kept up unceasingly between Clive and the fort. In this the garrison had the best of it, silenced some of the English guns, killed many of the assailants, and would certainly have beaten off the land attack had the fleet not been able to interfere in the struggle.

All this time the governor was hoping that aid would arrive from the nabob. The latter, indeed, did send a force under Rajah Dulab Ram, but the governor of Hoogly, bribed by Omichund, sent messages to this officer urging him to halt, as Chandranagore was about to surrender, and he would only incur the anger of the English uselessly. On the morning of the 23d, having ascertained that a channel was free, the fleet advanced. The *Tiger* leading, made her way through the passage and taking up a position abreast of the northeast bastion of the fort, opened a heavy fire upon it with her guns, and harassed the besieged with a musketry fire from her tops. The *Kent* was on the point of anchoring opposite the water-gate, when so heavy a fire was poured upon her, that in the confusion the cable ran out and the ship dropped down till she anchored at a point exposed to a heavy cross fire from the southeast and southwest bastions. Owing to this accident the *Salisbury* was forced to anchor a hundred and fifty yards below the fort. The French fought with extreme bravery. Vastly superior as were the English force and guns, the French fire was maintained with the greatest energy and spirit, the gunners being directed and animated by M. De Vignes, captain of one of the ships which had been sunk. No advantage was gained by the *Tiger* in her struggle with the northeast bastion, and the guns of the southwest bastion galled the *Kent* so severely, that the admiral, neglecting the southeast bastion, was forced to turn the whole of his guns upon it. De Vignes concentrated his fire against one point in the *Kent*, and presently succeeded in setting her on fire. The conflagration spread, a panic ensued, and some seventy or eighty men jumped into the boats alongside. The officers, however, rallied the rest of the crew. The fire was extinguished, the men returned to their duty, and the cannonade was recommenced.

After the battle had raged for two hours the fire of the fort began to slacken, as one after another of the guns was dismounted. M. Renault saw that the place could be no longer defended. Of his hundred and forty-six soldiers, over ninety had been killed and wounded. Collecting the remainder and their officers, with twenty Sepoys, the governor ordered them to leave the fort immediately, making a detour to avoid the English who were aiding the fleet by attacking the land side, and to march to Kossimbazar to join M. Law who commanded there. Then, there remaining in the fort only the clerks, women, and wounded, he hoisted a flag of truce. Terms were speedily arranged. The governor and all the civilians and natives were allowed to go where they chose with their clothes and linen. The wounded French soldiers were to remain as prisoners of war.

Chandranagore cost the English two hundred and six men. The attack upon the French colony was blamed by many at the time, for in the hour of English distress they had offered to remain neutral instead of joining the nabob in crushing us. Upon the other hand there was force in the arguments with which Admiral Watson had defended his refusal to sign the treaty of neutrality. That treaty would not be binding unless ratified by Pondicherry, and to Pondicherry it was known that the most powerful fleet and army France had ever sent to India was on its way. It was also known that Bussy, at the court of the Nizam of the Deccan, was in communication with the nabob. Thus then in a short time English interests in India might be menaced more formidably than ever before, and the crushing out of the French colony, almost at the gates of Calcutta, was a measure of extreme importance. It was hard upon the gallant governor of Chandranagore, but public opinion generally agreed that the urgency of the case justified the course adopted by the English authorities at Calcutta.

Suraja-u-Dowlah was filled with fury at the news of the capture of Chandranagore, but hearing a rumor two days later that the Afghans were upon their march to attack him, he wrote letters to Clive and Watson congratulating them upon their success, and offering to them the territory of Chandranagore on the same terms upon which it had been held by the French. But the young tyrant of Moorshedabad was swayed by constantly fluctuating feeling. At one moment his fears were uppermost, the next, his anger and hate of the English. Instead of recalling the army of Rajah Dulab Ram, as he had promised, he ordered it to halt at Plassey, a large village twenty-two miles south of Moorshedabad. The English were represented at his court by Mr. Watts, who had the greatest difficulty in maintaining his position in the constantly changing moods of the nabob. One day the latter would threaten to order him to be led to instant execution, the next he would load him with presents.

Besides Mr. Watts, the English affairs were conducted by Omichund, who, aided by the Sets or native bankers whom Suraja-u-Dowlah had plundered and despoiled, got up a conspiracy among the nabob's most intimate followers. The history of these intrigues is the most unpleasant feature in the life of Clive. Meer Jaffier, the nabob's general, himself offered to Mr. Watts to turn traitor if the succession to the kingdom was bestowed upon him. This was agreed to upon his promise to pay not only immense sums to the Company, but enormous amounts to the principal persons on the English side. So enormous, indeed, were these demands that even Meer Jaffier, anxious as he was to conclude the alliance, was aghast.

The squadron was to have two million and a half rupees and the same amount was to be paid for the army, presents amounting to six millions of rupees were to be distributed between Clive, Major Kilpatrick, the governor, and the members of the council. Clive's share of these enormous sums amounted to two million eighty thousand rupees. In those days a rupee was worth half a crown. Never did an English officer make such a bargain for himself.

But even this is not the most dishonorable feature of the transaction. Omichund had for some time been kept in the dark as to what was going forward, but obtaining information through his agents he questioned Mr. Watts concerning it. The latter then informed him of the whole state of affairs, and Omichund, whose services to the English had been immense, naturally demanded a share of the plunder. Whether or not he threatened to divulge the plot to the nabob, unless his demands were satisfied, is doubtful. At any rate, it was considered prudent to pacify him, and he was accordingly told that he should receive the sum he named. Clive and the members of the council, however, although willing to gratify their own extortionate greed at the expense of Meer Jaffier, determined to rob Omichund of his share. In order to do this two copies of the treaty with Meer Jaffier were drawn up on different colored papers. They were exactly alike, except that in one the amount to be given to Omichund was entirely omitted. This was the real treaty. The other was intended to be destroyed after being shown to a friend of Omichund in order to convince the latter that all was straight and honorable. All the English authorities placed their signatures to the real treaty, but Admiral Watson indignantly refused to have anything to do with the fictitious one, or to be a party in any way to the deceit practiced on Omichund. In order to get out of the difficulty, Clive himself forged Admiral Watson's signature to the fictitious treaty.

A more disgraceful transaction was never entered into by a body of English gentlemen. That Mr. Drake and the members of his council, the pitiful cowards who fled from Calcutta and refused to allow the ships to draw off its brave garrison, should consent to such a transaction was but natural, but that Clive, the gallant and dashing commander, should have stooped to it, is sad indeed. It may be said that to the end of his life Clive defended his conduct in this transaction, under the excuse that Omichund was a scoundrel. The Indian was not, indeed, an estimable character. Openly he was the friend and confidant of the nabob, while all the time he was engaged in bribing and corrupting his officers and in plotting with his enemies. This, however, in no way alters the facts that he rendered inestimable service to the English, and that the men who deceived and cheated him were to the full as greedy and grasping as himself, without, in the case of the governor and his council, having rendered any service whatever to the cause.

At last the negotiations were complete. More and more severely did Clive press upon the nabob. Having compelled him to expel Law and the French, first from Moorshedabad and then from his dominions, he pressed fresh demands upon him, until the unfortunate prince, driven to despair, and buoyed up with the hope that he should receive assistance from Bussy, who had just expelled the English from their factory at Vizapatam, ordered Meer Jaffier to advance with fifteen thousand men to reinforce Rajah Dulab Ram at Plassey. Clive, in fact, forced on hostilities. His presence, with that of a considerable portion of his army, was urgently required at Madras. He was sure, however, that the instant he had gone, and the English force was greatly weakened, the nabob would again commence hostilities; and the belief was shared by all in India. He was, therefore, determined to force on the crisis as soon as possible, in order that, the nabob being disposed of, he should be able to send reinforcements to Madras.

While these negotiations had been going on Charlie Marryat had remained in Calcutta. He had been severely wounded in the attack on Chandranagore, and was carried down to Calcutta in a boat. On arriving there he heard that the *Lizzie Anderson* had just cast anchor off the fort. He caused himself at once to be conveyed on board, and was received with the greatest heartiness and pleasure by his old friend, the captain, and assiduously attended by the doctor of the ship. In order that he might have as much air as possible the captain had a sort of tent, with a double covering, erected on deck. During the daytime the sides of this were lifted so that the air could pass freely across the bed. Charlie's wound was a severe one, and had he been nursed in a hospital on shore, it is probable that it would have been fatal. Thanks, however, to the comforts on board ship, the freshness and coolness of the situation, and the care of all surrounding him, he was, after some weeks' illness, pronounced convalescent, and was sufficiently recovered to join the force with which Clive marched against Plassey.

This force consisted of nine hundred and fifty European infantry, a hundred artillerymen, fifty sailors, and two thousand one hundred Sepoys. The artillery consisted of eight six pounders and two small howitzers. The army of the nabob was fifty thousand strong, and against such a force it was indeed an adventurous task for an army of three thousand men, of whom only one-third were Europeans, to advance to the attack. Everything depended, in fact, upon Meer Jaffier and his two colleagues in treachery, Rajah

Dulab Ram and Yar Lutf Khan. The nabob on hearing of Clive's advance had sent to M. Law, who was with a hundred and fifty men at a place over a hundred miles distant, to which he had in accordance with the orders of Clive been obliged to retire, and begged him to advance to join him with all speed. The nabob had with him forty or fifty Frenchmen commanded by M. St. Frais, formerly one of the council of Chandranagore. These had some field-pieces of their own, and also directed the native artillery of fifty-three guns, principally thirty-two, twenty-four, and eighteen pounders.

Had Clive been sure of the co-operation of Meer Jaffier and his confederates, who commanded three out of the four divisions of the nabob's army, he need not have hesitated. But he was till the last moment in ignorance whether to rely upon them. The nabob, having become suspicious of Meer Jaffier, had obtained from him an oath sworn on the Koran of fidelity, and although the traitor continued his correspondence with Clive his letters were of a very dubious character, and Clive was in total ignorance as to his real intentions. So doubtful, indeed, was he, that when only a few miles of ground and the river Bhagirathi lay between him and the enemy, Clive felt the position so serious that he called a council of war, and put to them the question whether they should attack the nabob or fortify themselves at Katwa, and hold that place until the rainy season, which had just set in with great violence, should abate. All the officers above the rank of subalterns, twenty in number, were present. Clive himself, contrary to custom, gave his vote first in favor of halting at Katwa. Major Kilpatrick, who commanded the Company's troops, Major Grant of the 37th, and ten other officers voted the same way. Major Eyre Coote declared in favor of an immediate advance. He argued that the troops were in high spirits and had hitherto been everywhere successful, and that a delay would allow M. Law and his troops to arrive. He considered that if they determined not to fight they should fall back upon Calcutta. Charlie Marryat supported him, as did five other officers, all belonging to the Indian service. The decision taken, the council separated, and Clive strolled away to a grove and sat down by himself. There he thought over in his mind the arguments which had been advanced by both sides. He saw the force of the arguments which had been adduced by Major Eyre Coote and Charlie Marryat, and his own experience showed him that the daring course is always the most prudent one in fighting with Asiatics. At last he came to a conclusion. Rising, he returned to the camp, and meeting Major Coote on the way informed him that he had changed his mind and would fight the next day.

Charlie returned to his tent after the council broke up disheartened at the result. He was greeted by Tim.

"Shure, yer honor, Hossein is in despair. The water has filled up the holes where he makes his fires and the rain has soaked the wood. Yer dinner is not near cooked yet, and half the dishes are spoilt."

"It does not matter a bit, Tim," Charlie said. "You know I'm not particular about my eating, though Hossein will always prepare a dinner fit for an alderman."

"We are going to fight them to-morrow, yer honor, I hope," Tim said. "It's sick to death I am of wading about here in the wet like a duck. It's as bare as the bogs of ould Ireland, without the blessings of the pigs and potatoes, to say nothing of the colleens."

"No, Tim, I'm afraid we're going to stop where we are for a bit. The council of war have decided not to fight."

"Shure and that's bad news," Tim said, "the worst I've heard for many a day. What if there be fifty thousand of 'em, Mister Charles, haven't we bate 'em at long odds before, and can't we do it agin?"

"I think we could, Tim," Charlie replied; "but the odds of fifty-three heavy cannon, which the spies say they've got, to our ten pop-guns is serious. However, I'm sorry we're not going to fight, and I'm afraid that you must make up your mind to the wet, and Hossein his to giving me bad dinners for some weeks to come, that is to say if the enemy don't turn us out of this."

A few minutes later Lieutenant Peters entered the tent. "Is it true, Charlie, that we are not going to fight after all?"

"True enough," Charlie said. "We are to wait till the rains are over."

"Rains!" Peters said in disgust; "what have the rains got to do with it. If we had a six weeks' march before us I could understand the wet weather being a hindrance. Men are not water-rats, and to march all day in those heavy downpours, and to lie all night in the mud would soon tell upon our strength. But here we are within a day's march of the enemy, and the men might as well get wet in the field as here. Every one longs to be at the enemy, and a halt will have a very bad effect. What have you got to drink, Charlie?"

"I have some brandy and rum; nothing else," Charlie said. "But what will be better than either for you is a cup of tea; Hossein makes it as well as ever. I suppose you have dined?"

"Yes, half an hour ago."

Just as Charlie finished his meal, Major Eyre Coote put his head into the tent. "Marryat, the chief has changed his mind. We cross the river the first thing in the morning and move at once upon Plassey."

"Hurrah!" Charlie shouted; "Clive is himself again. That is good news indeed."

"You will move your Sepoys down to the river at daybreak, and will be the first to cross. There is no chance of any opposition, as the spies tell us that the nabob has not arrived yet at Plassey."

Several other officers afterwards dropped into the tent, for the news rapidly spread through the camp. There was, as had been the case at the council, considerable differences of opinion as to the prudence of the measure, but among the junior officers and men the news that the enemy were to be attacked at once was received with hearty satisfaction.

"Here, major," a fellow subaltern of Peters' said, as he entered the tent followed by a servant, "I have brought in half a dozen bottles of champagne. I started with a dozen from Calcutta, and had intended to keep these to celebrate our victory. But as in the first place all heavy baggage is to be left here, and in the second, it has occurred to me that possibly I may not come back to help to drink it; we may as well turn it to the good purpose of drinking success to the expedition."

Some of the bottles were opened and a merry evening was spent, but the party broke up early, for they had a heavy day's work before them on the morrow.

At daybreak the troops were in movement towards the banks of the Bhagirathi. They had brought boats with them from Chandranagore, and the work of crossing the river continued without intermission until four in the afternoon, when the whole force was landed on the left bank. Here Clive received another letter from Meer Jaffier, informing him that the nabob had halted at Mankarah and intended to intrench himself there. He suggested that the English should undertake a circuitous march and attack him in the rear;

but as this march would have exposed Clive to being cut off from his communications, and as he was still very doubtful of the good faith of the conspirators, he determined to march straight forward, and sent word to Meer Jaffier to that effect.

From the point where Clive had crossed the Bhagirathi it was fifteen miles to Plassey, following as they did the curves of the river. It was necessary to do this as they had no carriage, and the men were obliged to tow their supplies in boats against the stream. Orders were issued that as soon as the troops were across they should prepare to eat their dinners, as the march was to be resumed at once. The rain was coming down in a steady pour as the troops, drenched to the skin, started upon their march. The stream, swollen by the rains, was in full flood, and the work of towing the heavy-laden barges was wearisome in the extreme. All took a share in the toil. In many cases the river had overflowed its banks, and the troops had to struggle through the water, up to their waists, while they tugged and strained at the ropes.

Charlie, as a mounted officer, rode at the head of his Sepoys who formed the advance of the force. Three hundred men preceded the main body who were towing the boats, to guard them from any sudden surprise. Tim marched beside him, occasionally falling back and taking a turn at the ropes. "This is dog's work, Mister Charles," he said. "It's lucky that it's raining, for the river can't make us wetter than we are. My hands are fairly sore with pulling at the ropes."

"Ah, Tim, you're not fond of ropes, you know. You remember that night at Moorshedabad."

"Faith, yer honor, and I'll not forget it if I live to be as old as Methuselah. Well, yer honor, it will be hard on us if we do not thrash them niggers to-morrow after all the trouble we are taking to be at them."

At one o'clock in the morning the weary troops reached the village of Plassey. They marched through it, and halted and bivouacked in a large mango grove a short distance beyond.

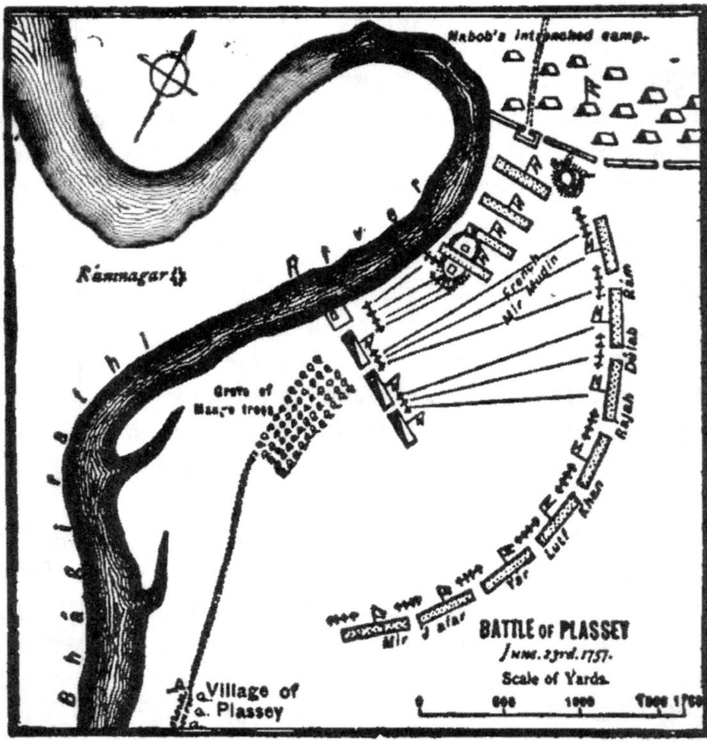

CHAPTER XXIII.

PLASSEY.

SCARCELY had the soldiers taken off their packs when the sound of martial music was heard. Charlie was speaking at the time to Major Coote. "There are the enemy, sure enough," the latter said. "That old rascal Meer Jaffier must have been deceiving us when he said that the nabob had halted at Mankarah. I'm afraid he means to play us false."

"I expect," Charlie remarked, "that he does not know what he means himself. These Asiatics are at any time ready to turn traitors, and to join the strongest. At present Jaffier does not know which is the stronger, and I think it likely enough that he will take as little share as he can in the battle to-morrow till he sees which way it is going. Then if we are getting the best of it the rascal will join us for the sake of the advantages which he expects to gain. If the day is going against us he will do his best to complete his master's victory; and should proofs of his intended treachery ever come to light he will clear himself by saying that he intended to deceive us all along, and merely pretended to treat with us in order to throw us off our guard, and so deliver us into the hands of his master."

"Yes," Major Eyre Coote replied. "These Mahommedan chiefs are indeed crafty and treacherous rascals. The whole history of India shows that gratitude is a feeling altogether unknown to them, and that whatever favors a master may have lavished upon them they are always ready to betray him if they think that by so doing they will better their position. Now I shall lie down and try to get a few hours' sleep before morning. I am wet to the skin, but fortunately in these sultry nights that matters little."

"I must go my rounds," Charlie said, "and see that the sentries are on the alert. If the men were not so tired I should have said that the best plan would have been to make a dash straight at the enemy's camp. It would take them quite unprepared, even if they know, as I dare say they do, that we are close at hand, and they would lose all the advantage of their artillery."

"Yes, if we had arrived an hour before sunset so as to be able to learn something of the nature of the ground, that would be our best course," Major Coote agreed. "But, even if the troops had been fresh, a night attack on an unknown position is a hazardous undertaking. Good-night, I must see Clive and take his last orders."

At daybreak the English were astir, and the position of the enemy became visible. He occupied strongly intrenched works which the Rajah Dulab Ram had thrown up during his stay. The right of these works rested on the river, and extended inland at a right angle to it for about two hundred yards, and then swept round to the north at an obtuse angle for nearly three miles. At the angle was a redoubt mounted with cannon. In advance of this was a mound covered with jungle. Half-way between the intrenchments and the mango grove were two large tanks near the river surrounded by high mounds of earth. These tanks were about half a mile from the English position. On the river bank, a little in advance of the grove, was a hunting-box belonging to the nabob, surrounded by a masonry wall. Clive took possession of this immediately he heard the sound of the nabob's music on his arrival.

Soon after daylight the nabob's troops moved out from their intrenchments, and it was evident that he was aware of the position of the English. The French with their four field-guns took up their post on the mound of the tank nearest to the grove, and about half a mile distant from it, and in the narrow space between them and the river two heavy guns under a native officer were placed. Behind the French guns was the division of Mir Mudin Khan, the one faithful general of the nabob. It consisted of five thousand horse and seven thousand foot. Extending in the arc of a circle towards the village of Plassey, were the troops of the three traitor generals, Rajah Dulab Ram, Yar Lutf Khan, and Meer Jaffier. Thus the English position was almost surrounded, and in advancing against the camp they would have to expose themselves to an attack in the rear by the troops of the conspirators. These generals had between them nearly thirty-eight thousand troops.

From the roof of the hunting-box Clive watched the progress of the enemy's movements. He saw at once that the position which they had taken up was one which would entail the absolute destruction of his force should he be defeated, and that this depended entirely upon the course taken by the conspirators. Against such a force as that opposed to him, if these remained faithful to their master, success could hardly be hoped for. However, it was now too late to retreat, and the only course was to show a bold front. Clive accordingly moved his troops out from the mango trees to a line with the hunting-box. The Europeans were formed in the centre with three field-pieces on each side. The native troops were on either flank. Two field-guns and the two howitzers were placed a little in advance of the hunting-box facing the French position on the mound.

At eight o'clock in the morning of the 23d of June, a memorable day in the annals of India, the preparations on both sides were complete, and St. Frais opened the battle by the discharge of one of his guns at the English. At the signal the whole of the artillery round the long curve opened their fire. The ten little guns replied to this overwhelming discharge, and for half an hour continued to play on the dense masses of the enemy. But however well they might be handled they could do little against the fire of the fifty pieces of cannon concentrated upon them. Had these been all served by European artillerymen the British force would have been speedily annihilated as they stood. The natives of India, however, were extremely clumsy gunners. They fired but slowly, and had the feeblest idea of elevation. Consequently their balls, for the most part, went far over the heads of the English, and the four field-guns of St. Frais did more execution that the fifty heavy pieces of the nabob. At the end of half an hour, however, Clive had lost thirty of his men, and determined to fall back to the mango grove.

Leaving a party in the hunting-box and in the brick kilns in front of it, in which the guns had been posted, to harass St. Frais battery with their musketry fire, he withdrew the rest of his force into the grove. Here they were in shelter, for it was surrounded by a high and thick bank. Behind this the men sat down, while parties set to work piercing holes through the banks as embrasures for the guns.

The enemy, on the retreat of the British within the grove, advanced with loud shouts of triumph, and bringing their guns closer, again opened fire. The British had by this time pierced the holes for their field-pieces, and these opened so vigorously that several of the enemy's cannon were disabled, numbers of their gunners killed, and some ammunition wagons blown up. On the other hand the English, now in perfect shelter, did not suffer at all, although the tops of the trees were cut off in all directions by the storm of cannon balls which swept through them.

Although the English fire was producing considerable loss among the enemy, this was as nothing in comparison to his enormous numbers, and at eleven o'clock Clive summoned his principal officers around him, and it was agreed that as Meer Jaffier and his associates, of whose position in the field they were ignorant, showed no signs of drawing off or of treachery to their master, it was impossible to risk an attack upon the front, since they would, as they pressed forward, be enveloped by the forces in the rear. It was determined, therefore, that unless any unexpected circumstance occurred they should hold their present position till nightfall, and should at midnight attack the enemy's camp.

A quarter of an hour later a tremendous tropical shower commenced, and for an hour the rain came down in torrents. Gradually the enemy's fire slackened. The English had tarpaulins to cover their ammunition, which, therefore, suffered no injury. The natives had no such coverings, and their powder was soon completely wetted by the deluge of rain. Mir Mudin Khan, knowing that his own guns had been rendered useless, believed that those of the English were in a similar condition, and leading out his cavalry, made a splendid charge down upon the grove.

The English were in readiness. As the cavalry swept up a flash of fire ran from a thousand muskets from the top of the embankments, while each of the field-guns sent its load of grape-shot through the embrasures into the throng of horsemen. The effect was decisive. The cavalry recoiled before the terrible fire, and rode back with their brave leader mortally wounded.

This blow was fatal to the fortunes of Suraja-u-Dowlah. When the news of the death of his brave and faithful general reached him he was struck with terror. He had long suspected Meer Jaffier of treachery, but he had now no one else to rely upon. Sending for that general he reminded him in touching terms of the benefits which he had received at the hands of his father, and conjured him to be faithful to him. Throwing his turban upon the ground, he said, "Jaffier, you must defend that turban."

Jaffier responded with assurances of his loyalty and sincerity, and promised to defend his sovereign with his life. Then riding off he at once despatched a messenger to Clive informing him of what had happened, and urging him to attack at once. As long as Mir Mudin Khan lived it is probable that Meer Jaffier was still undecided as to the part he should play. While that general lived it was possible, even probable, that the English would be defeated, even should the traitors take no part against them. His death, however, left the whole management of affairs in the hands of the three conspirators, and their course was now plain.

Scarcely had Meer Jaffier left the nabob than the unhappy young man, who was still under twenty years old, turned to Rajah Dulab Ram for counsel and advice. The traitor gave him counsel that led to his destruction. He told him that the English could not be attacked in their position, that his troops exposed to the fire of their guns were suffering heavily and losing heart, and he advised him at once to issue orders for them to fall back within their intrenchments. He also advised him to leave the field himself, and to retire to Moorshedabad, leaving it to his generals to annihilate the English should they venture to attack them. Suraja-u-Dowlah, at no time capable of thinking for himself, and now bewildered by the death of the general he knew to be faithful to him, and by his doubts as to the fidelity of the others, fell into the snare. He at once issued orders for the troops to retire within their intrenchments, and then mounting a swift camel, and accompanied by two thousand horsemen, he left the field and rode off to Moorshedabad.

The movement of retirement at once commenced. The three traitor generals drew off their troops, and those of Mir Mudin Khan also obeyed orders and fell back. St. Frais, however, refused to obey. He saw the ruin which would follow upon the retreat, and he pluckily continued his fire.

Clive, after the council had decided that nothing should be done till nightfall, had lain down in the hunting-box to snatch a little repose, his thoughts having kept him awake all night. Major Kilpatrick, seeing the retirement of the enemy, and that the French artillerymen remained unsupported on the mound, at once advanced with two hundred and fifty Europeans and two guns against it, sending word to Clive what he was doing. Clive, angry that any officer should have taken so important a step without consulting him, at once ran after the detachment and severely reprimanded Major Kilpatrick for moving from the grove without orders. Immediately, however, that he comprehended the whole position he recognized the wisdom of the course Kilpatrick had taken, and sent him back to the grove to order the whole force to advance.

St. Frais, seeing that he was entirely unsupported, fired a last shot, and then limbering up fell back in perfect order to the redoubt at the corner of the intrenchment, where he again posted his field-pieces in readiness for action.

Looking round the field Clive saw that two of the

divisions which formed the arc of the circle were marching back towards the intrenchments, but that the third, that on the left of their line, had wheeled round and was marching towards the rear of the grove. Not having received the letter which Meer Jaffier had written to him, he supposed that this movement indicated an intention to attack his baggage, and he therefore detached some European troops with a field-gun to check the advance. Upon the gun opening fire the enemy's division halted. It ceased its advance but continued apart from the rest of the enemy. In the mean time Clive had arrived upon the mound which St. Frais had left, and planting his guns there opened fire upon the enemy within their intrenchments.

The Indian soldiers and inferior officers, knowing nothing of the treachery of their chiefs, were indignant at being thus cannonaded in their intrenchments by a foe so inferior in strength, and horse, foot, and artillery poured out again from the intrenchments and attacked the British.

The battle now raged in earnest. Clive posted half his infantry and artillery on the mound of the tank nearest to the enemy's intrenchments, and the greater part of the rest on rising ground two hundred yards to the left of it, while he placed a hundred and sixty picked shots, Europeans and natives, behind the tank close to the intrenchments, with orders to keep up a continuous musketry fire upon the enemy as they sallied out.

The enemy fought bravely. St. Frais worked his guns unflinchingly at the redoubt, the infantry poured in volley after volley, the cavalry made desperate charges right up to the British lines. But they had no leader, and were fighting against men well commanded and confident in themselves. Clive observed that the division on the enemy's extreme left remained inactive and detached from the army, and it for the first time struck him that this was the division of Meer Jaffier. Relieved for the safety of his baggage, and from the attack which had hitherto threatened in his rear, he at once determined to carry the hill in advance of St. Frais's battery, and the redoubt occupied by the French leader. Strong columns were sent against each position. The hill was carried without opposition, and then so heavy and searching a fire was poured into the intrenched camp that the enemy began to fall back in utter confusion. St. Frais finding himself isolated and alone in the redoubt, as he had before been on the mound, was forced to retire.

At five o'clock the battle was over, and the camp of the Nabob of Bengal in the possession of the English. The British loss was trifling. Seven European and sixteen native soldiers were killed, thirteen Europeans and thirty-six natives wounded. It was one of the decisive battles of the world, for the fate of India hung in the balance. Had Clive been defeated and his force annihilated, as it must have been if beaten, the English would have been swept out of Bengal. The loss of that presidency would have had a decided effect on the struggle in Madras, where the British were with the greatest difficulty maintaining themselves against the French. Henceforth Bengal, the richest province in India, belonged to the English, for although for a time they were content to recognize Meer Jaffier and his successors as its nominal rulers, these were but puppets in their hands, and they were virtual masters of the province.

After the battle Meer Jaffier arrived. Conscious of his own double-dealing he by no means felt sure of the reception he should meet with. It suited Clive, however, to ignore the doubtful part he had played, and he was saluted as Nabob of Bengal. It would have been far better for him had he remained one of the great chiefs of Bengal. The enormous debt with which Clive and his colleagues had saddled him crushed him. The sum was so vast that it was only by imposing the most onerous taxation upon his people that he was enabled to pay it, and the discontent excited proved his destruction.

Omichund had no greater reason for satisfaction at the part which he had played in the ruin of his country. The fact that he had been deceived by the forged treaty was abruptly and brutally communicated to him and the blow broke his heart. He shortly afterward became insane and died before eighteen months were over.

Suraj-u-Dowlah fled to Moorshedabad, where the remnants of his army followed him. At first the nabob endeavored to secure their fidelity by issuing a considerable amount of pay. Then, overpowered by his fears of treachery, he sent off the ladies of the zenana and all his treasures on elephants, and a few hours afterwards he himself, accompanied by his favorite wife and a slave with a casket of his most valuable jewels, fled in disguise. A boat had been prepared and lay in readiness at the wharf of the palace. Rowing day and night against the stream the boat reached Rajmahal, ninety miles distant, on the night of the fourth day following his flight. Here the rowers were so knocked up by their exertions that it was impossible to proceed farther, and they took refuge in a deserted hut by the bank.

The following morning, however, they were seen by a fakir, whose ears the young tyrant had had cut off thirteen months previously, and this man, recognizing the nabob even in his disguise, at once took the news to Meer Jaffier's brother, who happened to reside in the town. The latter immediately sent a party of his retainers, who captured the nabob without difficulty. He was again placed in the boat and taken back to Moorshedabad, where he was led into the presence of

Meer Jaffier. The wretched young man implored the mercy of his triumphant successor, the man who owed station and rank and wealth to his grandfather, and who had nevertheless betrayed him to the English.

His entreaties so far moved Meer Jaffier that he was irresolute for a time as to the course he should pursue. His son, however, Mirav, a youth of about the same age as the deposed nabob, insisted that it was folly to show mercy, as Meer Jaffier would never be safe so long as Suraj-u-Dowlah remained alive, and his father at last assigned the captive to his keeping, knowing well what the result would be. In the night Suraj-u-Dowlah was murdered. His mangled remains were in the morning placed on an elephant and exposed to the gaze of the populace and soldiery.

Suraj-u-Dowlah was undoubtedly a profligate and rapacious tyrant. In the course of a few months he alienated his people and offended a great number of his most powerful chiefs. The war which he undertook against the English, although at the moment unprovoked, must still be regarded as a patriotic one, and had he not soiled his victory by the massacre of the prisoners, which he first permitted and then approved, the English would have had no just cause of complaint against him. From the day of the arrival of Clive at Calcutta he was doomed. It is certain that the nabob would not have remained faithful to his engagements when the danger which wrung the concessions from him had passed. Nevertheless the whole of the circumstances which followed the signature of the treaty, the manner in which the unhappy youth was alternately cajoled and bullied to his ruin, the loathsome treachery in which those around him engaged with the connivance of the English, and lastly the murder in cold blood, which Meer Jaffier, our creature, was allowed to perpetrate, rendered the whole transaction one of the blackest in the annals of English history.

CHAPTER XXIV.

MOUNTED INFANTRY.

A FEW days after Plassey Colonel Clive sent for Charlie.

"Marryat," he said, "I must send you back with two hundred men to Madras. The governor there has been writing to me by every ship which has come up the coast, begging me to move down with the bulk of the force as soon as affairs are a little settled here. That is out of the question. There are innumerable matters to be arranged. Meer Jaffier must be sustained. The French under Law must be driven entirely out of Bengal. The Dutch must be dealt with. Altogether I have need of every moment of my time, and of every man under my orders, for at least two years. However, I shall at once raise a Bengal native army, and so release the Sepoys of Madras. If there be any special and sore need I must, of course, denude myself here of troops to succor Madras; but I hope it will not come to that. In the mean time I propose that you shall take back two hundred of the Madras Europeans. Lawrence will be glad to have you, and your chances of fighting are greater there than they will be here. Bengal is overawed, and so long as I maintain the force I now have, it is unlikely in the extreme to rise; whereas battles and sieges, great and small, are the normal condition of Madras."

The next day Charlie, with two hundred European troops, marched down towards Calcutta. Clive had told him to select any officer he pleased to accompany him as second in command, and he chose Peters, who, seeing that there were likely to be far more exciting times in Madras than in Bengal at present, was very glad to accompany him. Three days after reaching Calcutta Charlie and his party embarked on board a ship, which conveyed them without adventure to Madras. The authorities were glad indeed of the reinforcement, for the country was disturbed from end to end. Since the departure of every available man for Calcutta the Company had been able to afford but little aid to Muhammud Ali, and the authority of the latter had dwindled to a mere shadow in the Carnatic. The Marattas made incursions in all directions. The minor chiefs revolted and refused to pay tribute, and many of them entered into alliance with the French. Disorder everywhere reigned in the Carnatic, and Trichinopoli was again the one place which Muhammud Ali held.

The evening after landing Charlie Marryat had a long chat with Colonel Lawrence, who, after explaining to him exactly the condition of affairs in the country, asked him to tell him frankly what command he would like to receive.

"I have thought for some time," Charlie said, "that the establishment of a small force of really efficient cavalry, trained to act as infantry also, would be invaluable. The Maratta horsemen, by their rapid movements, set our infantry in defiance, and the native horse of our allies are useless against them. I am convinced that two hundred horsemen, trained and drilled like our cavalry at home, would ride through any number of them. In a country like this, where every petty rajah has his castle, cavalry alone could, however, do little. They must be able to act as infantry, and should have a couple of little four-pounders to take about with them. A force like this would do more to keep order in the Carnatic than one composed of infantry alone of ten times its strength. It could act as a police force, call upon petty chiefs who refuse to pay their share of the revenue, restore order in disturbed places, and permit the peasants to carry on their agricultural work upon which the revenue of the Company depends, and altogether render valuable services. Among the soldiers who came down with me is a sergeant who was at one time a trooper in an English regiment. He exchanged to come out with the 39th to India, and has again exchanged into the Company's service. I would make him drill instructor, if you will give him a commission as ensign. Peters I should like as my second in command, and, if you approve of the plan, I should be very much obliged if you would get him his step as captain. He's a good officer, but has not had such luck as I have."

Colonel Lawrence was very much pleased at the idea, and gave Charlie full authority to carry it out. The work of enlistment at once commenced. Hossein made an excellent recruiting sergeant. He went into the native bazaars, and by telling of the exploits of Charlie at Ambur and Suwarndrug, and holding out bright prospects of the plunder which such a force would be likely to obtain, he succeeded in recruiting a hundred and fifty of his co-religionists. In those days fighting was a trade in India, and in addition to the restless spirits of the local communities, great numbers of the hardy natives of northern India, Afghans, Pathans, and others, were scattered over India, ever ready to enlist in the service of the highest bidder. Among such men as these Hossein had no difficulty in obtaining a hundred and fifty picked horsemen.

Charlie had determined that his force should consist

of four troops, each of fifty strong. Of these one would be composed of Europeans, and he was permitted to take this number from the party he had brought down. He had no difficulty in obtaining volunteers, for as soon as the nature of the force was known the men were eager to engage in it. To this troop the two little field-pieces would be committed.

A few days after the scheme had been sanctioned Ensign Anstey was at work drilling the recruits as cavalry. Charlie and Peters were instructed by him also in the drill and words of command, and were soon able to assist. Two months were spent in severe work, and at the end of that time the little regiment were able to execute all simple cavalry manœuvres with steadiness and regularity. The natives were all men who had lived on horseback from their youth, and therefore required no teaching to ride. They were also, at the end of that time, able to act as infantry with as much regularity as the ordinary Sepoys. When so engaged four horses were held by one man, so that a hundred and fifty men were available for fighting on foot. The work had been unusually severe but as the officers did not spare themselves, and Charlie had promised a present to each man of the troop when fit for service, they had worked with alacrity, and had taken great interest in learning their new duties. At the end of two months they were inspected by Colonel Lawrence and Governor Pigot, and both expressed their highest gratification and surprise at their efficiency, and anticipated great benefits would arise from the organization.

So urgent, indeed, was the necessity that something should be done for the restoration of order, that Charlie had with difficulty obtained the two months necessary to attain the degree of perfection which he deemed necessary. The day after the inspection the troop marched out from Madras. Ensign Anstey commanded the white troop, the other three were led by native officers. Captain Peters commanded the squadron composed of the white troop and one of the others. A Lieutenant Hallowes, whom Peters knew to be a hard-working and energetic officer, was at Charlie's request, appointed to the command of the other squadron. He himself commanded the whole.

They had been ordered in the first place to move to Arcot, which was held by a garrison of Muhammud Ali. The whole of the country round was greatly disturbed. French intrigues and the sight of the diminished power of the English had caused most of the minor chiefs in that neighborhood to throw off their allegiance. A body of Maratta horse were ravaging the country districts, and it was against these that Charlie determined in the first place to act. He had been permitted to have his own way in the clothing and arming of his force. Each man carried a musket, which had been shortened some six inches, and hung in slings from the saddle, the muzzle resting in a piece of leather, technically termed a bucket. The ammunition pouch was slung on the other side of the saddle, and could be fastened in an instant by two straps to the belts which the troopers wore round their waists. The men were dressed in brown, thick cotton cloth, called karkee. Round their black forage caps was wound a long length of blue and white cotton cloth, forming a turban, with the ends hanging down to protect the back of the neck and spine from the sun.

Having obtained news that the Maratta horse, two thousand strong, were pillaging at a distance of six miles from the town, Charlie set off the day following his arrival to meet them. The Marattas had notice of his coming; but hearing that the force consisted only of two hundred horse, they regarded it with contempt. When Charlie first came upon them they were in the open country, and seeing that they were prepared to attack him, he drew up his little force in two lines. The second line he ordered to dismount to act as infantry. The two guns were loaded with grape, and the men of the first line were drawn up at sufficient intervals to allow an infantryman to pass between each horse.

With shouts of anticipated triumph the Maratta horse swept down. The front line of English horsemen had screened the movements of those behind, and when the enemy were within fifty yards, Charlie gave the word. The troopers already sat musket in hand, and between each horse an infantry soldier now stepped forward, while towards each end the line opened and the two field-pieces were advanced. The Maratta horsemen were astonished at this sudden manœuvre, but, pressed by the mass from behind, they still continued their charge. When but fifteen yards from the English line, a stream of fire ran along this from end to end, every musket was emptied into the advancing force, while the guns on either flank swept them with grape. The effect was tremendous. Scarcely a man of the front line survived the fire, and the whole mass halted and recoiled in confusion. Before they could recover themselves another volley of shot and grape was fired into them. Then Charlie's infantry ran back, and the cavalry, closing up, dashed upon the foe, followed half a minute afterwards by the lately dismounted men of the other two troops, ten white soldiers alone remaining to work and guard the guns. The effect of the charge of these two hundred disciplined horse upon the already disorganized mob of Maratta horsemen was irresistible, and in a few minutes the Marattas were scattered and in full flight over the plain, pursued by the British cavalry, now broken up into eight half troops. The rout was complete, and in a very short time the last Maratta had fled, leaving behind them three hundred dead upon the plain. Greatly gratified with their success, and feeling confident now in their own powers, the British force returned to Arcot.

Charlie now determined to attack the fort of Vellore, which was regarded as impregnable. The town lay at the foot of some very steep and rugged hills, which were surmounted by three detached forts. The rajah, encouraged by the French, had renounced his allegiance to Muhammud Ali, and had declared himself independent. As, however, it was certain that he was prepared to give assistance to the French when they took the field against the English, Charlie determined to attack the place. The French had received large reinforcements, and had already captured many forts and strong places around Pondicherry. They were, however, awaiting the arrival of still larger forces, known to be on the way, before they made a decisive, and, as they hoped, final attack upon the English.

The rajah's army consisted of some fifteen hundred infantry and as many cavalry. These advanced to meet the English force. Charlie feigned a retreat as they came on, and retired to a village some three miles distant. The cavalry pursued at full speed, leaving the infantry behind. Upon reaching the village Charlie at once dismounted all his men, lined the inclosures, and received the enemy's cavalry, as they galloped up, with so heavy a fire that they speedily drew rein. After trying for some time to force the position they began to fall back, and the English force again mounted, dashed upon them and completed their defeat. The broken horsemen, as they rode across the plain, met their infantry advancing, and these, disheartened at the defeat of the cavalry, fell back in great haste, and abandoning the town, which was without fortification, retired at once to the forts commanding it. Charlie took possession of the town, and spent the next two days in reconnoitering the forts. The largest and nearest of these faced the right of the town. It was called Suzarow. The second, on an even steeper hill, was called Guzarow. The third, which lay some distance behind this, and was much smaller, was called Mortz Azur. Charlie determined to attempt in the first place to carry Guzarow, as in this, which was considered the most inaccessible, the rajah himself had taken up his position, having with him all his treasure. Charlie saw that it would be next to impossible with so small a force to carry it by a direct attack by the road which led to it, as this was completely covered by its guns. It appeared to him, however, that the rocks upon which it stood were by no means inaccessible.

He left twenty men to guard his guns, placed a guard of ten upon the road leading up to the fort, to prevent the inhabitants from sending up news of his intentions to the garrison, who had, with that of Suzarow, kept up a fire from their guns upon the town since his arrival there. The moon was not to rise until eleven o'clock, and at nine Charlie marched with a hundred and seventy men from the town. Making a considerable detour, he found himself, at half-past ten at the foot of the rocks, rising almost sheer from the upper part of the hill. He was well provided with ropes and ladders. The most perfect silence had been enjoined upon the men, and in the darkness the march had been unseen by the enemy. While waiting for the moon to rise the troopers all wound pieces of cloth, with which they had come provided, round their boots to prevent these from making a noise by slipping or stumbling on the rocks. When the moon rose the ascent of the rocks began at the point which Charlie had, after a close inspection through a telescope, judged to be most accessible. The toil was very severe. One by one the men climbed from ledge to ledge, some of the most active hill men from northern India leading the way, and aiding their comrades to follow them by lowering ropes, and placing ladders at the most inaccessible spots. All this time they were completely hidden from the observation of the garrison above.

At last the leaders of the party stood at the foot of the walls, which rose a few feet from the edge of the cliff. The operation had been performed almost noiselessly. The ammunition pouches had been left behind, each man carrying ten rounds in his belt. Every piece of metal had been carefully removed from their uniforms, the very buttons having been cut off, lest these should strike against the rocks, and the muskets had been swathed up in thick coverings. The men, as they gained the upper ridge, spread along at the foot of the walls until the whole body had gathered there. They could hear the voices of the sentries thirty feet above them, but these having no idea of the vicinity of an enemy, did not look over the edge of the wall. Indeed, the parapets of the Indian fortifications were always so high that it was only from projecting towers that the foot of the wall could be seen. When the English force were assembled, the ladders, which, like everything else, had been muffled, were placed against the walls, and headed by their officers, the troops ascended. The surprise was complete. Not until the leaders of the storming party stood upon the parapet was their presence perceived. The guards discharged their firelocks and fled hastily.

As soon as twenty men were collected on the wall Charlie took the command of these and hurried forward towards the gate. Hallowes was to lead the next party along the opposite direction, Peters was to form the rest up as they gained the wall, and to follow Charlie with fifty more, while Anstey was to hold the remainder in reserve, to be used as circumstances might demand. The resistance, however, was slight. Taken absolutely by surprise the enemy rushed out from their sleeping places. They were immediately fired upon from the walls. The greater part ran back into shelter, while some of the more determined, gathering together, made for the gate. But of this Charlie had already taken possession, and received them with so vigorous a fire that they speedily fell back. When the whole circuit of the walls was in his possession, Charlie took a hundred of his men and descended into the fort. Each building as he reached it was searched, and the garrison it contained made to come out and lay down their arms, and were then allowed to depart through the gate. Upon reaching the rajah's quarters he at once came out and surrendered himself. Two guns were discharged to inform the little body in the town of the complete success of the movement; and the guard on the road then fell back and joined the party with the guns.

Thus, without losing a man, the fort of Guzarow, regarded by the natives as being impregnable, was carried. Fifteen lacs of rupees were found in the treasury. Of these, in accordance with the rules of the service, half was set aside for the Company, the remainder became the property of the force. Of this half fell to the officers, in proportion to their rank, and the rest was divided among the men. The share of each trooper amounted to nearly two hundred pounds. Knowing how demoralizing the possession of such a sum would be, Charlie assembled his force next morning. He pointed out to them that as the greater part of the plunder was in silver, it would be impossible for them to carry it on their persons. He advised them, then, to allow the whole sum to remain in the treasury, to be forwarded under an escort to Madras, each soldier to receive an order for the amount of his share upon the treasury there. This was agreed to unanimously, and Charlie then turned his attention to the other forts.

The guns of Guzarow were turned against these, and a bombardment commenced. Suzarow, which extended partly down the slope, was much exposed to the fire from Guzarow, and, although no damage could be done to the walls at so great a distance, the garrison, suffering from the fire, and intimidated by the fall of Guzarow, lost heart. Large numbers deserted, and the governor, in the course of two days, thought it prudent to obey the orders which the rajah had, upon being made captive, sent to him to surrender. The next day the governor of Mortz Azur followed his example, and Vellore and its three strong forts were thus in the possession of the English.

At Vellore Charlie nearly lost one of his faithful followers. Early in the morning Hossein came into Charlie's room.

"Sahib," he said, "something is the matter with Tim."

"What is the matter?" Charlie said, sitting up in his bed.

"I do not know, sahib. When I went to him he did not move. He was wide awake and his eyes are staring. When I went beside him he shook his head a little and said, 'S-s-s-h.' He seems quite rigid, and is as pale as death."

Charlie leaped out and hurried to Tim. The latter was lying on the ground in the next room. He had carried off three or four cushions from the rajah's divan and had thrown these down, and had spread a rug over him. He lay on his back exactly as Hossein had described. As Charlie hurried up Tim again gave vent to the warning "S-s-s-h."

"What is the matter, Tim? What is the matter, my poor fellow?"

Tim made a slight motion with his head for his master to bend towards him. Charlie leant over him, and he whispered:

"There is a sarpent in bed with me."

"Are you quite sure, Tim?"

"He woke me with his cold touch," Tim whispered. "I felt him crawling against my foot, and now he is laying against my leg."

Charlie drew back for a minute and consulted with Hossein. "Lie quite still, Tim," he said, "and don't be afraid. We will try to kill him without his touching you; but even if he should bite you, with help ready at hand there will be no danger."

Charlie now procured two knives, the one a sharp surgical knife, from a case which he had brought, the other he placed in a charcoal fire, which one of the men speedily fanned until the blade had attained a white heat. Charlie had decided that if the snake bit Tim he would instantly make a deep cut through the line of the punctures of the fangs, cutting down as low as these could penetrate, and immediately cauterize it by placing the hot knife in the gash so made. Six men were called in with orders to seize Tim on the instant and hold his leg firm, to enable the operation to be performed. Two others were to occupy themselves with the snake. These were armed with sticks. Hossein now approached the bed, from which hitherto they had all kept well aloof. The snake, Tim said, lay against his leg, between the knee and the ankle, and the spot was marked by a slight elevation of the rug. Hossein drew his tulwar, examined the edge to see that nothing had blunted its razor-like keenness, and then took his stand at the foot of the bed. Twice he raised his weapon, and then let it fall with a drawing motion. The keen blade cut through the rug as if it had been pasteboard, and at the same instant Tim sprang from the other side of the bed, and fainted in the arms of the men. Hossein threw off the rug, and there, severed in pieces, lay the writhing body of a huge cobra. Tim soon recovered under the administration of water sprinkled in his face, and brandy poured down his throat. But he was some time ere he thoroughly recovered from the effects of the trying ordeal through which he had passed. Many of the buildings in the fort were in a very bad condition, and Charlie had several of the most dilapidated destroyed, finding in their walls several colonies of cobras, which were all killed by the troops.

CHAPTER XXV.

BESIEGED IN A PAGODA.

A FEW days later Charlie received a message from the Rajah of Permacoil, saying that he was besieged by a strong native force aided by the French. He at once moved his force to his assistance. He found that the besiegers, among whom were two hundred French troops, were too strong to be attacked. He therefore established himself in their rear, attacked and captured convoys and prevented the country people from bringing in provisions. Several times the besieging infantry advanced against him, but before these he at once fell back, only to return as soon as they retired to their camp. Whenever their horse ventured out against him, he beat them back with considerable loss.

Ten days after his arrival, the enemy, finding it impossible to maintain themselves in the face of so active an enemy, and suffering greatly from want of provisions, raised the siege and fell back. As soon as they had drawn off Charlie entered the fort. The rajah received him with the greatest warmth. He was, however, much distressed at the capture of a hill fort at some distance from Permacoil. In this he had stowed his wives and treasure, thinking that it would be unmolested. The French, however, had, just before Charlie's arrival, detached a strong force with some guns and these had captured the place. The force which had accomplished this had, he now heard, marched to Trinavody, a fort and town thirty miles away, upon the road by which the force which had besieged the town was retiring. The treasure was a considerable one, amounting to seven lacs of rupees, and as the rajah stated his willingness that the troops should take possession of this if they could but rescue his women, Charlie at once determined to attempt the feat. The main body of the enemy would not reach the place until the afternoon of the following day. Charlie soon collected his men, and making a detour through the country arrived next morning within a mile of Trinavody.

The town was a small one, and the fort one of the ordinary native forts, built in a parallelogram with flanking towers. The place, however, contained a very large and solidly built pagoda or temple. It was surrounded by a wall forty feet high, and at the gateway stood an immense tower with terraces rising one above the other. Capturing a native, Charlie learnt that the fort was tenanted only by the troops of the native rajah of the place, the French detachment being encamped in the pagoda. He at once rode forward with his troops, dashed through the native town, and in through the wide gateway of the tower into the courtyard within. Beyond two or three straggling shots from the sentries he had so far encountered no opposition, and the native troops in the courtyard, thrown into wild confusion by this sudden appearance of a hostile force, threw down their arms and cried for mercy. From the temple within, however, the French infantry, a hundred strong, opened a brisk fire.

Charlie sent some of his men on to the tower, whence their fire commanded the flat roof of the temple, and these speedily drove the defenders from that post. The field-pieces were unlimbered and directed towards the gate of the inner temple, while a

CHARLIE SURPRISED BY THE FRENCH AT TRINAVODY.

musketry fire was kept up against every window and loophole in the building. The gate gave way after a few shots had been fired, and Charlie led his party to the assault. The French defended themselves bravely, but they were outnumbered, and were driven fighting from room to room until the survivors laid down their arms. The assault, however, had cost the British a loss of twenty-five men.

The Rajah of Permacoil's treasure and his women fell into the hands of the captors. Charlie ordered the chests to be brought down and placed in bullock wagons. Just as he was about to order his men, who were scattered through the temple looting, to form up, he heard a shout from the tower, and looking up saw one of his men there gesticulating wildly. He ran up the tower, and on reaching the first terrace saw to his surprise the whole of the force which he believed to be fifteen miles distant already entering the town. The French officer in command, knowing the activity and dash of his opponent, and fearing that an attempt might be made to carry Trinavody and recapture the rajah's treasure, had marched all night. When within a mile of the place he heard what had happened, and at once pushed forward.

Charlie saw that already his retreat was cut off, and running to the edge of the terrace shouted to Peters to hurry out with all the men already in the courtyard, to occupy the houses outside the gate, and to keep back the advancing enemy. Summoning another party to the tower, four guns upon the terrace were at once loaded, and these opened upon the head of the enemy's column as they entered the street leading to the temple. In a short time a brisk fight began. The enemy planted guns to bear upon the tower. The cannon of the fort joined in the assault, the infantry pressed forward through the houses and inclosures to the temple and were soon engaged with the men under

Captain Peters, while the guns and musketry from the tower also opened upon them.

Having seen that the preparations to repulse an immediate attack were complete, Charlie again ran down to the courtyard. The weak point of the defences was the gateway. This was fifty feet wide and unprovided with gates, and Charlie at once set a strong party to work to form a barricade across it. For some hours the party outside the gates maintained their position, but they were gradually driven back, and towards evening, by Charlie's orders, they retired within the temple.

The barricade was now eight feet high, the face was formed of large slabs of stone piled one upon another backed by a considerable thickness of earthwork. This, however, although capable of resisting a sudden rush of infantry, would, Charlie knew, be incapable of resisting artillery. During the night he divided his men in two parties, which alternately slept and worked at the inner defences which he had designed. These consisted of two walls running from each side of the gateway to the temple. They were placed a few feet farther back than the edge of the gateway, so that an enemy advancing to the storm would not see them until within the gate. These walls he intended to be eight feet high, and to be backed with earth four feet high, so as to form a bank on which the defenders could stand and fire into the space between them. To obtain materials he pulled down several buildings forming a part of the temple. The distance from the gateway to the temple was fifty yards, and although the men worked without ceasing the wall had made but little progress when daylight dawned. During the night Charlie lowered one of his men from the wall farthest from the enemy with instructions to make his way as fast as possible to Madras to ask for succor.

In the morning Charlie found that the enemy had

on their side been also busy. A house which faced the end of the street leading to the temple had been pulled down and a battery of four guns erected there. As soon as it was light the combat began. The enemy had sixteen pieces of artillery besides those on the fort, and while the four guns in front played unceasingly upon the barricade across the gateway, the others cannonaded the tower, whence the English guns kept up a fire on the battery in front. So well were these directed, and so heavy was the musketry, that the enemy's guns were several times silenced and the artillerymen driven from them.

Behind the barricade a working party threw up fresh earth, to strengthen the part most shaken by the enemy's fire, and then set to work to form a similar barricade in a line with the back of the gateway. This was completed by nightfall, by which time the enemy's guns had completely shattered the stone facing of the outer barricade, rendering it possible for it to be carried with a rush. As from the windows of the houses they could see the new work behind it, they would, Charlie judged, not attempt an assault until this also was destroyed. During the night large quantities of fresh earth were piled on the outer barricade, which was now useful as forming a screen to that behind it from the guns. All night the work at the parallel walls continued, and by morning these had reached a height of three feet.

During the next two days the fight continued without much advantage on either side. Each day the enemy's guns shattered the outer barricade, but this was as regularly repaired at night in spite of the heavy artillery and matchlock fire which they kept up towards the spot. On the fourth day the enemy pulled down a house standing just in the rear of their battery, and Charlie found that behind it they had erected another.

It was a solidly built work of fifteen feet in height, and the enemy must have labored continuously at it every night. It had a strong and high parapet of sand-bags protecting the gunners from the musketry fire of the tower. The muzzles of four guns projected through embrasures which had been left for them, and these opened fire over the heads of the gunners in the lower battery.

In spite of the efforts of the besieged the enemy kept up so heavy a fire that by the afternoon the inner as well as the outer barricade was knocked to pieces. By this time, however, the inner walls were completed, and the English awaited the storm with confidence. The doorway of the temple had been closed and blocked up behind, but the doors had been shattered to pieces by the shot which had passed through the gateway, and the entrance now stood open. Inside the temple, out of the line of fire, Charlie had the two little field-pieces, each crammed to the muzzle with bullets, placed in readiness to fire. The lower floor of the tower had been pierced above the gateway, and here two huge caldrons filled with boiling lead, stripped from the roof, stood ready for action.

At three in the afternoon, after a furious cannonade, the fire of the enemy's battery suddenly ceased. They had formed communications between the houses on either side of the street, and at the signal the troops poured out from these in large bodies and rushed to the assault. The guns from the tower, which had been awaiting the moment, poured showers of grape among them, but, believing that the temple now lay at their mercy, the enemy did not hesitate but rushed at the gateway. Not a shot was fired as they entered. Scrambling over the remains of the two barricades the enemy poured with exulting shouts into the courtyard. Then those in front hesitated. On either hand, as far as the doorway of the temple, extended a massive wall eight feet high, roughly built certainly, but far too strong to be battered down, too steep to be scaled. They would have retreated, but they were driven forward by the mass which poured in through the gateway behind them; and seeing that their only safety was in victory they pressed forward again.

Not a defender showed himself until the head of the column had reached a point two-thirds of the distance across the courtyard. Then suddenly on either side the wall was lined by the British, who at once opened a tremendous fire on the mass below. At the same moment the guns were run into the doorway and poured their contents into the struggling mass. Pent up between the walls, unable to return the fire poured down upon them, with lanes torn through them by the discharge of the cannon, the greater portion of the mass strove to turn and retire. The officer in command, a gallant Frenchman, called upon the survivors of the fifty French infantry who had led the attack to follow him, and rushed forward upon the guns. Here, however, Charlie had posted his Europeans, and these, swarming out from the temple, poured a volley into the advancing French and then charged them with the bayonet.

The pressure from behind had now ceased. Streams of boiling lead poured through the holes above the archway had effectually checked the advance, and through this molten shower the shattered remnants of the assaulting column now fled for their lives, leaving two hundred and fifty of their best men dead behind them. As the last of the column issued out the guns of the battery again angrily opened fire. As Charlie had anticipated, the enemy, finding how strong were the inner defences, abandoned all further idea of attack by the gateway; and leaving only two guns there to prevent a sortie, placed their whole artillery on the western side of the pagoda, and opened fire to prevent a breach there.

For a week the siege continued, and then Charlie determined to evacuate the place. The rajah's treasure was made up into small sacks which were fastened to the horse's croups. Had it not been for these animals he would have defended the place to the last, confident in his power to devise fresh means to repel fresh assaults. The store of forage, however, collected by the enemy for their own use in the temple was now exhausted. Charlie directed Peters with twenty men to sally out from the gate at midnight, to enter the nearest house on the right hand side, and to follow the communications made by the enemy before the assault until they came to the end of the street. Lieutenant Hallowes with a similar party was to take the left side. If they found any guards within the houses they were to overpower these, and rushing straight on, to attack the battery and spike the guns. Should they find the houses deserted they were to gather in the houses nearest the battery, when Peters was to fire his pistol as a signal to Hallowes and both parties were to attack the battery. One of the inner walls had been pulled down, and the main body of the force, having the wounded and the ladies of the rajah's zenana in their centre, were to sally out the instant the guns were taken.

The plan was carried out with the greatest success. The houses on both sides of the street were found to be deserted, and as Peters fired his pistol, the party dashed at the flanks of the battery. The French gunners leaped to their feet, and, believing that they were attacked in front, discharged their cannon. The grape-shot swept along the empty street and through the gateway, and Charlie, leading one of the troops, at once dashed down the street. At their first rush Peters and Hallowes had carried the battery, cutting down the gunners. Immediately behind, however, the enemy had posted a support several hundred strong, and these speedily advanced to recover the battery. Leaving their horses in charge of a small party, Charlie dismounted his men and joined Peters, and his fire quickly checked the assault. In the mean time the rest of the defenders of the temple rode down the street; and leaving a few men with the horses of Peters' and Hallowes' detachments, rode out into the open country. After driving back his assailants Charlie led his party back to their horses, mounted them, and speedily rejoined the main body. An hour later they were well on their way towards Permacoil, which they reached next day.

The rajah was delighted at recovering his family. The treasure was divided, and the portion belonging to the troops was, with the Company's share, sent down under a strong escort to Madras.

For a considerable time Charlie's force were occupied with small undertakings. Lally had now arrived from France and had taken the command. He had at his orders a European force considerably exceeding any that had hitherto been gathered in India, and he boasted that he was going to capture Madras and drive the English out of India. Nothing could have been more unfortunate for the French than the choice of such a man, and his appointment was destined to give the last blow to French influence in India, as the supercession of Dupleix had given the first. M. Lally had one virtue, he was personally brave; but he was arrogant, passionate and jealous. He had no capacity whatever for either awing or conciliating those with whom he came in contact. He treated the natives with open contempt, and was soon as much hated by them as by his own soldiers. His first step had been to order Bussy down from Hyderabad with the whole of his force.

Bussy, a man of great genius, of extreme tact, of perfect knowledge of the Indian character, had for eight years maintained French influence supreme at that court, and had acquired for France the Northern Sirkars, a splendid and most valuable province on the sea-coast north of Madras. Salabut Jung, the ruler of Hyderabad, the protégé of the French, heard with dismay the order which Bussy had received. To Bussy himself the blow was a heavy one, and he saw that his departure would entail the ruin of the edifice of French influence, which he had built up by so many years of thought and toil. However, he obeyed at once, and marched with two hundred and fifty Europeans and five hundred native troops into the Sirkars. He made over the charge of this treaty to the Marquis de Conflans, whom although but just arrived from Europe and entirely new to Indian affairs, Count de Lally had sent to replace M. Moracin, who had for years ably managed the province. He then marched with his troops to join the main army under Count de Lally. This force having taken Fort St. David had operated against Tanjore, where it had suffered a repulse. The news of this reached the Northern Sirkars soon after the departure of Bussy, and Anandraz, the most powerful chief of the country, rose in rebellion, and sent a messenger to Calcutta begging the assistance of the English to drive out the French.

While the rest of the Bengal council, seeing that Bengal was at the time threatened with invasion from the north and menaced with troubles within, considered that it would be an act little short of madness to send troops at a time when they could be so little spared to assist a chief, who, even from his own accounts, was only able to raise three thousand irregular followers, Clive thought otherwise. He saw the great value of the Northern Sirkars, whose possession would complete the line of British territory along the sea-coast from Calcutta down to Madras. He saw, too, that a movement here would effect a diversion in favor of Madras. The situation there appeared very serious, and he could spare no troops which would suffice to turn the scale. But even should Madras be lost the gain of the Northern Sirkars would almost compensate for the disaster. Having gained the council to his views he sent Lieutenant-Colonel Forde, who commanded the Company's troops in Bengal, with five hundred Europeans, two thousand natives, and six six-pounders by sea to Vizagapatam, a port which Anandraz had seized. These landed on the 20th of October, 1758.

Had Conflans been an efficient officer he could have crushed Anandraz long before the arrival of the English. He had under his orders a force composed of five hundred European troops, men trained by Bussy and accustomed to victory, four thousand native troops, and a brigade of artillery. Instead of marching at once to crush the rebellion, he sent messenger after messenger to Lally begging for assistance. It was only when he heard from Lally that he had directed Moracin with three hundred European troops to support him that he moved against Anandraz. His opportunity had, however, slipped from his hands. He had thrown away six weeks, and when upon the march the news reached him of the landing of the English, he took up the very strong position within sight of the fort Peddapur and intrenched himself there.

Clive had sent to Madras the news that he was despatching Colonel Forde to the Sirkars, and begged that any body of troops who might be available might be forwarded. Charlie's corps had already been recalled towards Madras to keep the bodies of French who were converging in that direction at a distance as long as possible, so as to allow the victualling of

Madras to go on uninterrupted. Mr. Pigot now instructed Charlie to hand over the command of that force to Peters, and with fifty men to make his way north and to effect a junction with Forde, who was entirely deficient in cavalry. Avoiding the French force, Charlie reached Vizagapatam upon the 2d of December, and found that Forde had marched on the previous day. He started at once, and on the evening of the 3d came up to Forde, who had arrived in sight of the French position.

Charlie had already made the acquaintance of Colonel Forde in Bengal, and Forde was glad to obtain the assistance and advice of an officer who had seen so much service. An hour after arriving Charlie rode out with his commander and reconnoitred the French position, which was, they concluded, too strong to be attacked. In point of numbers the forces were about even. Conflans had, in addition to his five hundred Europeans, six thousand native infantry, five hundred native cavalry, and thirty guns. Forde had four hundred and seventy Europeans, one thousand nine hundred Sepoys, and six guns. Anandraz had forty Europeans, five thousand infantry, five hundred horsemen, and four guns. These five thousand men were, however, a mere ragged mob, of whom very few had fire-arms, and the rest were armed with bows and arrows. His horsemen were equally worthless, and Forde could only rely upon the troops he had brought with him from Calcutta and the troop of fifty natives under Charlie Marryat.

Finding that the French position was too strong to be attacked, Forde fell back to a strong position at Chambol, a village nearly four miles from the French camp. Here for four days the two armies remained watching each other, the leaders of both sides considering that the position of the other was too strong to be attacked.

CHAPTER XXVI.

THE SIEGE OF MADRAS.

AT last, weary of inactivity, the Marquis de Conflans and Colonel Forde arrived simultaneously, on the 8th of December, at a determination to bring matters to a crisis. Conflans had heard from a deserter that Forde had omitted to occupy a mound which, at a short distance from his camp, commanded the position. He determined to seize this during the night, and to open fire with his guns, and that his main army should take advantage of the confusion which the sudden attack would occasion to fall upon the English. Forde on his part had determined to march at four o'clock in the morning to a village named Condore, three miles distant, whence he could threaten the French flank. Ignorant of each other's intentions the English and French left their camps at night. Forde marched at a quarter past four, as arranged with Anandraz; but the rajah and his people, with the usual native aversion to punctuality, remained quietly asleep, and a few minutes after daybreak they were roughly awakened by a deadly fire poured by six guns into the camp. The rajah sent messenger after messenger to Forde urging him to return, and he himself with his frightened army hurried towards Condore. Forde had, indeed, retraced his steps immediately he heard the fire of the guns, and soon met the rajah's rabble in full flight, and uniting with them marched back to Condore.

Conflans supposed that the fire of his guns had driven the whole of his opponents in a panic from Chambol, and determining to take advantage of the confusion marched with his force against them. Forde at once prepared for the battle. In the centre he placed the English, including the rajah's forty Europeans. Next to these, on either side, he placed his Sepoys, and posted the troops of Anandraz on the right and left flanks. He then advanced towards the enemy. The French guns opened fire. Forde halted. In the position in which he found himself his centre occupied a field of Indian corn, so high that they were concealed from the enemy. Conflans had moved towards the English left, with the intention apparently of turning that flank, and after the artillery battle on both sides had continued for forty minutes he ordered his troops to advance.

In Madras both the English and French dress their Sepoys in white. In Bengal, however, since the raising of Sepoy regiments after the recapture of Calcutta the English had clothed them in red. Conflans, therefore, thought that the force he was about to attack was the English contingent, and that if he could defeat this the rout of his enemy would be secured. The French advanced with great rapidity and attacked the Sepoys in front and flank so vigorously that they broke in disorder. The rajah's troops fled instantly, and in spite of the exhortations of Forde the Sepoys presently followed their example, and fled with the rajah's troops to Chambol pursued by the enemy's horse. They would have suffered even more severely than they did in this pursuit had not Charlie Marryat launched his little squadron at the enemy's horse. Keeping his men well together he made repeated charges, several times riding through and through them, until at last they desisted from the pursuit, and forming in a compact body fell back towards the field of battle, Charlie who had already lost twelve men, not thinking it prudent again to attack so strong a force.

Conflans' easy success over the Sepoys was fatal to him. Believing that he had defeated the English he gave orders to several companies of the French troops to press on in pursuit without delay. They started off in hot speed, proceeding without much order or regularity, when they were suddenly confronted by the whole line of English troops in solid order advancing from the high corn to take the place lately occupied by the Sepoys. In vain the scattered and surprised companies of the French endeavored to re-form and make head against them. So heavy was the fire of musketry opened by the British line, immediately they had taken up their position, that the French broke their ranks and ran back as fast as they could to regain their guns, which were fully half a mile in the rear.

In the mean time the French Sepoys on their left had been gradually driving back the English right; but Forde, disregarding this, pressed forward in hot pursuit of the French with his English, behind whom the greater portion of the beaten Sepoys had already rallied. Keeping his men well together he advanced at the fullest speed, following so closely upon the enemy that the latter had only time to fire one or two rounds with their thirteen guns before the English were upon them. The French, who had already lost heart by the serious check which had befallen them, were unable to stand the shock, and at once retreated, leaving their guns behind them.

As Forde had anticipated, the French Sepoys, seeing their centre and right defeated, desisted from their attack on the English right and fell back upon their camp. The English Sepoys at once marched forward and joined Forde's force. The rajah's troops, however, the whole of whom had fled, remained cowering in the shelter of a large dry tank. Forde did not wait for them, but, leaving his guns behind him, pressed forward an hour after the defeat of the French against their camp. To reach this he had to pass along a narrow valley commanded by the French heavy guns. These opened fire, but the English pressed forward without wavering. The defenders, not yet recovered from the effects of their defeat in the plain, at once gave way, and retreated in the utmost confusion towards Rajahmahendri. Had the cavalry of Anandraz been at hand to follow up the advantage great numbers might have been captured. As it was, Charlie Marryat with his little force harassed them for some miles, but was unable to effect any serious damage on so strong a body. The English captured thirty-two pieces of cannon, and all the stores, ammunition, and tents of the French.

Forde at once despatched a battalion of Sepoys under Captain Knox in pursuit, and this officer pressed on so vigorously that he approached Rajahmahendri the same evening. Two more native battalions reached Knox during the night.

So thoroughly dispirited were the enemy that the sight of the red-coated Sepoys of Knox, whom they could not distinguish from English, induced them to abandon Rajahmahendri in all haste, although it contained a strong mud fort with several guns. The Godavery is two miles wide, and all night the passage of the river in boats continued, and when at daybreak next morning Knox broke into the town he found fifteen Europeans still on the banks expecting a returning boat. These he captured; and seeing upon the opposite bank a party about to disembark guns and stores from another boat, he opened fire from the guns of the fort towards it, and although the shot could scarcely reach half-way across the river, such was the terror of the enemy that they forsook the boat and fled. Knox at once sent a boat across and brought back that containing the guns. The French retreated to Masulipatam, the capital of the province, a port which rivalled Madras in its commerce. Forde determined to follow them there, but he was hindered by want of money to pay his troops. This the Rajah Anandraz, who had promised to supply money, now excited and arrogant by the victory which he had done nothing towards gaining, refused to supply, and many weeks were spent in negotiations before Forde was able to move forward.

Charlie was no longer with him. The very day before the fight of Condore letters had arrived from Madras stating the urgency of the position there, and upon the night after the battle Colonel Forde ordered Charlie to return to aid in the defence of that city, before which the French had appeared on the 29th of November. Several skirmishes took place outside the city, and the English then retired within the fort. The force consisted of sixteen hundred white troops and two thousand three hundred Sepoys. The nabob, who had also retired into the town, had two hundred horse and a huge retinue of attendants.

On the morning of the 14th the French occupied the town, and the next day the English made a sortie with six hundred men. These, for a while, drove the French before them through the streets of Madras; but as the French gradually rallied, the fire upon the English was so heavy that the sortie was repulsed with a loss of two hundred soldiers and six officers, killed, wounded, and prisoners. The French loss had been about the same. Had not a large quantity of the French troops broken into the wine-stores on their arrival and drunk to a point of intoxication it is probable that none of the British party would have returned to the fort. The sortie had, however, the effect that Saubinet, one of the best of the French officers, was killed, and Count D'Estaign, an able general, taken prisoner. For some time the siege proceeded slowly, the French waiting for the arrival of their siege artillery by ship from Pondicherry.

The fort of Madras was now a far more formidable post than it had been when the French before captured it. In the year 1743 Mr. Smith, an engineer, had marked out the lines for a considerable increase in the fortifications. The ditch was dug and faced with brick, but on account of the expense nothing further had been done. The French had added somewhat to the fortifications during their stay there in 1750. Nothing had been done by the English when they recovered the town until the news of the preparations which the French were making for the siege of the place had been received. Four thousand natives were then set to work, and these in eighteen months had completed the fortifications, as designed by Mr. Smith, just before the arrival of the French.

The latter determined to attack from the northern side. Here the fort was protected by a demi-bastion next to the sea, and by the Royal Bastion, the wall between the two being covered by a work known as the North Ravelin. The defence was also strengthened by the fire of the north-west lunette and Pigot's Bastion. Against these the French threw up four batteries. Lally's Battery, erected by the regiment of that name, was on the sea-shore directly facing the demi-bastion. To its right was the Burying-ground Battery, facing the Royal Bastion. Against the western face of this position the French regiment of Lorraine erected a strong work, while farther round to the west, on a rising ground, they threw up a battery called the Hospital Battery, which kept up a cross-fire on the English position. To prevent the French from pressing forward along the strip of shore between the fort and the sea, the English erected a strong stockade, behind which was a battery called the Fascine Battery.

A few days after the siege began it was found that the numbers crowded up in the fort could scarcely be accommodated, and the rajah was, therefore, invited to leave by sea, on board a ship which would land him at the Dutch settlement of Negapatam, whence he might journey through the Tanjore country to Trichinopoli. This proposal he willingly accepted, and embarked with his wife, women, and children, his other followers leaving by the land side opposite to that invested by the French. Thus the garrison were relieved of the embarrassment and consumption of food caused by four hundred men and two hundred horse.

Charlie rode with his troop without interruption through the country, avoiding all bodies of the enemy until he reached the sea fifteen miles north of Madras. Here he hired a native boat, and leaving the troops under the command of Ensign Anstey, sailed for Madras in order to inform the garrison of Forde's victory over the French, and to concert with the governor as to the measures which he wished him to carry out to harass the enemy. He was accompanied only by Tim and Hossein. The wind was fair, and starting an hour before sunset the boat ran into Madras roads two hours later. The *Harlem*, which had that day arrived with artillery for the French from Pondicherry, fired at the little craft, and the native boatmen were about to turn the head of their craft northward again. Charlie, however, drew his pistol, and Hossein took his place with his drawn tulwar by the helmsman. The boatmen, thereupon, again continued their course, and though several shots fell near them they escaped untouched, and anchored just outside the surf abreast of the fort. The English had taken the precaution of erecting a number of huts under the walls of the fort for the boatmen, in order to be able to communicate with any ship arriving, or to send messages in or out. As soon as the boat anchored a catamaran put out and brought Charlie and his followers to shore. There was great joy at the receipt of his news, and the guns of the fort fired twenty-one shots towards the enemy in honor of the victory.

Governor Pigot was in general command of the defence, having under him Colonel Lawrence in command of the troops. The latter, after inquiring from Charlie the character of the officer he had left in command of his troop, and finding that he was able and energetic, requested Charlie to send orders to him to join either the force under Captain Preston at Chingalpatt, or that of a native leader, Mahommed Issoof, both of whom were ravaging and destroying the country about Conjeveram, whence the French besieging Madras drew most of their provisions. Charlie himself was requested to remain in the fort, where his experience in sieges would render him of great value.

At daybreak on the 2d of January the Lorraine and Lally Batteries opened fire. The English guns, however, proved superior in weight and number, dismounted two of the cannon, and silenced the others. The French mortars continued to throw heavy shell into the fort, and that night most of the European women and children were sent away in native boats. The French batteries, finding the superiority of the English fire, ceased firing until the 6th, when seven guns and six large mortars from Lally's Battery, and eight guns and two mortars from the Lorraine Battery opened upon the town. The cannonade now continued without intermission, but the enemy gained but little advantage. Every day, however, added to their strength, as fresh vessels with artillery continued to arrive from Pondicherry. They were now pushing their approaches from Lally's Battery towards the demi-bastion. The losses on the part of the besieged were considerable, many being killed and wounded each day. This continued to the end of the month in spite of many gallant sorties by parties of the besiegers, who repeatedly killed and drove out the working parties in the head of the French trenches. These progressed steadily and reached to the outworks of the demi-bastion.

On the 25th the *Shaftesbury*, one of the Company's trading vessels, commanded by Captain Inglis, was seen approaching. The five French ships hoisted English colors. A catamaran was sent out to warn her, and at nine o'clock in the evening she came to anchor. She had on board only some invalids, but brought the welcome news that three other ships with troops would soon be up. She had on board, too, thirty-seven chests of silver and many military stores, among them hand-grenades and large shell, which were most welcome to the garrison, who had nearly expended their supply. The native boats went off from the fort and brought on shore the ammunition and stores. In the afternoon the *Shaftesbury* was attacked by the two French ships the *Bristol* and the *Harlem*. She fought them for two hours, and then sailed in and anchored again near the fort. The French ships lay off at a distance, and these and one of their batteries played upon the *Shaftesbury* after she had anchored, and continued to do so for the next three days.

Many of the guns of the fort were dismounted by the artillery fire, which had continued with scarcely any intermission for a month. The parapets of the ramparts were in many places beaten down, and the walls exposed to the enemy's fire greatly damaged. The enemy now opened their breaching battery close to the works, and on the 7th two breaches had been effected, and Lally ordered his principal engineer and artillery officers to give their opinion as to the practicability of an assault. These, however, considered that the assault would have no prospect of success, as the guns commanding the ditch were still uninjured, and the palisades which stormers must climb over before reaching the breach untouched. So heavy a cross-fire could be brought to bear by the besieged upon an assaulting column that it would be swept away before it could mount the breach. These officers added their opinion that, considering the number of men defending the fort in comparison with those attacking it, final success could not be looked for, and further prosecution of the works would only entail a useless loss of life.

On the 9th of February the French attacked Mahommed Issoof's men and those of Captain Preston, the whole under the command of Major Calliaud, who had come up from Trichinopoli and had taken station three miles in the rear of the French position. The greater part of the natives, as usual, behaved badly, but Calliaud with the artillery and a few Sepoys defended himself till nightfall and then drew off.

For the next week the French continued to fire, and their approaches were pushed on. Several sorties were made, but matters remained unchanged until the 14th, when six English ships were seen standing into the roads, and that night the French drew out from their trenches and retreated. The next morning six hundred troops landed from the ships, and the garrison who had so stoutly resisted the assaults made upon them for forty-two days, sallied out to inspect the enemy's works. Fifty-two cannon were left in them, and so great was the hurry with which the French retreated that they left forty-four sick in the hospital behind. The fort fired during the siege 26,554 rounds from their cannon, 7502 shells, threw 1990 hand-grenades, and expended 200,000 musketry cartridges. Thirty pieces of cannon and five mortars had been dismounted during the siege. Of the Europeans the loss in killed, wounded, and prisoners, was five hundred and seventy-nine. Three hundred and twenty-two Sepoys were killed and wounded, and four hundred and forty deserted during the siege.

In spite of the resolution with which the French had pushed the siege it was from the first destined to failure. The garrison were well provisioned, had great stores of ammunition, and plenty of spare cannon to replace those disabled or dismounted. The works were strong and the garrison not greatly inferior in number to the besiegers. The French, on the other hand, had to bring their artillery, ammunition and stores by water from Pondicherry, and the activity of the English parties in their rear rendered it extremely difficult for them to receive supplies of food by land. Lally had disgusted even the French officers and soldiers by his arrogance and passionate temper, while by the Sepoys he was absolutely hated.

During the siege Charlie had been most active in the defence. Colonel Lawrence had assigned no special post to him, but used him as what would now be called his chief of the staff. He was ever where the fire was thickest, encouraging the men and during the intervals of comparative cessation of fire he went about the fort seeing to the comforts of the men in their quarters, to the issue of stores, and other matters. Upon the very morning after the French had withdrawn he asked to be allowed to rejoin his troop, which was with Major Calliaud, and at once started to rejoin Colonel Forde. He wished to take the whole of his corps with him; but Colonel Lawrence considered that these would be of extreme use in following up the French and in subsequent operations, as cavalry was an arm in which the English were greatly deficient.

Colonel Forde had been terribly delayed by the conduct of Rajah Anandraz, and the delay enabled the French again to recover heart. He was not able to move forward until the 1st of March. On the 6th he arrived before Masulipatam, and the following day Charlie joined him with his troop. The fort of Masulipatam stood in an extremely defensible position. It was surrounded by a swamp on three sides. The other face rested on the river. From the land side it was only approachable by a causeway across the

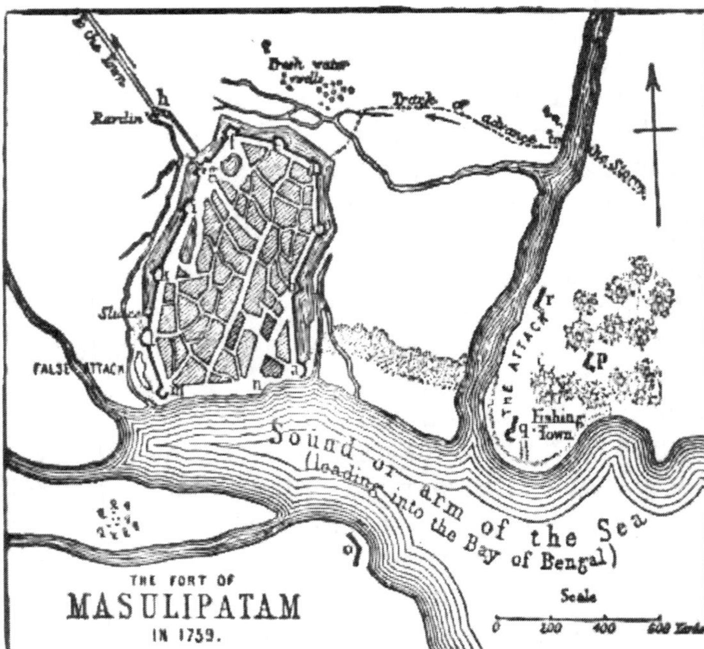

BASTIONS AND DEFENCES.
a, François, . . 8 guns.
b, Dutch, . . . 5 „
c, St. John's, . 18 „
d, Chameleon, . 10 „
e, Small gate, . 8 „
f, Churchyard, . 8 „
g, Great gate, . 8 „
h, Ravelin, . . 5 guns.
i, Pettah, . . . 6 „
k, Engodour, . 8 „
l, Saline, . . . 8 „
m, St. Michael, . 8 „
n, Watergate, 4 „
o, Battery on other side of the water to flank

English batteries, 4 guns.
THE ATTACK.
p, 2 guns 12-pounders.
q, 2 „ 18 „
2 „ 24 „
and 2 mortars.
r. 2 guns, 18-pounders, and 2 guns 24-pounders.

swamp, and this was guarded by a strong ravelin, which is the military name for an outwork erected beyond the ditch of a fortress. It was in all respects capable of a prolonged defence. In form it was an irregular parallelogram about eight hundred yards in length and six hundred yards wide, and on the walls were eleven strong bastions. The morass which surrounded it was of from three to eighteen feet in depth. On the approach of Forde, Conflans evacuated the town, which, also surrounded by swamps and lying two miles to the northwest of the fort, was itself a most defensible position, and retired across the narrow causeway, more than a mile long, to the fort.

CHAPTER XXVII.

MASULIPATAM.

"I AM heartily glad that you have come, Marryat," Colonel Forde said as Charlie rode up. "I have got here at last, as you see, but that is a very different thing from getting in. An uglier place to attack I never saw; and in other respects matters are not bright. Anandraz is a constant worry and trouble to me. He has everything to gain by our success, and yet will do nothing to aid it. His men are worse than useless in fight, and the only thing which we want and he could give us—money—he will not let us have. Will you ride with me to the spot where I'm erecting my batteries, and you will see the prospect for yourself?"

The prospect was, as Charlie found when he saw it, the reverse of cheerful. The point which Forde had selected to erect his batteries was on some sandbanks eight hundred yards from the eastern face of the fort. It would be impossible to construct approaches against the walls, and should a breach be made, there still remained a wide creek to be crossed, beyond which lay the deep, and in most parts absolutely impassable, swamp. Charlie and his men were employed in bringing in provisions from the surrounding country; but a short distance in the rear a French column under Du Rocher, with two hundred European and two thousand native troops, with four field-pieces, watched the

British and rendered the collection of provisions difficult. Du Rocher had several strong places with European and Sepoy garrisons near him, in which to retire in case Forde should advance against him.

"Well, Mister Charles," Tim said one morning, "this is altogether a quare sort of a siege. Here we are with a place in front of us with ten times as many guns as we have got, and a force well nigh twice as large. Even if there were no walls and no guns, I don't see how we could get at 'em barring we'd wings, for this bog is worse than anything in the ould country. Then behind us we've got another army, which is, they say, with the garrisons of the forts, as strong as we are. We've got little food and less money, and the troops are grumbling mightily, I can tell you."

On the 18th of March, while his batteries were still incomplete, Forde received certain news that the Nizam of the Deccan, the old ally of the French, was advancing with an army of forty thousand men to attack him. No British commander ever stood in a position of more imminent peril. This completed the terror of Anandraz. Du Rocher had caused reports to be circulated that he intended to march against that chief's territories, and the news of the approach of the nizam, who was his suzerain lord, completed his dismay. He refused to advance another penny. Colonel Forde had already expended the prize-money gained by the troops, his own private funds, and those of his officers, in buying food for his troops, and the men were several months in arrear of their pay.

"I'm afraid, yer honor," Tim said that evening to Charlie, "that there's going to be a shindy."

"What do you mean by a shindy, Tim?"

"I mane, yer honor, that the men are cursing and swearing, and saying the devil a bit will they fight any longer. It's rank mutiny and rebellion, yer honor; but there's something to be said for the poor boys.

They have seen all the prize-money they had taken spent. Not a thraneen have they touched for months. Their clothes are in rags, and here they are before a place which there's no more chance of their taking than there is of their flying up to the clouds. And now they hear that besides the French behind us, there's the nizam with forty thousand of his men marching aginst us. It's a purty kettle of fish altogether, yer honor. It isn't for myself I care, Mr. Charles. Haven't I got an order in my pocket on the treasury at Madras for three hundred pound and over; but it's mighty hard, yer honor, just when one has become a wealthy man, to be shut up in a French prison."

"Well, Tim, I hope there will be no trouble; but I own that things look bad."

"Hossein has been saying, yer honor, that he thinks that the best way would be for him and me to go out and chop off the heads of half a dozen of the chief ringleaders. But I thought I'd better be asking after yer honor's pleasure in the affair before I set about it."

To Tim's great disappointment Charlie told him that the step was one to which he could hardly assent at present.

The next morning the troops turned out with their arms and threatened to march away. Forde spoke to them gently but firmly. He told them that he could not believe that men who had behaved so gallantly at Condore would fail now in their duty. He begged them to return to their tents, and to send two of their number as deputies to him. This they did. The deputies came to the colonel's tent and told him that all were resolved to fight no more unless they were immediately paid the amount of prize-money due to them, and were assured of the whole booty in case Masulipatam should be taken. Colonel Forde promised that they would receive their prize-money out of the very first funds which reached him. As to the booty which might be taken in Masulipatam, he said he had no power to change the regulations of the Company; but that he would beg them, under consideration of the hardships which the troops had endured and their great services, to forego their half of the plunder. Directly Masulipatam was taken, he said, he would divide one half among them, and hold the other until he obtained the Company's answer to his request. Then he would distribute it at once. With this answer the troops were satisfied, and returned at once to their duty.

On the 25th the guns of the battery opened fire upon the fort, but the damage which they did was inconsiderable. On the 27th news came that the French army of observation had retaken Rajamahendri and that the nizam with his army had arrived at Baizwara, forty miles distant. Letters came in from the nizam to Anandraz ordering him instantly to quit the English camp and join him. The rajah was so terrified that that night he started with his troops without giving any information of his intentions to Colonel Forde; and dilatory as were his motions in general, he on this occasion marched sixteen miles before daybreak.

The instant Colonel Forde heard that he had left he sent for Charlie Marryat. "I suppose you have heard, Marryat, that that scoundrel Anandraz has bolted. Ride off to him with your troop and do your best to persuade him to return."

"I will do so, sir," Charlie said; "but really it seems to me that we are better without him than with him. His men only consume our provisions and cause trouble, and they are no more good fighting than so many sheep."

"That is so," Colonel Forde said. "But in the first place his five thousand men, absolutely worthless as they are, swell our forces to a respectable size. If Conflans and Du Rocher saw how small is our really fighting body, they would fall upon us together and annihilate us. In the second place, if Anandraz goes to the nizam he will at once, of course, declare for the French, and will give up Vizapatam and the rest of the ground we won by the battle of Condore. The whole of the fruits of the campaign would be lost, and we should only hold that portion of the Northern Sirkars on which our troops here are encamped."

"I beg your pardon, Colonel," Charlie said; "you are right and I am wrong. I will start at once."

Putting himself at the head of his five-and-twenty men Charlie rode off at once in pursuit of the rajah. He found him encamped in a village. Charlie had already instructed his men as to the course which they were to pursue, and halted them at a distance of fifty yards from the rajah's tent. Then dismounting, and followed by Tim as his orderly and Hossein as his body-servant, he walked to the tent. He found Anandraz surrounded by his chief officers. The rajah received him coldly; but Charlie, paying no attention to this, took a seat close to him. "I am come, Rajah," he said, "from Colonel Forde to point out to you the folly of the course which you have pursued. By the line which you have taken so far, it is evidently your intention to cross the Godavery and retire to your own country. What chance have you of accomplishing this? By this time the cavalry of the nizam will be scattered over the whole country between this and the Godavery. At Rajahmahendri is Du Rocher with his army, who will take you in flank. Even supposing that you reach your own country, what is the future open to you? If the English are finally successful they will deprive you of your rank and possessions for deserting them now. If the French are victorious they and the nizam will then turn their atten-

THE SUDDEN CONVERSION OF A FAITHLESS ALLY.

tion to you, and you cannot hope to escape with life when your treason has brought such troubles upon them."

The rajah looked for a minute doubtful, and then, encouraged by the murmurs of the officers around him, who were weary of the expedition and its labors although their troops had not fired a single shot, he said obstinately: "No more words are needed. I have made up my mind."

"And so have I," Charlie said, and with a sudden spring he leaped upon the rajah, seized him by the throat, and placed a pistol to his ear. Hossein drew his sword and rushed to his side. Tim ran outside and held up his arm, and the little body of cavalry at once rode up and half of them dismounting, entered the tent with drawn swords.

So astounded were the officers of the rajah at Charlie's sudden attack, that for a moment they knew not what to do, and before they could recover from their surprise Charlie's troopers entered.

"Take this man," Charlie said, pointing to the rajah, "to that tree and hang him at once. Cut down any of these fellows who move a finger." The rajah was dragged to the tree almost lifeless with terror. "Now, Rajah," Charlie said, "you either give instant orders for your army to march back to Masulipatam, or up you go on that branch above there."

The terrified rajah instantly promised to carry out Charlie's orders and to remain faithful to the English. The officers were brought out from the tent and received orders from the rajah to set his troops instantly in motion on their way back. The rajah was led to his tent and there kept under a guard until the army was in motion. When the whole of it was well on its way Charlie said: "Now, Rajah, we will ride on. We will say no more about this little affair, and I will ask Colonel Forde to forgive your ill-behavior in leaving him. But mind, if at any future time you attempt to disobey his orders or to retire from the camp, I will blow out your brains, even if I have to follow you with my men into the heart of your own palace."

Upon their return to the British camp Charlie explained to Colonel Forde the measures which he was obliged to take to convince the rajah of the soundness of his arguments, and of these Colonel Forde entirely approved. He told Charlie that he had sent off to open negotiations with Salabut Jung, so as to detain him as long as possible at Baizwara. Without any intermission the batteries continued to play on the fort from the 25th of March to the 6th of April. Several houses had been destroyed and some breaches effected, but these the French repaired in the night as fast as they were made. They were aware of the position of the English, and regarded the siege with contempt.

On the morning of the 7th news came that the nizam was advancing from Baizwara to attack the English, and that Du Rocher was hurrying from Rajahmahendri to effect a junction with him. The same morning the senior artillery officer reported to Colonel Forde that only two days ammunition for the batteries remained in store. He learned, too, that a ship with three hundred French soldiers would arrive in the course of a day or two. The position was, indeed, a desperate one, and there remained only the alternatives of success against the fort or total destruction. He determined to attack. All day his batteries kept up a heavier fire than ever, maintaining an equal fire against all the bastions in order that, if the enemy should obtain any information of the projected attack, they would not know against which point it was directed. Colonel Forde had ascertained that fishermen were in the habit of making their way across the swamp to the southwest angle of the fort, that on the sea face opposite to the British frontiers; he determined to effect a diversion by an attack upon that side and therefore ordered Captain Knox, with seven hundred Sepoys, to make a detour to cross the swamp and to attack upon that side. Still further to distract the attention of the garrison he instructed Anandraz to advance with his men along the causeway and to open fire against the ravelin. The main attack, which consisted of the rest of the force, composed of three hundred and twenty European infantry, thirty gunners, thirty sailors, and seven hundred Sepoys, was to be delivered against the breach in the bastion, mounting ten guns, in the northeast angle of the fort.

At ten o'clock the force drew up under arms. The fire of the batteries was kept up much later than usual in order that the enemy should have no time to repair the breaches. The hour of midnight was fixed for the attack, as at that time the tide was at its lowest and the water in the ditches round the ramparts not more than three feet deep. Captain Knox and his party started first. The main body should have set out half an hour later, but were detained owing to the unaccountable absence of Captain Callender, the officer who was to command it. As this officer was afterwards killed the cause of his absence was never explained. The party started without him, and before they could reach the ditch they heard the sound of firing from the farther corner of the fort, telling that Knox was already at work.

"Shure, yer honor," muttered Tim, as he made his way through the swamp knee-deep beside his master, "this is worse than the day before Plassey. It was water then but this thick mud houlds one's legs fast at every step. I've lost one of my boots already."

It was indeed hard work; but at last the head of the column reached the ditch just as a fresh burst of firing told that the Rajah Anandraz was attacking the ravelin. The French, in their belief in the absolute security of the place, had taken but few precautions against an attack, and it was not until the leading party had waded nearly breast-high through the ditch and began to break down the palisade beyond it, that they were discovered. Then a heavy artillery and musketry fire from the bastions on the right and left was opened upon the assailants. Captain Fisher with the first division attacked the breach; Captain Maclean with the second covered them by opening fire upon the bastion on their right; while the third, led by Captain Yorke, replied to that on their left. Charlie, although superior in rank to any of these officers, had no specific command, but accompanied the party as a simple volunteer.

The storming party soon mounted the breach, and Yorke's division joined it on the top. Yorke, turning to the left, seized the bastion which was firing on Maclean; while Fisher turned along the ramparts to the right to secure the bastions in that direction. Just as Yorke was setting out he saw a strong body of French Sepoys advancing between the foot of the ramparts and the buildings of the town. These had been sent directly the firing was heard, to reinforce the bastion just carried. Without a moment's hesitation Yorke ran down the rampart, seized the French officer who commanded, and ordered him to surrender at once, as the place was already taken. Confused and bewildered the officer gave up his sword and ordered the Sepoys to lay down their arms. They were then sent as prisoners into the bastion. Yorke now pushed forward with his men at the foot of the rampart and carried two out of three of the bastions on that side. The men, however, separated from the rest and alone in the unknown town, were beginning to lose heart. Suddenly they came upon a small magazine, and some of the men called out, "A mine!" Seized with a sudden panic the whole division ran back, leaving Yorke alone with two native drummer boys, who continued to beat the advance. The soldiers, however, did not stop running until they reached the bastion. Captain Yorke went back, and found that many of the soldiers were proposing to leave the fort together. He swore that he would cut down the first man who moved, and some of the men who had served with him in the 39th, ashamed of their conduct, said that they would follow him. Heading the thirty-six men who had now come to their senses, Captain Yorke again advanced with the drummer boys. Just as he was setting out, Charlie, who had at first gone with Fisher's division, hearing an entire cessation of fire on the other side, ran up to see what was going on.

"Major Marryat," Captain Yorke said, "will you rally these fellows and bring them after me. They've been frightened with a false alarm of a mine and have lost their heads altogether."

Charlie, aided by Tim, exerted himself to the utmost to encourage and command the soldiers, shaming them by telling them that while they, European soldiers, were cowering in the bastion, their Sepoy comrades were winning the town. "Unless," he said, "in one minute the whole of you are formed up ready to advance I will take care that not one shall have a share in the prize-money that will be won to-night."

The men now fell in, and Charlie led them after Captain Yorke. The first retreat of the latter's division had given the French time to rally a little, and as he now made along the rampart towards the bastion on the river, the French officer in command there having turned a gun and loaded it with grape discharged it when the English were within a few yards.

Captain Yorke fell badly wounded. The two black drummer boys were killed, as were several of the men, and sixteen others were wounded. Charlie, hurrying along with the rest of the party, met the survivors of Captain Yorke's little band coming back carrying their wounded officer.

"There," Charlie shouted to his men, "that is your doing. Now retrieve yourselves. Show you are worthy of the name of British soldiers." With a shout the men rushed forward and carried the bastion, and this completed the capture of the whole of the wall from the northeast angle to the river.

In the mean time Captain Fisher with his division was advancing to the right along the rampart. Maclean's men had joined him, and they were pushing steadily forward. Colonel Forde continued with the reserve at the bastion first taken, receiving reports from both divisions as they advanced, and sending the necessary orders. As fast as the prisoners were brought in they were sent down the breach into the ditch where they were guarded by Sepoys, who threatened to shoot any that tried to climb up.

Meanwhile all was disorder in the town. Greatly superior as were the besieged to their assailants in number, they could, if properly handled, have easily driven them back. Instead, however, of disregarding the attack by Knox at the southwest angle, which was clearly only a feint, and that of Anandraz on the ravelin, which might have been disregarded with equal safety, and concentrating all their forces against the main attack, they made no sustained effort against either of the columns which were rapidly carrying bastion after bastion. Conflans appeared to have completely lost his head as messenger after messenger arrived at his house by the river with news of the progress of the English columns. As Fisher's division advanced toward the bastion in which was the great gate, the French who had gathered there again attempted to check his progress. But his men reserved their fire until close to the enemy, and then discharging a volley at a few yards distance they rapidly cleared the bastion. Fisher at once closed the great gates, and thus cut off all the defenders of the ravelin and prevented any of the troops within from joining these and cutting their way through the rajah's troops, which would have been no difficult matter. Just as the division were again advancing, Captain Callender, to the astonishment of every one, appeared and took his place at its head. A few shots only were fired after this, and the last discharge killed Captain Callender.

By this time Conflans, bewildered and terrified, had sent a message to Colonel Forde offering to surrender on honorable terms. Colonel Forde sent back to say that he would give no terms whatever; that the town was in his power and further resistance hopeless, and that if it continued longer he would put all who did not surrender to the sword. On the receipt of this message Conflans immediately sent round orders that all his men were to lay down their arms and to fall in in the open space by the water. The English assembled on the parade by the bastion of the gateway. Captain Knox's column was marched round from the southwest into the town. A strong body of artillery kept guard over the prisoners till morning. Then the gate was opened and the French in the ravelin entered the fort and became prisoners with the rest of the garrison. The whole number of prisoners exceeded three thousand, of whom five hundred were Europeans and the rest Sepoys. The loss of the English was twenty-two Europeans killed and sixty-two wounded. The Sepoys had fifty killed and a hundred and fifty wounded. The rajah's people, who had kept up their false attack upon the ravelin with much more bravery and resolution than had been expected, also lost a good many men.

Considering the natural strength of the position, that the garrison was, both in European troops and Sepoys, considerably stronger than the besiegers, that the fort mounted a hundred and twenty guns, and that a relieving army enormously superior to that of the besiegers was within fifteen miles at the time the assault was made, the capture of Masulipatam may claim to rank among the very highest deeds ever performed by British arms.

CHAPTER XXVIII.

THE DEFEAT OF LALLY.

A LARGE quantity of plunder was obtained at Masulipatam. Half was at once divided among the troops, according to promise, and the other half retained until the permission, applied for by Colonel Forde, was received from Madras for its division among them. The morning after the capture of the town the Maratta horse of Salabut Jung appeared. The nizam was furious when he found that he had arrived too late; but he resolved that when the three hundred French troops, daily expected by sea, arrived, he would besiege Forde in his turn, as with the new arrivals Du Rocher's force would alone be superior to that of Forde, and there would be in addition his own army of forty thousand men. The ships arrived off the port three days later, and sent a messenger on shore to Conflans. Finding that no answer was returned and that the fire had entirely ceased, they came to the conclusion that the place was captured by the English, and sailed away to Pondicherry again. Had Du Rocher taken the precaution of having boats in readiness to communicate with them, inform them of the real state of affairs, and order them to land farther along the coast, and join him, Forde would have been besieged in his turn, although certainly the siege would have been ineffectual. Rajah Anandiaz, greatly terrified at the approach of the nizam, had, two days after the capture of the place, received a portion of the plunder as his share, and marched away to his own country, Forde, disgusted with his conduct throughout the campaign, making no effort whatever to retain him.

When Salabut Jung heard that the French had sailed away to Pondicherry, he felt that his prospects of retaking the town were small, and at the same time receiving news that his own dominions were threatened by an enemy, he concluded a treaty with Forde, granting Masulipatam and the Northern Sirkars to the English, and agreeing never again to allow any French troops to enter his dominions. He then marched back to his own country.

Colonel Forde sailed with a portion of the force to Calcutta, where he shortly afterwards commanded at the battle of Chinsurah, where the Dutch who had made vast preparations to dispute the supremacy of the English, were completely defeated, and thenceforth they, as well as the French, sunk to the rank of small trading colonies under British protection in Bengal.

Charlie returned to Madras, and journeying up the country he joined the main body of his troop, under Peters. They had been engaged in several dashing expeditions, and had rendered great service; but they had been reduced in numbers by action and sickness, and the whole force when reunited only numbered eighty sabres—Lieutenant Hallowes being killed. Peters had been twice wounded. The two friends were greatly pleased to meet again, and had much to tell each other of their adventures since they parted.

The next morning a deputation of four of the men waited upon Charlie. They said that from their share of the booty of the various places they had taken, all were now possessed of sums sufficient in India to enable them to live in comfort for the rest of their lives; they hoped, therefore, that Charlie would ask the authorities at Madras to disband the corps, and allow them to return home. Their commander, however, pointed out to them that the position was still a critical one; that the French possessed a very powerful army at Pondicherry, which would shortly take the field; and that the English would need every one of their soldiers to meet the storm. If victorious there could be no doubt that a final blow would be dealt to French influence, and that the Company would then be able to reduce its forces. A few months would settle the event, and it would, he knew, be useless to apply for their discharge before that time. He thought he could promise them, however, that by the end of the year at latest their services would be dispensed with. The men, although rather disappointed, retired, content to make the best of the circumstances. Desertions were very frequent in the Sepoy force of the Company, as the men, returning to their native villages and resuming their former dress and occupation, were in no danger whatever of discovery. But in Charlie's force not a single desertion had taken place since it was raised, as the men knew that by leaving the colors they would forfeit their share of the prize-money, held for them in the Madras treasury.

"Have you heard from home lately?" Peters asked.

"Yes," Charlie said. "There was a large batch of letters lying for me at Madras. My eldest sister, who has now been married three years, has just presented me with a second nephew. Katie and my mother are well."

"Your sister is not engaged yet?" Peters asked.

"No. Katie says she's quite heart-whole at present. Let me see—how old is she now? It is just eight years and a half since we left England, and she was twelve years old then. She is now past twenty. She would do nicely for you, Peters, when you go back. It would be awfully jolly if you two were to fall in love with each other."

"I feel quite disposed to do so," Peters said, laughing, "from your descriptions of her. I've heard so much of her in all the time we've been together, and she writes such bright merry letters, that I seem to know her quite well."

For Charlie, during the long evenings by the campfires, had often read to his friend the lively letters which he received from his sisters. Peters had no sisters of his own, and he had more than once sent home presents, from the many articles of jewelry which fell to his share of the loot of captured fortresses, to his friend's sisters, saying to Charlie that he had no one in England to send things to, and that it kept up his tie with the old country; for he had been left an orphan as a child.

The day after the deputation from his men had spoken to Charlie, Tim said:

"I hope, yer honor, that whin the troops disbanded you will be going home for a bit yerself."

"I intend to do so, Tim. I have been wanting to get away for the last two years, but I did not like to ask for leave until everything was settled here. And what is more, when I once get back I don't think they will ever see me in India again. I have sufficient means to live as a wealthy man in England, and I've seen enough fighting to last a lifetime.

"Hooroo! shouted Tim. "That's the best word I've heard for a long time. And I shall settle down as yer honor's butler, and look after the grand house and see that you're comfortable."

"You must never leave me, Tim, that's certain," Charlie said; "at least till you marry and set up an establishment of your own."

"If I can't marry without leaving yer honor, divil a wife will Tim Kelly ever take."

"Wait till you see the right woman, Tim. There is no saying what the strongest of us will do when he's once caught in a women's net. However, we'll talk of that when the time comes."

"And there's Hossein, your honor. Fire and water wouldn't keep him away from you, though what he'll do in the colds of the winter at home is more than I know. It makes me laugh to see how his teeth chatter and how the creetur shivers of a cold morning here. But cold or no cold he'd follow you to the north pole, and climb up it if yer honor told him."

Charlie laughed. "He is safe not to be put to the test there, Tim. However you may be sure that if Hossein is willing to go to England with me, he shall go. He has saved my life more than once; and you and he shall never part from me so long as you are disposed to stay by my side."

For some months no great undertaking was attempted on either side. Many petty sieges and skirmishes took place, each party preparing for the great struggle which was to decide the fate of Southern India. At last in January, 1760, the rival armies approached each other. Captain Sherlock, with thirty Europeans and three hundred Sepoys, were besieged by the French in the fort of Vandivash, which had shortly before been captured by them from the French.

Lally was himself commanding the siege, having as his second in command M. Bussy, of whom, however, he was more jealous than ever. Lally's own incapacity was so marked that the whole army, and even Lally's own regiment recognized the superior talent of Bussy. But although Lally constantly asked the advice of his subordinate, his jealousy of that officer generally impelled him to neglect it.

When the English under Colonel Coote, who now commanded their forces in Madras, were known to be advancing against him, Bussy strongly advised that the siege should be abandoned and a strong position taken up for a battle. The advice was unquestionably good, but Lally neglected it, and remained in front of Vandivash until the English were seen approaching. The French cavalry, among whom were three hundred European dragoons, and a cloud of Maratta horse moved forward against the English, whose troops were scattered on the line of march. Colonel Coote brought up two guns, and these, being kept concealed from the enemy until they came within two hundred yards, opened suddenly upon them, while the Sepoys fired heavily with their muskets. The Marattas rapidly turned and rode off, and the French cavalry, finding themselves alone, retired in good order. Colonel Coote now drew up his army in order of battle, and marched his troops so as to take up a position in front of some gardens and other inclosures which extended for some distance from the foot of the mountains out on to the plain. These inclosures would serve as a defence in case the army should be forced to retire from the open.

The French remained immovable in their camp. Seeing this, Colonel Coote marched his troops to the right, the infantry taking up their post in the stony ground at the foot of the mountain, at a mile and a half from the French camp. Some of the French cavalry came out to reconnoitre, but being fired upon returned. Finding that the French would not come out to attack, Colonel Coote again advanced until he reached a point where, swinging round his right, he faced the enemy in a position of great strength. His right was now covered by the fire of the fort, his left by the broken ground at the foot of the hills.

As soon as the English had taken up their position

the French sallied out from their camp and formed in line of battle. The French cavalry were on their right; next to these was the regiment of Lorraine, four hundred strong; in the centre the battalion of India, seven hundred strong. Next to these was Lally's regiment, four hundred strong, its left resting upon an intrenched tank, which was held by three hundred marines and sailors from their fleet, with four guns. Twelve other guns were in line, three between each regiment. Four hundred Sepoys were in reserve at a tank in rear of that held by the marines. Nine hundred Sepoys held a ridge behind the position, but in front of the camp, and at each end of this ridge was an intrenchment guarded by fifty Europeans. A hundred and fifty Europeans and three hundred Sepoys remained in the batteries facing Vandivash. The whole force consisted of two thousand four hundred Europeans and sixteen hundred Sepoys. The Marattas, three thousand strong, remained in their own camp and did not advance to the assistance of their allies.

The English army consisted of nineteen hundred Europeans, of whom eighty were cavalry, two thousand one hundred Sepoys, twelve hundred and fifty irregular horse, and twenty-six field guns. The Sepoys were on the flanks, the Company's two battalions in the centre, with Coote's regiment on their right and Draper's on their left. The four grenadier companies of the white regiments were withdrawn from the fighting line, and with two hundred Sepoys on each flank were held as a reserve. Ten field-pieces were in line with the troops; two, with two companies of Sepoys were posted a little on the left; the rest were in reserve. The English line was placed somewhat obliquely across that of the French, their left being the nearest to the enemy.

As the English took up their position Lally led out

his cavalry, made a wide sweep round the plain, and then advanced against the English horse, who were drawn up some little distance behind the reserve. Upon seeing their approach the whole of the irregular horse fled at once, leaving only Charlie's troop remaining. The Sepoys with the two guns on the left were ordered to turn these round so as to take the advancing French in flank; but the flight of their horse had shaken the natives, and the French cavalry would have fallen unchecked on Charlie's little troop, which was already moving forward to meet them, had not Captain Barlow, who commanded the British artillery, turned two of his guns and opened fire upon them. Fifteen men and horses fell at the first discharge, throwing the rest into some confusion, and at the next deadly discharge the whole turned and rode off. Seeing the enemy retreating, many of the irregular horse rode back, and joining Charlie's troop, pursued them round to the rear of their own camp.

For a short time a cannonade was kept up by the guns on both sides, the English fire, being better directed, causing some damage. Upon Lally's return to his camp with the cavalry he at once gave the order to advance. Coote ordered the Europeans of his force to do the same, the Sepoys to remain on their ground. The musketry fire began at one o'clock. The English, according to Coote's orders, retained theirs until the enemy came close at hand. Following the tactics which were afterwards repeated many times in the Peninsula, the Lorraine regiment, forming a column twelve deep, advanced against that of Coote, which received them in line. The French came on at the double. When within a distance of fifty yards, Coote's regiment poured a volley into the front and flanks of the column. Although they suffered heavily from this fire the French bravely pressed on with levelled bayonets, and the head of the column, by sheer weight.

broke through the English line. The flanks of the English, however, closed in on the sides of the French column, and a desperate hand-to-hand fight ensued. In this the English had all the advantage, attacking the French fiercely on either side, until the latter broke and ran back to the camp.

Colonel Coote, who was with his regiment, ordered it to form in regular order again before it advanced, and rode off to see what was going on in the rest of the line. As he was passing on a shot struck an ammunition wagon in the intrenched tank held by the French. This exploded, killing and wounding eighty men, among whom was the commander of the post. The rest of its occupants, panic-stricken by the explosion, ran back to the next tank. Their panic communicated itself to the Sepoys there, and all ran back together to the camp. Colonel Coote at once sent orders to Major Brereton, who commanded Draper's regiment, to take possession of the tank before the enemy recovered from the confusion which the explosion would be sure to cause. The ground opposite that which Draper's regiment occupied was held by Lally's regiment, and in order to prevent his men being exposed to a flanking fire from these, Draper ordered them to file off to the right. Bussy, who commanded at this wing, endeavored to rally the fugitives, and gathering fifty or sixty together, added two companies of Lally's regiment to them, and posted them in the tank; he then returned to the regiment. As Major Brereton, moving up his men, reached the intrenchment a heavy fire was poured upon him. Major Brereton fell, mortally wounded, and many of his men were killed. The rest, however, with a rush carried the intrenchment, and firing down from the parapet on the guns on Lally's left, drove the gunners from them. Two companies held the intrenchment, and the rest formed in the plain on its left to prevent

Lally's regiment attacking it on this side. Bussy wheeled Lally's regiment, detached a portion of it to recover the intrenchment, and with the rest marched against Draper's troops in the plain.

A heavy musketry fire was kept up on both sides until the two guns, posted by Draper's regiment, and left behind when they attacked the intrenchment, came up and opened on the French. These began to waver. Bussy, as the only chance of gaining the day, put himself at their head, and endeavoured to lead them forward to attack the English with the bayonet. His horse, however, was struck with a ball and soon fell; the English fire was redoubled, and but twenty of Lally's men kept round him. Two companies of the English rushed forward and surrounded the little party, who at once surrendered. Bussy was led a prisoner to the rear, and as he went was surprised at the sight of the three hundred grenadiers, the best troops in the English army, remaining quietly in reserve. While on either flank the French were now beaten, the fight in the centre, between the European troops of the English and French companies, had continued, but had been confined to a hot musketry and artillery fire. But upon seeing the defeat of their flanks the enemy's centre likewise fell back to their camp.

From the moment when the Lorraine regiment had been routed, four field-pieces kept up an incessant fire into their camp to prevent them from rallying. The three English regiments now advanced in line and entered the enemy's camp without the least opposition. The Lorraine regiment had passed through it a mass of fugitives, the India regiment and Lally's went through rapidly, but in good order. Lally had in vain endeavored to bring the Sepoys forward to the attack to restore the day. The French cavalry, seeing the defeat of Lorraine's regiment, advanced to cover it.

their appearance completely intimidating the English regular horse. Charlie's troop were too weak to charge them single-handed. Reanimated by the attitude of their cavalry, the men of the Lorraine regiment rallied, yoked up four field-pieces which were standing in the rear of the camp, and moved off in fair order. They were joined in the plain by Lally's regiment and the India battalion, and the whole, setting fire to their tents, moved off in good order. The four field-pieces kept in the rear, and behind these moved the cavalry. As they retired they were joined by the four hundred and fifty men from the batteries opposite Vandivash.

Colonel Coote sent orders to his cavalry to harass the enemy. These followed them for five miles, but as the native horse would not venture within range of the enemy's field-guns, Charlie, to his great disappointment, was able to do nothing.

Upon neither side did the Sepoys take any part in the battle of Vandivash. It was fought entirely between the two thousand two hundred and fifty French, not including those in their battery, and sixteen hundred English, excluding the grenadiers, who never fired a shot. Twenty-four pieces of cannon were taken and eleven wagons of ammunition, and all the tents, stores, and baggage that were not burned. The French left two hundred dead upon the field. A hundred and sixty were taken prisoners, of whom thirty died of their wounds before the next morning. Large numbers dropped upon the march and were afterwards captured. The English had sixty-three killed and a hundred and twenty-four wounded.

The news of this victory reached Madras, on the following morning, and excited as much enthusiastic joy as that of Plassey had done at Calcutta and the event was almost as important a one. There was no longer the slightest fear of danger, and the Madras authorities began to meditate an attack upon Pondicherry. So long as the great French settlement remained intact, so long would Madras be exposed to fresh invasions, and it was certain that France, driven now from Bengal, would make a desperate effort to regain her shaken supremacy in Madras. The force, however, at the disposal of the Madras authorities was still far too weak to enable them to undertake an enterprise like the siege of Pondicherry, for their army did not exceed in numbers that which Lally possessed for its defence. Accordingly, urgent letters were sent to Clive to ask him to send down in the summer as many troops as he could spare, other reinforcements being expected from England at that time. The intervening time was spent in the reduction of Chittapett, Karical, and many other forts which held out for the French.

After the battle of Vandivash Charlie kept his promise to his men. He represented to Mr. Pigot that they had already served some months over the time for which they were enlisted, that they had gone through great hardships, and performed great services, and that they were now anxious to retire to enjoy the prize-money they had earned. He added that he had given his own promise that they should be allowed to retire if they would extend their service until after a decisive battle with the French. Mr. Pigot at once assented to Charlie's request, and ordered that a batta of six months' pay should be given to each man upon leaving. The troop, joined by many of their comrades, who had been at different times sent down sick and wounded to Madras, formed up there on parade for the last time. They responded with three hearty cheers to the address which Charlie gave them, thanking them for their services, bidding them farewell, and hoping that they would long enjoy the prize-money which they had gallantly won. Then they delivered over their horses to the authorities, drew their prize-money from the treasury, and started for their respective homes, the English portion taking up their quarters in barracks until the next ship should sail for England.

"I am sorry to leave them," Charlie said to Peters as they stood alone upon the parade. "We have gone through a lot of stirring work together, and no fellows could have behaved better."

"No," Peters agreed. "It is singular that, contemptible as are these natives of India when officered by men of their own race and region, they will fight to the death when led by us."

CHAPTER XXIX.

THE SIEGE OF PONDICHERRY.

AS the health of the two officers was shaken by their long and arduous work, and their services were not for the moment needed, they obtained leave for three months, and went down in a coasting ship to Columbo, where several English trading stations had been established. Here they spent two months, residing for the most part among the hills, at the town of a rajah very friendly to the English, and with him they saw an elephant hunt, the herd being driven into a great inclosure formed by a large number of natives who had for weeks been employed upon it. Here the animals were fastened to trees by natives who cut through the thick grass unobserved, and were one by one reduced to submission, first by hunger and then by being lustily belabored by the trunks of tamed elephants. Tim highly appreciated the hunt, and declared that tiger shooting was not to be compared to it.

Their residence in the brisk air of the hills completely restored their health, and they returned to Madras perfectly ready to take part in the great operations which were impending. Charlie on his return was appointed to serve as chief of the staff to Colonel Coote, Captain Peters being given the command of a small body of European horse, who were, with a large body of irregulars, to aid in bringing in supplies to the

British army, and to prevent the enemy from receiving food from the surrounding country.

Early in June the British squadron off the coast was joined by two ships of the line, the *Norfolk* and *Panther*, from England, and a hundred Europeans and a detachment of European and native artillery came down from Bombay. Around Pondicherry ran a strong cactus hedge strengthened with palisades, and the French retired into this at the beginning of July. They were too strongly posted there to be attacked by the force with which the English at first approached them, and they were expecting the arrival of a large body of troops from Mysore with a great convoy of provisions.

On the 17th these approached. Major Moore, who was guarding the English rear, had a hundred and eighty European infantry, fifty English horse, under Peters, sixteen hundred irregular horse, and eleven hundred Sepoys. The Mysoreans had four thousand good horse, a thousand Sepoys, and two hundred Europeans, with eight pieces of cannon.

The fight lasted but a few minutes. The British native horse and Sepoys at once gave way, and the English infantry retreated in great disorder to the fort of Trivadi, which they gained with a loss of fifteen killed and forty wounded. Peters' horse alone behaved well. Several times they charged right through the masses of Mysorean horse, but when five and twenty were killed and most of the rest, including their commander, severely wounded, they also fell back into the fort.

Colonel Coote, when the news of the disaster reached him, determined, if possible, to get possession of the fort of Vellenore, which stood on the river Ariangopang, some three miles from Pondicherry, and covered the approaches of the town from that side. The English encampment was at Perimbé on the main road leading through an avenue of trees to Pondicherry. Colonel Coote threw up a redoubt on the hill behind Perimbé and another on the avenue, to check any French force advancing from Pondicherry. These works were finished on the morning of the 19th of July. The next morning the French army advanced along the river Ariangopang, but Coote marched half his force to meet them, while he moved the rest as if to attack the redoubts interspersed along the line of hedge. As the fall of these would have placed the attacking force in his rear Lally at once returned to the town. The same evening the Mysoreans, with three thousand bullocks carrying their artillery and drawing their baggage and three thousand more laden with rice and other provisions, arrived on the other bank of the Ariangopang river, crossed under the guns of the redoubt of that name and entered the town.

The fort of Vellenore was strong, but the road had been cut straight through the glacis to the gate, and the French had neglected to erect works to cover this passage. Coote took advantage of the oversight and laid his two eighteen-pounders to play upon the gate, while two others were placed to fire upon the parapet. The English batteries opened at daybreak on the 16th and at nine o'clock the whole of the French army with the Mysoreans advanced along the bank of the river. Coote at once got his troops under arms, and advanced towards the French, sending a small detachment of Europeans to reinforce the Sepoys firing at the fort of Vellenore. By this time the batteries had beaten down the parapet and silenced the enemy's fire. Two companies of Sepoys set forward at full run up to the very crest of the glacis.

The French commander of the place had really nothing to fear, as the Sepoys had a ditch to pass and a very imperfect breach to mount, and the fort might have held out for two days before the English could have been in a position to storm it. The French army was in sight, and in ten minutes a general engagement would have begun. In spite of all this the coward at once hoisted a flag of truce and surrendered. The Europeans and Sepoys ran in through the gate, and the former instantly turned the guns of the fort upon

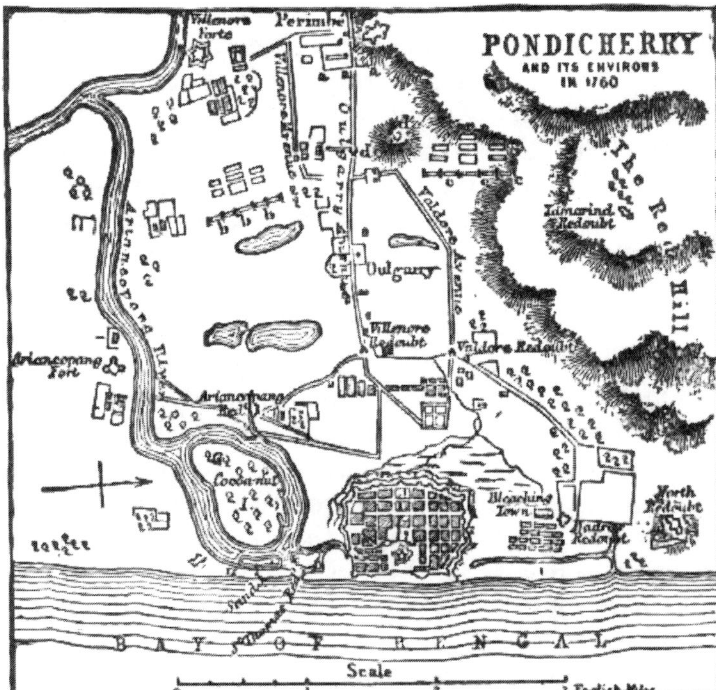

a a a, First encampment, July 17. | b b b, Second encampment, Sept. 10.
d d d, Redoubts erected, July 18. | c c c, Third encampment, Oct. 6.

the French army. This halted, struck with amazement and anger, and Lally at once ordered it to retire upon the town.

A week afterward six ships with six hundred fresh troops from England arrived.

The Mysoreans who had brought food into Pondicherry made many excursions in the country, but were sharply checked. They were unable to supply themselves with food, and none could be spared them from the stores in the magazines. Great distress set in among them, and this was heightened by the failure of a party with two thousand bullocks with rice to enter the town. This party, escorted by the greater portion of the Mysorean horse from Pondicherry, was attacked and defeated, and nine hundred bullocks laden with baggage captured. Shortly afterwards the rest of the Mysorean troops left Pondicherry and marched to attack Trinomany.

Seeing that there was little fear of their returning to succor Pondicherry the English now determined to complete the blockade of that place. In order to have any chance of reducing it by famine it was necessary to obtain possession of the country within the hedge, which with its redoubts extended in the arc of a circle from the river Ariangopang to the sea. The space thus included contained an area of nearly seven square miles, affording pasture for the bullocks, of which there were sufficient to supply the troops and inhabitants for many months. Therefore, although the army was not yet strong enough to open trenches against the town, and indeed the siege artillery had not yet sailed from Madras, it was determined to get possession of the hedge and its redoubts.

Before doing this, however, it was necessary to capture the fort of Ariangopang. This was a difficult undertaking. The whole European force was but two thousand strong, and if eight hundred of these were detached across the river to attack the fort, the main body would be scarcely a match for the enemy should he march out against them. If on the other hand the whole army moved round to attack the fort the enemy would be able to send out and fetch in the great convoy of provisions collected at Jinji. Mr. Pigot therefore requested Admiral Stevens to land the marines of the fleet. Although, seeing that a large French fleet was expected, the admiral was unwilling to weaken his squadron, he complied with the request, seeing the urgency of the case, and four hundred and twenty marines were landed.

On the 2d of September two more men-of-war, the *America* and *Medway*, arrived, raising the fleet before Pondicherry to seventeen ships of the line. They convoyed several Company's ships which had brought with them the wing of a Highland regiment.

The same evening Coote ordered four hundred men to march to invest the fort of Ariangopang, but Colonel Monson, second in command, was so strongly against the step that at the last moment he countermanded his orders. The change was fortunate, for Lally, who had heard from his spies of the English intentions, moved his whole army out to attack the —as he supposed—weakened force.

At ten at night fourteen hundred French infantry, a hundred French horse, and nine hundred Sepoys marched out to attack the English, who had no suspicion of their intent. Two hundred marines and five hundred Sepoys proceeded in two columns. Marching from the Valdore redoubt one party turned to the right to attack the Tamarind redoubt, which the English had erected on the Red Hill. Having taken this they were to turn to their left and join the other column. This skirted the foot of the Red Hill to attack the redoubt erected on a hillock at its foot on the 18th of July. Four hundred Sepoys and a company of Portuguese were to take post at the junction of the Valdore and Oulgarry avenues. The regiments of Lorraine and Lally were to attack the battery in this avenue, Lorraine's from the front, while Lally's marching outwards in the fields was to fall on its right flank. The Indian battalion with the Bourbon volunteers, three hundred strong, were to march from the fort of

Ariangopang across the river to the villages under the fort of Vellenore, and as soon as the fire became general were to fall upon the right rear of the English encampment.

At midnight a rocket gave the signal and the attack immediately commenced. The attack on the Tamarind redoubt was repulsed, but the redoubt on the hillock was captured and the guns spiked. At the intrenchment on the Oulgarry Road the fight was fierce, and Colonel Coote himself brought down his troops to its defence. The attack was continued, but, as, owing to some mistake, the column intended to fall upon the English rear had halted and did not arrive in time, the regiments of Lorraine and Lally drew off, and the whole force retired to the town.

The ships arriving from England brought a commission appointing Monson to the rank of colonel, with a date prior to that of Colonel Coote, ordering him, however, not to assert his seniority so long as Coote remained at Madras. Coote, however, considered that it was intended that he should return to Bengal, and so handing over the command to Monson he went back to Madras. Colonel Monson at once prepared to attack the hedge and its redoubts. Leaving sufficient guards for the camp he advanced at midnight with his troops divided into two brigades, the one commanded by himself, the other by Major Smith. Major Smith's division was first to attack the enemy outside the hedge in the village of Oulgarry, and, driving them hence, to carry the Vellenore redoubt, while the main body were to make a sweep round the Red Hill and come down to the attack of the Valdore redoubt.

Smith moving to the right of the Oulgarry avenue attacked that position on the left, and the advance led by Captain Myers carried by storm a redoubt in front of the village and seized four pieces of cannon. Major

Smith, heading his grenadiers, then charged the village, tore down all obstacles, and carried the place.

The day had begun to dawn when Colonel Monson approached the Valdore redoubt. But at the last moment, making a mistake in their way, the head of the column halted. At this moment the enemy perceived them and discharged a twenty-four pounder, loaded with small shot, into the column. Eleven men were killed and twenty-six wounded by this terrible discharge, among the latter Colonel Monson himself, his leg being broken. The grenadiers now rushed furiously to the attack, swarmed round the redoubt, and although several times repulsed, at last forced their way through the embrasures and captured the position.

The defenders of the village of Oulgarry had halted outside the Vellenore redoubt, but upon hearing the firing to their right retreated hastily within it. Major Smith pressed them hotly with his brigade, and followed so closely upon their heels that they did not stop to defend the position but retreated to the town. Major Smith was soon joined by the Highlanders under Major Scott, who had forced a way through the hedge between the two captured redoubts. Thus the whole line of the outer defence fell into the hands of the English, with the exception of the Ariangopang redoubt on the left which was held by the India regiment. Major Gordon, who now took the command, placed the Bombay detachment of three hundred and fifty men in the captured redoubts, and encamped the whole of the force in the fields to the right of Oulgarry. Major Smith advised that at least a thousand men should be left near at hand to succor the garrisons of the redoubts, which, being open at the rear, were liable to an attack. Major Gordon foolishly refused to follow his advice, and the same night the French attacked the redoubts. The Bombay troops, however, defended themselves with extreme bravery until assistance arrived. Three days later the French evacuated and blew up the fort of Ariangopang which the English were preparing to attack, and the India regiment retired into the town, leaving, however, the usual guard in the Ariangopang redoubt.

Colonel Coote had scarcely arrived at Madras when he received a letter from Colonel Monson saying that he was likely to be incapacitated by his wound for some months, and requesting that he would resume the command of the army. The authorities of Madras strongly urged Coote to return, representing the extreme importance of the struggle in which they were engaged. He consented and reached camp on the night of the 20th. He at once ordered the captured redoubts to be fortified to prevent the enemy again taking the offensive, and erected a strong work called the North Redoubt near the sea-shore and facing the Madras redoubt. A few days later, on a party of Sepoys approaching the Ariangopang redoubt, the occupants of that place were seized with a panic, abandoned the place, and went into the town. The English had now possession of the whole of the outward defences of Pondicherry, with the exception of the two redoubts by the sea-shore.

A day or two later Colonel Coote advancing along the sea-beach as if with a view of merely making a reconnaissance, pushed on suddenly, entered the village called the Blancherie, as it was principally inhabited by washerwomen, and attacked the Madras redoubt. This was carried, but the same night the garrison sallied out again and fell upon the party of Sepoys posted there. Ensign MacMahon was killed, but the Sepoys, although driven out from the redoubt, bravely returned and again attacked the French, who, thinking that the Sepoys must have received large reinforcements, fell back into the village, from which, a day or two later, they retired into the town. The whole of the ground outside the fort, between the river Ariangopang and the sea, was now in the hands of the English. The French still maintained their communications with the south by the sandy line of coast. By this time the attacks which the English from Trichinopoli and Madura had made upon the Mysoreans, had compelled the latter to make peace and recall their army which was still hovering in the neighborhood of Pondicherry.

Charlie, who had suffered from a slight attack of fever, had for some time been staying on board ship for change. In the road of Pondicherry three of the French Indiamen, the *Hermione*, *Baleine* and the *Compagnie des Indes*, were at anchor near the edge of the surf under the cover of a hundred guns mounted on the sea face of the fort. These ships were awaiting the stormy weather at the breaking of the monsoon, when it would be difficult for the English fleet to maintain their position off the town. They then intended to sail away to the south, fill up with provisions, and return to Pondicherry. Admiral Stevens, in order to prevent this contingency which would have greatly delayed the reduction of the place, determined to cut them out. Charlie's health being much restored by the sea breezes, he asked leave of the admiral to accompany the expedition as a volunteer. On the evening of the 6th, six-and-twenty of the boats of the fleet, manned by four hundred sailors, were lowered and rowed to the *Tiger*, which was at anchor within two miles of Pondicherry, the rest of the fleet lying some distance farther away.

When at midnight the cabin lights of the *Hermione* were extinguished, the expedition started. The boats moved in two divisions, one of which was to attack the *Hermione*, the other the *Baleine*. The third vessel lay nearer in shore, and was to be attacked if the others were captured. The night was a very dark one, and the boats of each division moved in line with ropes stretched from boat to boat to ensure their keeping together in the right direction. Charlie was in one of the boats intended to attack the *Hermione*. Tim accompanied him, but the admiral had refused permission for Hossein to do so, as there were many more white volunteers for the service than the boats would accommodate. They were within fifty yards of the *Hermione* before they were discovered, and a scattering musket fire was at once opened upon them. The crews gave a mighty cheer, and casting off the ropes, separated, five making for each side of the ship, while two rowed forward to cut the cables at her bows. The *Compagnie des Indes* opened fire upon the boats, but these were already alongside the ship, and the sailors swarmed over the side at ten points. The combat was a short one. The seventy men on board fought bravely for a minute or two, but they were speedily driven below. The hatches were closed over them, and the cables being already cut, the mizzen topsail, the only sail bent, was hoisted, and the boats, taking tow-ropes, began to row her away from shore.

The instant, however, that the cessation of fire informed the garrison the ship was captured, a tremendous cannonade was opened by the guns of the fortress. The lightning was flashing vividly, and this enabled the gunners to direct their aim upon the ship. Over and over again she was struck, and one shot destroyed the steering wheel, cut the tiller rope, and killed two men who were steering. The single sail was not sufficient to assist in steering her, and the men in the boats rowed with such energy that the ropes continually snapped. The fire continued from the shore, doing considerable damage, and the men in the boats, who could not see that the ship was moving through the water, concluded that she was anchored by a concealed cable and anchor. The officer in command, therefore, called up the Frenchmen from below, telling them that he was about to fire the ship. They came on deck and took their places in the boats, which rowed back to the *Tiger*. Upon arriving there Captain Dent, who commanded her, sternly rebuked the officer, and said that unless the boats returned instantly and brought the *Hermione* out he should send his own crew in their boats to fetch her. The division thereupon returned and met the ship half a mile off shore, the land wind having now sprung up. The *Baleine* had been easily captured, and having several sails bent she was brought out without difficulty. No attempt was made to capture the third vessel.

The rains had now set in, but the English labored steadily at their batteries. The French were becoming pressed for provisions, and Lally turned the whole of the natives remaining in the town, to the number of fourteen hundred men and women, outside the fortifications. On their arrival at the English lines they were refused permission to pass, as Colonel Coote did not wish to relieve the garrison of the consumption of food caused by them. They returned to the French lines and begged to be again received, but they were by Lally's orders, fired upon and several killed. For seven days the unhappy wretches remained without food, save the roots they could gather in the fields. Then Colonel Coote, seeing that Lally was inflexible, allowed them to pass.

On the 10th of November the batteries opened, and every day added to the strength of the fire upon the town. The fortifications, however, were strong, and the siege progressed but slowly. On the 30th of December a tremendous storm burst, and committed the greatest havoc both at land and sea. The *Newcastle*, man-of-war, the *Queenborough*, frigate, and the *Protector*, fire-ship, were driven ashore and dashed to pieces, but the crews, with the exception of seven, were saved. The *Duke* of *Aquitaine*, the *Sunderland*, and the *Duke*, store-ship, were sunk, and eleven hundred sailors drowned. Most of the other ships were dismasted.

CHAPTER XXX.

HOME.

THE fire of the batteries increased, and by the 13th of January the enemy's fire was completely silenced. The provisions in the town were wholly exhausted, and on the 15th the town surrendered, and the next morning the English took possession. Three days afterwards Lally was embarked on board ship to be taken a prisoner to Madras, and so much was he hated that the French officers and civilians assembled and hissed and hooted him, and had he not been protected by his guard, would have torn him to pieces. After his return to France he was tried for having, by his conduct, caused the loss of the French possessions in India, and being found guilty of the offence, was beheaded.

At Pondicherry two thousand and seventy-two military prisoners were taken, and three hundred and eighty-one civilians. Five hundred cannon and a hundred mortars fit for service, and immense quantities of ammunition, arms, and military stores fell into the hands of the captors. Pondicherry was handed over to the Company, who, a short time afterwards, entirely demolished both the fortress and town. This hard measure was the consequence of a letter which had been intercepted from the French government to Lally, ordering him to raze Madras to the ground, when it fell into his hands.

Charlie, after the siege, in which he had rendered great services, received from the Company, at Colonel Coote's earnest recommendation, his promotion to the step of lieutenant-colonel, while Peters was raised to that of major.

A fortnight after the fall of Pondicherry they returned to Madras and thence took the first ship for England. It was now just ten years since they had sailed, and in that time they had seen Madras and Calcutta rise from the rank of two trading stations, in constant danger of destruction by their powerful neighbors, to that of virtual capitals of great provinces. Not as yet, indeed, had they openly assumed the sovereignty of these territories, but Madras was, in fact, the absolute master of the broad tract of land extending from the foot of the mountains to the sea, from Cape Comorin to Bengal, while Calcutta was master of Bengal and Oressa, and her power already threatened to extend itself as far as Delhi. The conquest of these vast tracts of country had been achieved by mere handfuls of men, and by a display of heroic valor and constancy scarce to be rivalled in the history of the world.

The voyage was a pleasant one and was, for the times, quick, occupying only five months. But to the young men, longing for home after so long an absence, it seemed tedious in the extreme. Tim and Hossein were well content with their quiet, easy life after their long toils. They had nothing whatever to do, except that they insisted upon waiting upon Charlie and Peters at meals. The ship carried a large number of sick and wounded officers and men, and as these gained health and strength the life on board ship became livelier and more jovial. Singing and cards occupied the evenings, while in the daytime they played quoits, rings of rope being used for that purpose, and other games with which passengers usually while away the monotony of long voyages. It was late in June when the *Madras* sailed up the Thames, and as soon as she came to anchor the two officers and their followers landed. The din and bustle of the streets seemed almost as strange to Charlie as they had done when he came up a boy from Yarmouth. Hossein was astonished at the multitude of white people, and inquired of Charlie why, when there were so many men, England had sent so few soldiers to fight for her in India, and for once Charlie was unable to give a satisfactory reply.

"It does seem strange," he said to Peters, "that when such mighty interests were at stake, a body of even ten thousand troops could not have been raised and sent out. Such a force would have decided the struggle at once, and in three months the great possessions, which have cost the Company twelve years' war, would have been at their feet. It would not have cost them more, indeed, nothing like as much as it now has done, nor one tithe of the loss in life. Somehow England always seems to make war in driblets."

Charlie knew that his mother and Kate had for some years been residing at a house which their uncle had taken in the fashionable quarter of Chelsea. They looked in at the office, however, to see if Charlie's uncle was there, but found that he was not in the city, and, indeed, had now almost retired from the business. They therefore took a coach, placed the small articles of luggage which they had brought with them from the ship on the front seats, and then, Hossein and Tim taking their places on the broad seat beside the driver, they entered the coach and drove to Chelsea. Charlie had invited Peters, who had no home of his own, to stay with him, at least for a while. Both were now rich men, from their shares of the prize-money of the various forts and towns in whose capture they had taken part, although Charlie possessed some twenty thousand pounds more than his friend, this being the amount of the presents he had received from the Rajah of Ambur.

Alighting from the carriage, Charlie ran up to the door and knocked. Inquiring for Mrs. Marryat, he was shown into a room in which a lady, somewhat past middle age, and three younger ones were sitting. They looked up in surprise as the young man entered. Ten years had changed him almost beyond recognition, but one of the younger ones at once leaped to her feet and exclaimed, "Charlie!"

His mother rose with a cry of joy, and threw herself into his arms. After rapturously kissing her he turned to the others. Their faces were changed, yet all seemed equally familiar to him, and in his delight he equally embraced them all.

"Hullo!" he exclaimed, when he freed himself from their arms. "Why, there are three of you? What on earth am I doing? I have somebody's pardon to beg, and yet, although your faces are changed, they seem equally familiar to me. Which is it? But I need not ask," he said, as a cloud of color flowed over the face of one of the girls, while the others smiled mischievously.

You are Katie," he said, "and you are Lizzie, certainly, and this is—why, it is Ada! This is a surprise, indeed; but I sha'n't beg your pardon, Ada, for I kissed you at parting and quite intended to do so when I met again, at least if you had offered no violent objection. How you are all grown and changed, while you, mother, look scarcely older then when I left you. But, there, I have quite forgotten Peters. He has come home with me, and will stay till he has formed his own plans."

He hurried out and brought in Peters, who, not wishing to be present at the family meeting, had been paying the coachman, and seeing to the things being

WELCOME HOME!

brought into the house. He was warmly received by the ladies, as the friend and companion of Charlie in his adventures, scarcely a letter having been received from the latter without mention having been made of his comrade.

In a minute or two Mr. Tufton, who had been in the large garden behind the house, hurried in. He was now quite an old man, and under the influence of age and the cheerful society of Mrs. Marryat and her daughters, he had lost much of the pomposity which had before distinguished him.

"Ah! nephew," he said, when the happy party had sat down to dinner, their number increased by the arrival of Mrs. Haines, who had a house close by, "wilful lads will go their own way. I wanted to make a rich merchant of you, and you have made of yourself a famous soldier. But you've not done badly for yourself after all, for you have in your letters often talked about prize-money."

"Yes, uncle, I have earned in my way close upon a hundred thousand pounds, and I certainly shouldn't have made that if I had stuck to the office at Madras, even with the aid of the capital you offered to lend me to trade with on my own account."

There was a general exclamation of surprise and pleasure at the mention of the sum, although this amount was small in comparison to that which many acquired in those days in India.

"And you're not thinking of going back again, Charlie?" his mother said anxiously. "There can be no longer any reason for your exposing yourself to that horrible climate, and that constant fighting."

"The climate is not so bad, mother, and the danger and excitement of a soldier's life there at present render it very fascinating. But I have done with it. Peters and I intend, on the expiration of our leave, to resign our commissions in the Company's service, and to settle down under our own vines and fig-trees. Tim has already elected himself to the post of my butler, and Hossein intends to be my valet and body-servant."

Immediately after their arrival Charlie had brought in his faithful followers and introduced them to the ladies, who, having often heard of their devotion and faithful services, had received them with a kindness and cordiality which had delighted them.

Lizzie, whose appearance at home had been unexpected by Charlie, for her husband was a landed gentleman at Sevenoaks, in Kent, was, it appeared, paying a visit of a week to her mother, and her three children, two boys and a little girl, were duly brought down to be shown to, and admired by, their Uncle Charles.

"And how is it you haven't married, Katie? With such a pretty face as yours it is scandalous that the men have allowed you to reach the mature age of twenty-two unmarried."

"It is the fault of the hussy herself," Mr. Tufton said. "It is not from want of offers, for she has had a dozen, and among them some of the nobility at court; for it is well known that John Tufton's niece will have a dowry such as many of the nobles could not give to their daughters."

"This is too bad, Kate," Charlie said laughing. "What excuse have you to make for yourself for remaining single with all these advantages of face and fortune?"

"Simply that I didn't like any of them," Katie said. "The beaux of the present day are contemptible. I would as soon think of marrying a wax doll. When I do marry, that is, if ever I do, it shall be a man, and not a mere tailor's dummy."

"You are pert, miss," her uncle said. "Do what I will, Charlie, I cannot teach the hussy to order her tongue."

"Katie's quite right, uncle," Charlie laughed. "And I must make it my duty to find a man who will suit her taste, though, according to your account of her, he will find it a hard task to keep such a Xantippe in order."

Katie tossed her head.

"He'd better not try," she said saucily, "or it will be worse for him."

Two days later Charlie's elder sister returned with her family to her house at Sevenoaks, where Charlie promised before long, to pay her a visit. After she had gone, Charlie and Peters, with Katie, made a series of excursions to all the points of interest round London, and on these occasions Ada usually accompanied them. The natural consequences followed. Charlie had for years been the hero of Ada's thoughts, while Katie had heard so frequently of Peters, that she was from the first disposed to regard him in the most favorable light. Before the end of two months both couples were engaged, and as both the young officers possessed ample means, and the ladies were heiresses, there was no obstacle to an early union. The weddings took place a month later, and Tim was, in the exuberance of his delight, hilariously drunk for the first and only time during his service with Charlie. Both gentlemen bought estates in the country, and later took their seats in Parliament, where they vigorously defended their former commander, Lord Clive, in the assaults which were made upon him.

Tim married seven or eight years after his master, and settled down in a nice little house upon the estate. Although henceforth he did no work whatever, he insisted to the end of his life that he was still in Colonel Marryat's service. Hossein, to the great amusement of his master and mistress, followed Tim's example. The pretty cook of Charlie's establishment made no objection to his swarthy hue. Charlie built a snug cottage for them close to the house, where they took up their residence, but Hossein, though the happy father of a large family, continued to the end of a long life to discharge the duties of valet to his master. Both he and Tim were immense favorites with the children of Charlie and Peters, who were never tired of listening to their tales of the exploits of their fathers when with Clive in India.

THE END.